# 2014

*Your New Astrology™ Horoscopes*
*Chinese & Western Predictions*
*For the Wood Horse Year*

## By SUZANNE WHITE
### MONTHLY FORECASTS FOR ALL 24 ZODIAC SIGNS
*LOVE • MONEY • HEALTH • CAREER • FAMILY*

# 2014 Your New Astrology™ Horoscopes

## *Chinese & Western Predictions*

By Suzanne White

\*\*\*\*

Published by:
Suzanne White at Smashwords
Copyright (c) 2013 by Suzanne White

\*\*\*\*

# SUZANNE WHITE'S

## ANNUAL NEW ASTROLOGY™
## FORECASTS FOR
# 2014
# THE YEAR OF THE GREEN WOOD HORSE
### JANUARY 31, 2014 THROUGH FEBRUARY 19, 2015
## COMPLETE MONTHLY PREDICTIONS
# THE NEW ASTROLOGY™
# FULL YEAR HOROSCOPES
### FOR ALL 24 ASTROLOGICAL SIGNS
### WESTERN AND CHINESE

*The Black Water Snake slithers away out of reach and off our case on*
*January 31, 2014*
*The 2013 Snake Year brought much turmoil and strife.*
*It's been a strain on everyone and his or her budget.*
*In Snake Years the path is not easy for anyone*
*Except, of course, the Rich.*

*So we wave Bye Bye to the Luxury-Loving Lie-in-the Sun, Brainy,*
*Turbulence-Loving Water Snake. Ciao! Come back in 60 Years.*

*AND A HUGE HELLO AND WARM WELCOME TO OUR OLD FRIEND*
*(last visit 1954)*

### *THE WOOD HORSE!*

*PRACTICAL, HEADSTRONG, TALENTED AND SELF-RELIANT*
*WOOD HORSES WORK THEIR RUMPS OFF.*
*LET'S FACE IT READERS...*

### *HORSES ROCK!*

TABLE OF CONTENTS

# WHAT IS THE NEW ASTROLOGY™?

**THE NEW ASTROLOGY™** Combines Western signs with Chinese signs and comes up with 144 *new* signs. If you are a Sagittarius and were born in 1949, then you are a Sagittarius/Ox. It's simple. Take your regular, familiar astrological sign and match it with the animal sign of the year you were born. Now you know your **NEW ASTROLOGY™** sign

## HOW TO FIND YOUR NEW ASTROLOGY HOROSCOPE FOR 2013

Let's say you find out you are a Cancer/Tiger. First, read the monthly predictions for CANCER. After you have read your CANCER predictions, take a deep breath and turn to the Chinese Zodiac Signs half of the book. Read the month's predictions for TIGER. Then, switch on your mental blender. In a wink. the two months' forecasts will merge to keep you informed about what's going on in your New Astrology sign's life for the month ahead.

NB: **Capricorns and Aquarians**....For your exact Chinese Animal Sign, check the exact date (they vary) of the Chinese New Year on your birthday on the tables at the end of the book.

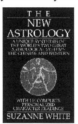

E-Book available at http://www.suzannewhite.com
and directly from Suzanne White on Facebook & Twitter & G+.

# 2014

## ALL ABOUT HORSES AND THE GREEN WOOD HORSE YEAR

### JANUARY 31, 2014 THROUGH FEBRUARY 19, 2015

**By Suzanne White**
**High Priestess of Chinese and Western Astrologies.**

Paris, France
October 2013

Dear Reader,

Get ready to rock and roll! The Year of the Horse means Get up an Go with a capital G. And we are the designated drivers. 2014 will certainly not be the most tranquil of years, it's a positive kind of year chockablock with real goals. Unlike 2013, a Water Snake Year, this Wood Horse year does not really favor intellectuals who lie about in *chaises longues,* sucking on expensive *bonbons* while philosophizing about the fate of the world at large. Decidedly, the Wood Horse does not encourage sloth or dissipation.

Horses are all about moving forward, running until they are exhausted and serving the world as useful vehicles for transport, agriculture or sport. So don't expect couch potatoes or goldbrickers to thrive in this coming Chinese Year. With Horses in charge, either you work and use your skills to move ahead or they are simply not interested in you. This means that everybody who wants to prosper in such an action-packed year, has to get up off their collective *derrières* and get busy being productive.

If you are unemployed , avoid whining. Instead, take a course to learn new skills so you can find work in that area of expertise. No matter if you hate computers and wish they would all simultaneously crash and leave you alone. Who cares if you hate getting your hands dirty and the only work you can find is landscaping? Not the Horse. The talented busy bee Horse does not give a whinny whether you have been a pipe fitter all these years, lost your job and are now faced with learning how to be a ballroom dance teacher. Horses are deaf to your cries of: "I don't want to." " Please Mommy don't make me." and "Do I have to, Dad?"

Fact is, this year you do *have to*. In 2014, you must make every effort to exit any and all stasis and move willingly toward fresh horizons. Your own boot straps want to be pulled up tight. You jump into the saddle. Both feet in the stirrups. Then give yourself a good kick in the ribs and off you will gallop toward certain success in the Wood Horse Year.

If you trot good-naturedly along your path, making steady headway toward worthy objectives, the headstrong Horse will applaud you with all four hooves. He or she wants you to move swiftly forward and realize as many of your dreams as you can concoct. But should the Horse get the hint that you are taking too many breaks, asking for excessive time off or flirting with floozies and mail room cuties at the water cooler, you will feel the pain of rejection from the speedy energy vector which characterizes Horse years. Keep moving ahead and you will be rewarded. Slack off and you may fall - and fall hard. Heed my advice and you will shine brighter in the 2014 Wood Horse Year than you ever could have hoped to in the slithering Snake Year 2013.

Although the Chinese New Year is January 31, 2014, The Horse Year doesn't officially begin until February 4, 2014. The start of the Tiger month is the first day of Chinese Spring when the sun enters the 315th degree on the tropical zodiac. Therefore, the 2014 Green Wood Horse year starts on February 3, 2014 in the United States and February 4 in other time zones. Why green? Because Wood is symbolized by plant color in Chinese Astrology. So between the New Year (Jan 31, 2014) and the start of the Horse year (Feb 3-4, 2014) we will enjoy a period of festivity devoted to welcoming Green Wood Horse and all that he or she stands for.

## WHAT TO EXPECT IN THE HORSE YEAR

In Horse years we are all called upon to shift into first gear and make it over the next hill almost every day. An all-out flurry of industry and social gathering will surge from out of nowhere. The Horse's mantras are: *Build. Rebuild. Make new friends. Leave worn out ones behind. Change your image. Clean up the existing picture of your life.*

In other words - get a move on!

Activity is everywhere in 2014. Join in, or go home and lock your door against those busy, busy Horse people who may just canter up and knock, saying, "We would like to invite you to join our cause or participate in our community theater event. Or we want give you a medal or teach you to dance the jitterbug or show you how to surf." Horses are unpredictable and headstrong and talented and irresistibly persuasive. They are also temperamental. You can't know ahead of time just what a Horse person will get up to. For the energetic soul, Horse years are sublime. For those of us addicted to lassitude and apathy, Horse years can prove nightmarish.

NB: Horse children born in winter will fare better than those who first see the light of day in a hot climate.

# THE HORSE CHARACTER

(1906,* 1918, 1930, 1942, 1954, 1966*, 1978, 1990, 2002, 2014, *2026)

(Capricorn & Aquarians Check Chinese Calendar End of Book for exact dates)

**THE HORSE IS YANG   THE HORSE'S MOTTO IS: "SELF RULE"**

HORSES ARE :

*Amiable • Eloquent • Skillful • Self-possessed*
*Quick-witted • Athletic • Entertaining • Charming • Independent*
*Powerful • Hard-working • Jolly • Sentimental • Frank • Sensual*

BUT THEY CAN ALSO BE:

**Selfish • Weak • Hotheaded • Ruthless**
**Rebellious • Pragmatic • Foppish • Tactless**
**Impatient • Unfeeling • Predatory**

Distinguished Horse,

High style is your style. Self-possessed and proud, you dream of cutting your own sweet swath through life, moving mountains and changing the shape of things. You are active and energetic. Yet, unless you feel like it, you may stubbornly refuse to do anything at all. Nobody can make you budge an inch. You're not lazy. You simply do precisely as you please. Nonetheless, Horse people are doers. You are a resolute achiever who cherishes his goals. You fear failure and will slave to save your career. Money is important to you. You are first pragmatic. Next emotional. Last foolhardy. You never let sentimentality get in your way. You are even willing to prance over a few cadavers to get what you want out of life.

Love is the only emotion that can turn your ruthlessness to mush. It may even cause you to give up the keys to your innermost soul, turn your back on family, desert friends and eradicate your past for the sake of pursuing an idyllic future with the object of your affection. Beware! Should it fail. Should a passionate love affair go sour and you be left bereft and alone, you could be utterly undone. Fall apart despondent. You might even be driven mad with regret. The kind of exclusive, 100% devotion you offer when you are madly in love can be the ruination of an otherwise hardy, practical and successful Horse. Where love is concerned, you are fragile.

Underneath a cloak of *coquetterie* and/or dandyism, you are oddly conservative. Your regulation-striped ties may boast a shocking pink background, but they are still regulation-striped ties. Your basic black dress may sport a sexy off-the-shoulder neckline, but it is still basic black. You think of yourself as a solid-citizen straight-arrow person. But verbally, you can be outrageous, outspoken and often out of line. To belong (and despite your rebellious streak, you long to belong) you will spend much of your life learning to control your outbursts. You're snappish and arrogant when riled - and you are frequently riled. You may suffer from nervous anxiety, tics and (obviously) back problems.

Childhood is easy for you. Kids are expected to be feisty and turbulent. Young adulthood will be a stormy, foot-dragging period. Although fitting in attracts you, responsibility dampens your high spirits. Maturity comes late to Horses. But once he has his common sense under control, the Horse progresses smoothly. Here's a piece of advice: don't break rules. Crime is not your strong suit. Should you try pulling off a bank robbery or go into burglary as a sideline, you will always get nabbed. For you hardy Horses the only real satisfaction will come from your own work. Anything from building a house to writing a book, to performing in theater or singing for your supper will suit you down to the ground. No more Horsing around. Let's get on with the show.

## THE HEADSTRONG HORSE

The handsome Horse is at his most attractive when he manages to be productive, enthusiastic, amusing, warm-hearted, talented, agreeable, industrious, generous, sociable, autonomous, strong-minded, sexy, curious, persuasive and logical.

But...when he fails to maintain control of himself, even the most delectable of Horses can become defiant, condescending, unscrupulous, anxious, moody, ruthlessly pragmatic, opportunistic, hard-nosed, self-serving and so obtuse as to seem to have gone both blind and deaf at once.

Horses cannot be forced into action. The old saying, "You can lead a Horse to water but you can't make him drink", suits this year's astrological subject. All the prodding and cajoling in the world won't spur these devotees of self-determination to advance, retreat, sidestep or jump hurdles. Horses are exasperatingly self-contained creatures whose sense of what is most expedient for them always comes first.

Horses are capable people, but they must be left to their own devices, allowed freedom of movement without interference or criticism. Except when they fall hopelessly in love, Horses remain entirely self-motivated, self-centered and self-propelled.

Horses are so fiercely autonomous that in many Asian societies where the family's welfare is a crucial priority, female Horse babies are considered undesirable. Sometimes prospective Asian mothers refuse to carry them to term because of the far-reaching consequences to the family circle. Even a young Horse woman is headstrong and self-reliant. She will not go gently into an arranged marriage. And if she is forced to get married, she will cause certain havoc in her new household.

Lesson? Never force a Horse.

In 1966 there was an upsurge of abortions in Asia, apparently to avoid hatching children in the year of the Fire Horse. This type of year traditionally produces the stormiest of Horse babies. And this Fire Horse year only comes around every sixty years. When it does, it drops millions of the most passionately self-minded of all Horses into society's lap. In the West nobody takes any notice of Fire Horse years, but Asian cultures fear the Fire Horse's presence, claiming it to be violent, intractable and disruptive. In Western cultures where the individual is highly regarded, spirited, individualistic children are prized. Docility and obedience are not necessarily qualities sought by Occidental parents.

Chinese astrology tells us that all Horses invariably leave home young. As soon as they are old enough to work, most Horses break out of their stalls and bolt, abandoning their parents and siblings without a backward glance, often leaving behind a trail of sorrowful memories. In Asia, a child who deserts his home and interrupts his devotion to parents and ancestors to pursue a personal destiny is a curse.

It would be folly to say that all Horse children are born home wreckers. But, no matter how integrated he seems to be, a Horse child's inner self remains powerfully rebellious, unusually sensitive to criticism and independent to a fault. The Horse despises being pressured to act for the good of the group or made to feel guilty. He has no time for recriminations, nor to display contrition for his wrongdoing. His motto? "Stay out of my way and I'll stay out of yours."

Although they have boundless energy and ambition, appear ebullient and optimistic and usually succeed at almost everything they do, Horses have a hard time belonging. They deplore the bounds of convention, feeling it limits their scope. They eschew the support of family and close ties in favor of what they see as freedom. In the process, they often lose what they most desire and need—the loving mirror of familiar folk who might afford them a clearer view of themselves. Yet—they cannot help it—they see all family intervention as undermining criticism. Even brotherly or sisterly love is often interpreted as sibling bullying or condescension.

Outside their disdain for the rigors of home and family, Horses willingly enter almost every race that catches their fancy, and they often win. Adventure delights them, as they enjoy evolving in an exciting whirlwind atmosphere where new things are always happening to keep them amused and titillated. They enjoy challenge and have a unique talent for undertaking arcane or unusual hobbies, such as cataloguing jazz musicians who played golf in the thirties or embroidering puppies on stationery for sale to SPCA members.

Horses are thunderous. They almost never know exactly how or when to keep their own counsel. They are not noisy and fire-breathing like Dragons. Horses appear dignified. Yet they are forever laughing too loudly in the wrong places or whispering aloud in company or making rude remarks about someone sitting next to them. This tendency to guffaw in the holiest parts of a church service could be called spontaneity. Nothing wrong with being irrepressible and uncontrived—who wants to be thought of as stuffy, rigid and predictable? Courtesy be damned!

Bottom line, the sudden, impassioned outbursts native to Horse behavior serve as a healthy security valve for the Horse's notoriously pent-up emotions.

Horses are wizards at speaking in public and influencing others. They can persuade a Laplander to buy a reconditioned air conditioner, eloquently defend a hopeless case in court and even get themselves brilliantly elected to public office. But, sadly, a Horse can hardly ever say what's buried in his heart. He cannot easily express his inner feelings. As a result of this blockage, his strongest emotions can cause him awful pain.

Yes, the Horse is emotionally hamstrung. In an attempt to communicate, when he goes to the theatre, he may burst into a patriotic folk song or leap up from a spellbound crowd of spectators and harangue the performer. He may fly at a loved one during a Christmas party, letting go with a strident verbal volley of wholly inappropriate proportion. In these circumstances, the Horse often does not realize that he or she is out of control. Rather, they assume they were never meant to be in control in the first place.

# SOME FAMOUS HORSES

## ARIES/HORSE – THE DAUNTLESS OPTIMIST

"There is something of the victorious athlete in all Aries/Horses. They are both fast on their feet and quick of wit. But they don't always carry through on their serve. Herein lies the first and most bothersome of Aries/Horse faults. Both Aries and Horse are pushy and active. Both signs are ego-oriented. Both Aries and Horse are guilty of willfulness. Couple them and you come up with a mighty character prone to demanding what he wants when he wants it, putting down his foot—after removing it from his mouth of course. The best part is however, that the Aries born Horse grows more kindly and sensitive with age. Nobody is ever bored in bed with an Aries/Horse. They approach sex with gusto and resolve."

17-Apr-1894  - Nikita Khrushchev

29-Mar-1918  - Pearl Bailey

29-Mar-1918  - Sam Walton

24-Mar-1930  - Steve McQueen

26-Mar-1930  - Sandra Day O'Conner

27-Mar-1930  - David Janssen

25-Mar-1942  - Aretha Franklin

26-Mar-1954  - Curtis Sliwa

07-Apr-1954  - Jackie Chan

09-Apr-1954  - Dennis Quaid

04-Apr-1966  - Nancy McKeon

19-Apr-1966  - Suge Knight

09-Apr-1978  - Rachael Stevens

13-Apr-1978  - Kyle Howard

15-Apr-1990  - Emma Watson

## TAURUS/HORSE – THE TALENTED TRAILBLAZER

The Taurus/Horse wants to play the *beau rôle* in all of life's dramas. He or she is bucking bronco in the somewhat stodgy persona of the earthbound Taurus. These people are often prodigies. The genius in Taurean Horses can however be compromised by the demands of a "normal" existence. The clever Taurus/Horse can never really find a *niche* amongst the ordinary. He is different - separate by virtue of his specialness. Taurus/Horses find satisfaction in greatness. If they don't get the Nobel Prize, they keep trying. Can this self-possessed demi-genius stop preening long enough to love anyone? Fact is, Love itself can be the undoing of the Taurus/Horse. Thunderous love-at-first-sight is not uncommon and its loss can lead this person to ruination. You see, this Horse may appear reserved, a bit distant and intellectual. But between the sheets and under the quilts this Horse rides high. He or she is a private dynamo in the sack.

27-Apr-1822  - Ulysses S. Grant

22-Apr-1870  - Vladimir Ilyich Lenin

09-May-1918  - Mike Wallace

10-May-1930  - Pat Summerall

24-Apr-1942  - Barbara Streisand

05-May-1942  - Tammy Wynette

23-Apr-1954  - Michael Moore

29-Apr-1954  - Jerry Seinfeld

12-May-1966  - Stephen Baldwin

16-May-1966  - Janet Jackson

22-Apr-1978  - Kim Elizabeth

10-May-1978  - Kenan Thompson

12-May-1978  - Jason Biggs

## GEMINI HORSE – THE STRUTTING ALTRUIST

The Horse's stylish bearing measured against the Gemini mutability gives us a multitalented person whose own worst enemy is himself. There's a nagging little gremlin wringing his hands inside the head of this goodhearted character who says, "I don't have to take this garbage! I don't have to put up with this nonsense! I want my freedom. I want my soul back." Of course we all know that our soul is never our own. But the Gemini/Horse works very hard to disprove that. He wants to be different, unusual, better than everybody else, cleverer, sexier, better dressed, and most of all, coolest. Yes, the Gemini/Horse wants desperately to be considered  a terrific fellow - a winner. Gemini/Horses can stick to their work. Normally, they choose a career that interests them and go ahead with that forever. They are often talented in music or graphic arts and are usually, in some very important way, involved in theater. Gemini/Horses are circus horses. Instead of walking, they prance. Their lovability quotient is high, but their ability to return love is often compromised by their ambition. However, Gemini/Horses find themselves in sizzling sexual situations, like all Horses, they perform brilliantly and willingly assuage their partners' most lascivious desires.

31-May-1930  - Clint Eastwood

03-June-1942  - Curtis Mayfield

07-June -1942 - Muammar Ghadaffi

10-June 1942 - Chantal Goya

18-Jun-1942  - Paul McCartney

20-Jun-1942  - Brian Wilson

02-June-1954 - Dennis Haysbert

19-June-1954  - Kathleen Turner

11-June - 1954 - Greta Van Susteren

15-Jun-1954  - Jim Belushi

26-May-1966 - Helena Bonham Carter

24-May-1966- Eric Cantona

# CANCER/ HORSE – THE MELANCHOLY WORKAHOLIC

The Horse, you may recall, is able to give himself up to a romantic passion and chuck everything —including his self-respect—for the sake of love. Cancer/Horses are, with their Scorpio counterparts, about the most self sacrificing of all the king's Horses and all the king's men. Love and its vicissitudes, the preservation of a home and kids and pets and insurance policies and telephone bills, can all be capably taken in hand by the Cancer/Horse. When questioned as to why he or she continues to struggle so hard and so seemingly alone without compassion or cooperation, the Cancer/Horse merely smiles: "It's for Janet. I love her." Or "I do it for the children, my home, my family." This Horse is a born workaholic. Keeping busy helps allay free floating fears and ward off frequent bouts of depression. Sexually unbeatable, Cancer born Horses make love the same way they work. With zeal, technique and devotion to duty. If you ever get into bed with one of these passionate Horse subjects, you won't want to get out.

15-Jul-1606  - Rembrandt Van Rijn

05-Jul-1810  - P.T. Barnum

23-Jun-1894  - Edward VIII, King of England

04-Jul-1918  - Ann Landers

18-Jul-1918  - Nelson Mandela

27-Jun-1930  - H. Ross Perot

04-Jul-1930  - George Steinbrenner

14-Jul-1930  - Polly Bergen

24-Jun-1942  - Mick Fleetwood

02-Jul-1942  - Vincente FOX

13-Jul-1942  - Harrison Ford

22-Jun-1954  - Freddie Prinze

28-Jun-1966  - John Cusack

30-Jun-1966  - Mike Tyson

06-Jul-1978  - Tia and Tamera Mowry

09-Jul-1990  - Steven Anthony Lawrence

## LEO/HORSE - THE PLUCKY CHAMPION

This good-natured steed rides high among his fellows and practically always passes muster with flying colors. The Leo/Horse is a born winner. No obstacle to his or her success is too daunting. He simply does not fear adversity. This person wants more than anything in life to achieve, to surpass himself in all areas of endeavor, and to do so in an atmosphere of good cheer. The Horse born Leo is not a sulker. His Leo imperiousness overrides any fears his skittish Horse side might harbor. Once the Leo/Horse knows what he wants, he harnesses himself to the phone, makes appointments, goes to meet the bankers, saddles himself with the regulation loans and starts painting the walls of his new shop or office. Leo/Horse is a doer. Sexually? Not surprisingly, this superlative person outperforms us all. He or she gives ample time and space to imaginative foreplay, then gets right down to the most erotic of details.

25-Jul-1870 - Maxfield Parrish

25-Jul-1894 - Walter Brennan

05-Aug-1930 - Neil Armstrong

13-Aug-1930 - Don Ho

16-Aug-1930 - Robert Culp

16-Aug-1930 - Frank Gifford

01-Aug-1942 - Jerry Garcia

20-Aug-1942 - Isaac Hayes

25-Jul- 1954 - Walter Payton

15-Aug-1954 - Steig Larsson

20-Aug-1954 - Al Roker

29-Jul-1966 - Martina McBride

31-Jul-1966 - Dean Cain

14-Aug-1966 - Halle Berry

19-Aug-1966 - LeAnn Womack

27-Jul-1990 - Cheyenne Kimball

06-Aug-1990 - Jon Benet Ramsey

## VIRGO/HORSE – THE PRANCING PRODUCER

The marriage of Virgo and Horse is one both lofty and elegant. Horses are self-motivated strivers, doers of grand deeds and sometimes—with all of their parading—a mite foolish and overly passionate. The Virgo, as we all know by now, is reserved. He takes care never to go outside the lines in the coloring book of life. Virgo is tasteful and a bit of a nit-picker to boot. He or she is also a borderline social climber. You won't find this subject hiding under any rocks or living among the homeless. His associations as well as his goals are high-minded and often intellectual. The love life of the Virgo born Horse is never dull. He is amiable and appealing. People literally fall at this alluring person's feet. In bed, he will be efficient – not cuddly or cozy – but effective and eager to achieve satisfaction by any and all means available. If ever you find yourself in bed with this entrancing creature, you might be shocked. But you won't be surprised by the remarkable skill.

25-Aug-1930 - Sean Connery

05-Sep -1942 - Werner Herzog

25-Aug-1954 - Elvis Costello

09-Sep- 1954 - Jeffrey Combs

02-Sep-1966 - Salma Hayek

09-Sep-1966 - Adam Sandler

17-Sep-1966- Tracy Dali

07-Sep- 1978- Devon Sawa

23-Aug-1978 - Kobe Bryant

25-Aug-1978 - Kel Mitchell

22-Sept -1978 - Daniella Alonso

29-Aug -1990 - Nicole Gale Anderson

08-Sep -1990 - Ella Rae Peck

## LIBRA/HORSE – THE MEASURED COMMANDER

A Horse born in gracious Libra will be genteel and dignified. Horses are sometimes rebellious and hardheaded. Libra practically never is. Libra wants peace and knows how to go after equilibrium. In this sign, Libra climbs on to the Horse's back and hangs on for dear life until she has tamed the self-propelled stallion into a better, more civilized person. When joined to Libra, the Horse retains full interest in his elegance and style. He wants to be popular and has the market cornered on idealism. Libra lends the Horse refined taste and balance. Libra knows that with her well-developed sense of measure the Horse will never totally buck the system. Passion is more important than tenderness in the love life of this person. Because of their elegantly sensitive approach to lovemaking, intimacy with a Libra/Horse is guaranteed bliss.

06-Oct-1846  - George Westinghouse

22-Oct-1882  - N.C. Wyeth

23-Sep-1930  - Ray Charles

15-Oct-1942  - Penny Marshall

29-Sep-1942 - Madeline Kahn

22-Oct-1942  - Annette Funicello

02-Oct-1954 -  Lorraine Bracco

03-Oct-1954  - Stevie Ray Vaughan

03-Oct-1954  - Al Sharpton

09-Oct-1954  - Scott Bakula

11-Oct-1966  - Luke Perry

02 -Oct -1966 - Samantha Barks

19-Oct - 1966 - John Favreau

28- Sep 1978 - Peter Cambor

03-Oct-1978 - Shannyn Sossamon

14- Oct 1978 - Usher Raymond

18-Oct-1990  - Carly Schroeder

22-Oct-1990  - Jonathan Lipnicki

## SCORPIO/HORSE – THE ROUGHSHOD PLODDER

This creature embodies most of the positive traits of the signs it combines. Scorpio/Horses are magnetic. And they are popular. They are disciplined and accomplished. They are persuasive and inspired, dedicated and fashionable. Scorpios born in Horse years are both independent and autonomous. There is little to prevent them from succeeding in a world class way. However, these strong-minded, sassy individuals are "can-do" people with immense personal power. Woe unto the associate who is not just as capable as they. Scorpio/Horse has no patience for lily-livered laggards. He rides himself hard and expects the same of partners and employees. Ironically, these feisty people love to do good works, assist the poor and heal the unwashed. Go figure. This is a hard sign to live with – for both the person wearing it and his or her entourage. Faithful in love (they ought to be cuz they ain't easy) the Scorpio/Horse adores his family, works overtime to protect and care for them. The Horse born in Scorpio makes love as often and as much he or she can with unbridled enthusiasm and fiery passion.

27-Oct-1858  - Theodore Roosevelt

07-Nov-1918  - Billy Graham

01-Nov-1942  - Larry Flynt

18-Nov-1942  - Linda Evans

19-Nov-1942  - Calvin Klein

23-Oct- 1954 - Ang Lee

13-Nov -1954 - Chris Noth

14-Nov-1954  - Condoleezza Rice

19-Nov-1954-  Kathleen Quinlan

12-Nov-1966  - David Schwimmer

17-Nov-1966  - Daisy Fuentes

17-Nov-1966 - Sophie Marceau

21-Nov-1966  - Troy Aikman

21-Dec-1966  - Kiefer Sutherland

07-Nov-1978 - Oliver Chris

17-Nov-1978 - Rachel McAdams

17-Nov-1978 - Zoe Bell

29-Oct -1990 - Megan Adelle

04-Oct- 1990 - Jean-Luc Bilodeau

## SAGITTARIUS/HORSE - THE KINDLY SPECULATOR

A great striding Horse figure, the Sagittarius/Horse is three-quarters Horse and only one part man. That indeed is a lot of horse! Interestingly, this person is more head than beast. The Sagittarian born Horse operates first out of homespun values, next in search of self-control, and thirdly he concentrates on finding and achieving a goal. Despite being born an adventurous Sagittarian, there is something of the plodder about this Horse. Works hard. Sticks to rules. Has grand plans and ambitions. The Sagittarian/Horse is a conventionally unconventional soul. He or she likes everything to "look good" on the surface. Prefers gold watches to trinkets. A practical person first, a romantic second. He usually marries and settles. But often leads a checkered double life in a quest for something a bit raunchier than just routine sex. This person's sexual prowess is legendary among his or her occasional partners. But her husband may not know about the seamier side of her sex life. And his wife might be very tired of the missionary position and wish she might meet someone more exciting to take to her bed.

25-Nov-1846  - Carrie Nation

11-Dec-1882  - Fiorello La Guardia

17-Dec-1930  - Bob Guccione

24-Nov-1942 - Billy Connolly

27-Nov-1942  - Jimi Hendrix

04-Dec-1942 - Gemma Jones

29 - Nov - 1954 - Joel Coen

30-Nov-1954 - Simonetta Stefanelli

11-Dec-1954  - Jermaine Jackson

18-Dec-1954- Ray Liotta

30-Nov-1978  - Clay Aiken

24-Nov-1978- Katherine Heigl

02-Dec-1978  - Nelly Furtado

18-Dec-1978  - Katie Holmes

24-Nov-1990 - Sarah Hyland

20-Dec-1990  - JoJo

## CAPRICORN/HORSE - THE CONSCIENTIOUS ENTREPRENEUR

"Count on me!" says the reliable Capricorn/Horse. And believe me, you can. Here is a marriage made in heaven. Capricorn lends solidity and staying power to the somewhat dandified and often insecure Horse character. In his turn, Horse gives this Capricorn manual dexterity and a finely developed sense of his or her own popularity. Always well turned-out and ready to attack new projects, this person rises above the madding crowd with aplomb. There is a crusader here. Here we have a person of high moral standards who is not afraid of hard work and has no time for trifling. Considering the lofty standards and well-developed moral sense, this Capricorn's sex life might prove to be a tad dull. But that is hardly the case. Why? Because this Horse born in Capricorn is so attractive, so poised and admirable that lovers will literally stalk him or her to the ends of the Earth. When properly approached (with dignity and *politesse*), the Capricorn born Horse melts. Then he or she trots right into the nearest paddock with the object of their affection where they proceed to perform some sexual circus tricks only a resourceful Capricorn/Horse could conjure.

25-Dec-1642  - Sir Isaac Newton

01-Jan-1895  - J. Edgar Hoover

14-Jan-1919  - Andy Rooney

05-Jan-1931  - Robert Duvall

17-Jan-1931  - James Earl Jones

19-Jan-1943  - Janis Joplin

28-Dec-1954  - Denzel Washington

12-Jan-1955  - Kirstie Alley

18-Jan-1955  - Kevin Costner

28-Dec-1978  - John Legend

16-Jan-1979  - Aaliyah

23-Dec-1990 - Anna Maria Perez de Tagle

27-Dec-1990 - Hayden Hawkens

## AQUARIUS/HORSE - THE GALLOPING VISIONARY

To this alert and energetic Aquarian, variety and movement represent freedom. The Horse lends rebellion to the clear-minded Aquarian, and pushes him to stride ahead. Horses are hasty and gifted for easy accomplishment. The Aquarian wants an original life. When the two are matched by birth, an eccentric, fleeting sort of being evolves. The Aquarius/Horse never lights for long. Sex, is of course, a must for this galloping visionary. However as he doesn't fancy settling down to raise up a herd of ponies, he will be more the type of lover who flits from flower to flower, loving and leaving onward and upward. This is not to say that the Aquarius born Horse is not a great lover. He or she will be an ardent and exciting partner in bed. But not for long. Something new and unusual will catch his eye and off he goes into the sunset.

15-Feb-1882  - John Barrymore

03-Feb-1894  - Norman Rockwell

14-Feb-1894  - Jack Benny

01-Feb-1895  - John Ford

06-Feb-1895  - Babe Ruth

03-Feb-1907  - James Michener

31-Jan-1919  - Jackie Robinson

30-Jan-1930  - Gene Hackman

10-Feb-1930  - Robert Wagner

18-Feb-1930  - Gahan Wilson

01-Feb-1931  - Boris Yeltsin

06-Feb-1931  - Rip Torn

06-Feb-1931  - Mamie Van Doren

08-Feb-1931  - James Dean

18-Feb-1954  - John Travolta

07-Feb-1966  - Chris Rock

19-Feb-1966  - Justine Bateman

07-Feb-1978  - Ashton Kutcher

24-Jan-1979  - Tatyana Ali

## PISCES/HORSE - THE BEGUILING ARTISTE

The apparent tranquility of this combination of Fish and Horse is but a façade. which masks a highly fragile and spiritual nature. Pisces/Horse people are clairvoyant. And they are often geniuses. In private, they willingly give of themselves without expecting more than a pat on the head in return. In this New Astrology™ sign, the Horse's ordinarily self-propelled push for autonomy is subdued. Peace-loving Pisces keeps the Horse's dander down, teaches him to be self-effacing, and clues to the wonders of second sight and empathy. The Pisces/Horse is well-advised to find a burning passion (music, dance, art, building or even business) while still quite young and then follow his or her chosen star a whole life through. If this Horse waits too long to find its path, he or she may become distracted. Myriad diversions will leave room for them to fritter away their energies looking for just the right profession or cause to espouse. Early focus and discipline will lead to certain success. In love, the Pisces born Horse has the capacity for undying devotion. He or she may be slightly on the shy side in bed. But the intuitive mate will know how to turn this charming creature on with tons of reassurance and endless tender smooches. In turn, the Pisces/Horse will admire and serve his mate for offering him or her such thrilling pleasure.

26-Feb-1846  - William "Buffalo Bill" Cody

25-Feb-1894  - Meher Baba

06-Mar-1906  - Lou Costello

20-Mar-1906  - Ozzie Nelson

09-Mar-1918  - Mickey Spillane

27-Feb-1930  - Joanne Woodward

08-Mar-1942 - Michael Eisner

02-Mar-1942 - John Irving

20-Feb-1954  - Patty Hearst

01-Mar-1954  - Ron Howard

20-Feb-1966  - Cindy Crawford

22-Feb-1978  - Jen Frost

01-Mar-1978 - Jensen Ackles

20-Feb-1978 - Lauren Ambrose

04-Mar-1990 - Andrea Bowen

13-Mar-1990 -  Emory Cohen

# YOUR MONTHLY FORECASTS
## for
# THE WESTERN SIGNS
### for 2014

# ARIES 2014

## OVERVIEW FOR THE WOOD HORSE YEAR

*Audacious Aries,*

*Horse Years are all about movement. Perpetual motion generally suits action-oriented Aries like you. Do be discriminating however. Don't go barreling blindly ahead. Stop. Look. Listen. The Horse sets a varied and sometimes uneven pace, which might leave you straight arrow Aries a bit perplexed. This Horse year will bring you new opportunities. But, if you don't snoop beneath the surface, the very rug could be pulled from under you. The key advice for you Aries this year is "Look deeper" and "Roll with the punches".*

*Remain alert to subtle signals both in your environment and from those around you. Learn to use those horns of yours as antennae. Sense approaching shifts before they come up and bite you on the snout. You tend to like change best when you initiate it. This year, prepare to adapt to sudden shifts that are not of your making. Know when to hang a U-turn and when to let up on the throttle. If you find yourself involved in conflict, pick your battles. Don't waste precious vitality tilting at windmills. Curb your impulsivity. Take breaks. Go on trips. Hide out from the crowd. Keep your nose clean and your shoulder to the wheel. The Horse bestows gifts on his fellow laborers. So don't slack off. Look busy at all times. sw*

————— ❦❦❦ —————

## THE CHINESE YEAR AHEAD

### ARIES 2014

### ARIES February 2014

The first week of February will mean conflict with your environment. If you're forging ahead in your career, relationship, or health matters, expect to be met with hardships everywhere you turn. Difficult or impossible tasks, spats over simple everyday things with your spouse or partner, and colds or headaches should be confronted quickly. Don't let any situation snowball out of control. Just because life is playing hardball , handing you a dozen dud projects, doesn't mean you can let go of your cherished objectives. Stay focused on your goals. Don't settle for complacency.

On the 6th of February, Mercury goes retrograde till Feb 28. Best laid plans as well as appliances, electronics and love affairs often go awry during Mercury retrograde. This particular period will bring a revelation. Maybe your current relationship isn't working out, or maybe you shouldn't have sent another man or woman chocolates on Valentine's day. Whether good or bad, you will need to come to terms with reality. This will also be a period where your career path is more clearly visible. What you're doing, what you could be doing, and what you should be doing, will all become clearer during Mercury Rx. The clarity may happen in a dream or in a flash you get during an otherwise stultifying business meeting. Don't sign anything till March.

The third week of February is an opportunity to meet someone who will have a significant impact on your life. You will not be lovers. So save yourself some heartache. Take a rain check on those candlelight dinner plans. You may be in conflict with this person at first, or actually feel an epidermic creepy crawly need to avoid them. Don't be afraid to step out of your comfort zone and start up a conversation. This character has value.

The last week of February is a time of inconvenience. You'll bring your umbrella to work but forget it in the car. Or you will accidentally call people by the wrong names. You might even drop some cash in the street, and let some lucky *finders keepers* person thank you for that slip up. Just bear in mind that, while frustrating for you, your mishaps will often bring a smile to others' lips. They may also teach you to be a tad more attentive.

## ARIES March 2014

Though they may be nothing more beguiling than sitting on the couch, watching the Nature Channel for hours at a time, you will have definite plans set for the first week of March. You'll be confronted by others who wish to change your agenda. They might propose a date, a vacation, or a few extra work shifts. Think carefully about how you respond. Your choice will affect how they view you as their friend, relative, or lover. Your values, as well as your lifestyle, will be brought into question. Don't be afraid to tell the world exactly how you feel. Speak your mind and stand your ground, but be careful not to alienate anyone. One extra word or misplaced opinion could cause you to lose an important contact.

The second week of March will lead you toward a joyful or encouraging event, likely relational. A new friend, or close friend, may draw closer to you than you ever thought possible. You may be on cloud nine, but the rest of your life isn't. Don't allow everything else to fall through the cracks.

Make sure you prepare accordingly, because the next week will be a spiritual dry season. You'll find a lack of sincerity, enthusiasm, or understanding in the words of others. You will be tempted to lay into them and change the situation. But know that your resources are limited. Make sure to catch yourself before you end up losing friends over minor things like leaving the refrigerator open. The last week of March will be relatively peaceful. There will be a small accident among coworkers or strangers. You might feel the need to add fuel to the fire by revealing your hunches about the origin of the mishap. Consider letting it go just this once. Your benevolence will be appreciated by your entourage.

## ARIES April 2014

Your Horse year will begin to take shape around the first week of April. The goals may not seem attainable at the rate things are going. You'll feel the need to pick up the pace. Don't act on impulse. Otherwise you'll end up in some awkward situations. April Fool's day events could convey a fairly high level of paranoia toward the beginning of the week. In the work place, be sure to pace yourself. Avoid burn out.

The year won't end for a while, so chill. The second week will involve the fulfillment of some short-term plans. You'll buy that new laptop you wanted, learn to execute a complex, tasty new recipe, or maybe even begin to learn pottery. Others might try to make you feel guilty for enjoying yourself. Just relax and do it your way. No use confronting them about your choices on their terms.

Use your ability to speak up without being ashamed of your own opinions now. Let everyone know your plans. But not so they can alter them for you. Just make sure they are aware of your intentions and do not imagine you're acting on a whim.

The third week of April might cause you to feel irked by those close to you. You'll find the very same individuals who were against your precious pleasures have decided to do as you do. Some may even try to show off to and arouse your jealousy streak. The wise thing would be not to fall for their manipulations. But you may tumble anyway - you are a naïve sort. There will be some bad blood between you and possibly even one or two vocal altercations.

Eventually everyone will forget what the petty arguments were even about, so try to keep from eliminating these characters from your life for good. The last week in April is the time to reorganize your priorities. Keep those intentions which are important to you and close to your heart. Try to create a day without any argument or shows of impatience with fools. You'll soon realize what needs to be done to correct your life path. But first, you must clear your head.

### ARIES May 2014

The pistol is cocked. The runners are set. The race is about to begin. But you have to keep in mind that it's a relay race, and you are the anchor. Your time to shine is coming up but don't jump the gun and disqualify your team. You'll know when you're handed the baton. It might be an important project at work, or a request to take care of your newly single neighbor's dog. Others might get their chance before you, but don't dismay. As soon as you're able, just take off running as fast as you can. Don't worry about restraints or conventional standards. Laws, however, are crucial so don't break any.

The second week could leave you exhausted, but you won't know it. You're not altogether fine. But all the excitement will make you feel great. It won't be easy to take things one step at a time, but it's of primary importance. Time will seem like it's flying by when you're working on your job or spending time with those you love. Take some part of each day to remember the last time you ate, slept, and showered. Notice that there was an "and" in the last sentence. This means you need to do all of the above every day.

The third week may bring an inevitable crash. The weather won't be to your liking. There won't be anything good on TV and no one will understand you. You'll consider snuffing out the candle light of a flame you've started with that person you felt sure was the one. Don't try to remember what you were thinking these past few weeks. In all likelihood you weren't thinking straight. It's best to go with the flow and let things unravel on their own.

The last week of May is where you start to backtrack. You'll find you have a lot of family issues this week. Don't be afraid to apologize or ask that they do the same in order to start picking up the pieces of feelings you may have trampled over this month.

### ARIES June 2014

In June, you will actually be able to have your cake and eat it too. Mercury goes retrograde on the 7th and stays that way till July 1st. The first week will be a great one for you and your career, but documents and major decisions could be delayed. You'll be responsible for making a breakthrough. Or maybe you will single-handedly secure that long term contract. Success with finances or the promise of future success will draw others to you. This is a good space in which to negotiate. But recoil from signing binding documents. Your social life will benefit as a result of this spate of small victories. Be careful about visibly spending large sums of money or telling others about your plans and ideas. Use caution or both may end up being stolen from you.

The second week of June is the perfect time to go somewhere you've never been before. Take a road trip or hop on a flight as a standby. Enjoy the journey as much as the destination. Be sure to grab a souvenir and a few pictures to bring home. The memories will greatly affect how you feel about people and places foreign to you.

Revive your artistic talent during the third week. The payoff will be on the effort, not the outcome. Let your imagination catch up to your native determination and stubbornness. A creative mind provides more options than do confrontation and conflict. Allow yourself the array of choices that comes with creativity.

The last week of June is a time to look for lost objects. Be prepared to find things you don't remember buying, or never bought at all. Yes, that includes year-old overdue library books. Even though many lost or forgotten items may reappear, don't expect to recover that which is most precious to you. What you're looking for most will only appear when you turn your back. Keep track of how you spend your time this week. You'll find yourself wandering through wave after wave of nostalgia. Allow the memories to take you in when you have the time. In any case, it's likely many of these old keepsakes and photographs will disappear again shortly. *C'est la vie!*

## ARIES July 2014

Mercury will still be retrograde on July 1. Hold off on making major decisions for a few more days. Clean up the house and equip yourself with seduction tools. The month of July will test your heart as well as your mind. Be on the lookout for that special someone the first week. You may not find them, but you'll be close. Ships sailing different courses gradually get further and further away. So it won't take long for you to realize there's a pretty big difference between a perfect match, a great one, and whatever kind of relationship temporarily engages your attention.

Intimacy and carnal desire will fill your head over the course of the first and second week. If you have an old flame or a new crush, expect a visit or message from them. The relationship won't be sexual, at first. At this point you might be asking yourself who would notice if you took advantage of the situation. Don't kid yourself. That sensual tug is a certainty. Even so, your body's and your conscience's choices will conflict. Why not go with how you feel physically? Break someone's heart (or your own). Have yourselves some sex and feel better. Now you must focus on one partner and your passion as well as stamina will increase. Quality over quantity.

Love invariably costs money. So it's a good idea to keep an eye on your finances over the third week of July. You might consider putting in extra work hours over the next few weeks, but hold off on it. You're forgetting an important event around the 25th. Change your schedule around to give you ample time before it starts. Chances are, you will be moving more slowly than usual.

The last week of the month is a good time to reconnect with friends. Your intimate relationship may have distanced them from you and many will be moving away soon. Inquire about their plans. Let them know they will be missed. Though painful, their separation is only temporary. There is always e-mail, text messages and wonder of wonders !!! There is Skype!

## ARIES August 2014

Work is in your future for the start of August. Expect most leisure time to vanish from your life. Don't bother trying to figure out how many hours you spent overworking. It will only depress you. Before the corporate world steals what little bit of your soul remains, take a moment to evaluate your health. Illness may spread around you during this week. Don't take any chances with questionable food, iffy weather, or snuffly kids.

The second and third week of August will leave you feeling slightly diminished. It would be best not to make things worse by indulging in worry. Mental exhaustion will test your social patience too. Don't feel guilty if a few calls go unanswered. Try to refrain from telling others you will get back to them. You're likely to forget. Friends and lovers will seem pushy over these two dicey weeks. Venting frustration on them is not a good idea. Tell them how exhausted you are of late. Don't reveal how little strength you can summon to care for their miseries right now.

Past memories will become clear and vivid over the last week of August. What you had in the past will seem more attractive than what you have now. Homesickness, nostalgia about exes, and former jobs will be glamorized and draw you to some previous version of your life. Remember your long term goals and make choices accordingly. Someone close to you will attempt to make you give up on a project because it differs from what they have in mind for your future. Even if you've made your decision about the matter, they will not relent. Show them the door as many times as it takes.

Toward the end of the month, consider getting a pet. Keep it simple. Choose a creature that lends tranquility rather than one which requires all your attention. Perhaps a goldfish or a turtle would do the trick. Something to care for can help re-connect us to what is truly important in our lives.

**ARIES September 2014**

September will provide a measure of relational and occupational security for the first and second week. Things may not seem to be going well, but at least the boat has ceased rocking. Take this becalmed time to get involved with the arts. Use visual stimulation through live performance, paintings, or even movies to explore the world around you. Expect praise for how well you've been doing at work. These kudos won't be awarded you for anything in particular - just for the quality of time and effort you contribute.

You may suspect that your coworkers and boss of insincerity. But that's not the case. They just can't put into words how much they need your help. Stay away from debates or heady discussion over the third week of September. Keep all of your uncanny insights and profound observations to yourself. Otherwise you may end up teaching yourself an embarrassing lesson in humility. Talk as little as possible this week. If you loosen your tongue, you're likely to lash out at others - especially those who seem to be leading a more felicitous life than yourself.

Why not take on a protegé over the last week? They will be attracted to you by your passion for a profession or a compelling hobby. This person will become a lifelong friend. Try to accept the fact that they ask questions every five minutes. Do not attempt to get them in bed with you. They're innocent. Let's keep it that way for a while. Take the time to get to know this person and understand their problems. The questions they ask are mere bandages covering the surface of some deep wound. Dig gently for information.

Your luck will increase over this time, but the improvement won't be enough to compensate for the dicey moments you'll have to go through. Focus on a personal project in order to stay busy. If not, the little annoyances present in your chart right now could drive you round the bend.

**ARIES October 2014**

From the 4th until the 25 th of October we will experience another of those trying Mercury retrograde periods. Allow extra time when driving to visit your friend on the other side of town. Back up your computer documents. And remember not to sign any contracts until after Mercury goes direct on the 25 th.

Keep your love life moving along this month, but don't hope for miracles. You usually prefer to get to know the other person before waking up beside them. Take time now to find out where you stand in order to avoid involving yourself in another disappointing passionate encounter which turns out to be little more than a one-night stand. You may be considering holding off telling your crush or love interest how you feel until the holiday season starts. If you're hoping to create some magical scenario around Christmas, do know well ahead that it probably won't work out the way you imagine. Stop thinking about waiting for the snow, lights, and that perfect chance. Keep an open mind so as to fend off eventual disillusion.

Starting with the second week and continuing over the course of the month, you will become afflicted with a bad case of deep-seated boredom. Not depression. Just plain boredom. Time will slow to almost a complete stop. Moreover you will get fed up pinching pennies saving up for that overpriced plane ticket or useless toy you imagined you couldn't live without. This is a good time to plan a weekend get-together with a few close friends. It's important that you plan this outing yourself. Pulling it off well will give you much-needed satisfaction and begin to extricate you from the stultifying monotony you've been suffering.

Don't be afraid to splurge a little over the last two weeks of October. Buy yourself some fancy duds. Spruce up your living quarters. Keep your schedule especially flexible over the last week. You will be invited to join in on some unusual activities. Anything from banana-boating to squirrel-watching is on the table. Don't be so quick to turn down these offers of exotic fun. While you may have little interests in squirrels, the personal relationships formed with those who invited you along will prove invaluable over the next few months. Some personalities you encounter may rub you the wrong way. But don't worry. The others will accept you almost as family. There will be very little interpersonal conflict over this time period.

**ARIES November 2014**

November will be a time of great financial success for you Aries. The 1$^{st}$ and 2$^{nd}$ in particular will turn out better than you might have expected. Now is when you need to increase savings for the holiday season. You will be tempted by friends to invest in their projects. Hear them out. But do not agree to anything binding right now. No need to increase your financial burden. Besides, they may be attempting to shrug some of their responsibilities off on to you.

Children around you, including your own, will grow increasingly excited during the second week. Do not become agitated or angry when you step on a few hard red plastic Lego pieces in your bare feet. Rage will make the pain worse. Children naturally become careless as the holiday season approaches. Try not to burden them with too many extra tasks just to keep everyone busy. Instead, why not make an evening of creating presents for Aunt Martha and Uncle Bill? Kids love projects they can make with their hands. The more gifts they make, the fewer Legos you will have to watch out for underfoot.

During the second and third weeks of November, it's important to focus on your health. Dieting is simply not on at this season. Also, refuse to try foods you've never tasted before or you may fall ill. Start nursing any health issues involving the head at this time. Migraines and dizziness may be prevalent now. You could be prone to a rolling cough and on-and-off headaches that may last the duration of the month. Keep relief medicine handy and do more exercise than usual. If you can't get to the gym or engage in sports activities, try taking walks - even on sidewalks in town. Keep the body agile and the blood coursing through your veins.

Relatives will visit at month's end. There will be some argument - possibly centered around or directed at you. Don't pipe up with your version. It will only add fuel to the flames. Instead of voicing your opinion, ask for opinions from those who challenge you. Their statements will provide information you have long been wondering about. Let them talk.

## ARIES December 2014

In December, your year's hard work will pay off. Take matters into your own hands when it comes to your love life. Waiting for just the right moment will only waste valuable time, so don't be afraid to just come out and say what your heart has been keeping inside. The first week of December will be perfect for that marriage proposal. You might be considering a magical Christmas Eve proposal. But if you're ready now, go ahead and make it happen. One of Aries' great strengths is in saying flat out what you mean.

In December's second week, avoid large groups of people. With Christmas coming, you may feel like mingling in crowds at the mall. Germs are everywhere in overheated places. Keep that in mind and shop locally. And of course holiday parties will come at you out of nowhere. Too much socializing may cause you to burn out. You will be tempted to give away some money to charity at this time. Donate as much as you are able. But don't overdo it. Aries generosity is a well-known source of dismay for even the sharpest among you. Stay close to those you care about now. Other less intimate friends and relatives will still be around after the holiday season has passed.

The last weeks of December are made for relaxation. When you're asked to help out with decorations and party planning, ask why they don't enlist the talents of those more creative than you. If pressed into service, even if you hate party decorating, keep smiling. But duck out early with a valid excuse. Tell them you are relaxing. There will be a gala event near the 19th. Decline the invitation. Late nights and party food will stress your newly toned body. You are relaxing. Remember?

Don't make too much of Christmas this year. You will benefit from having just a small gathering at home. Let others bring the food. Provide wine and soft drinks, but keep the celebrations to a minimum. Take the last week December to rest up from the festivities with your beloved. Read and watch TV programs you have recorded and never got around to viewing. Expect pleasant, but complex dreams over the course of this week. No need to take them as premonitions or signs. Just frolic in them. You will wake up refreshed.

## ARIES January 2015

Many Aries start the Western calendar New Year with a sense of purpose. They expect to try their best and resolve to make improvements in all areas of their lives. This passion is commendable. But more often than not, it is precisely what gets you into so much trouble. Ordinarily, your firm opinions may cause you to clash with Scorpio, Cancer, or possibly even Taurus. But this January 2014 is one of the few times you rams will butt heads with each other.

This month bodes conflict with others of your same sign. Let's say both you and your co-worker are Aries. Normally you are pals. You are always willing to tackle projects together. But this year, when you both have the Aries January resolve to work harder and get promoted, your pal may compete with you. If you put in fifty hours, they'll do sixty. If you have a new proposal for the executives, she'll be there to criticize it. Even if you only want to borrow their stapler, you'll may have to pry it from their cold, dead hands. This period of contention will pass. But not immediately. Refrain from bringing it up to your crony. He or she has taken this tack for a personal reason which, in fact, has nothing to do with you.

Maintain steady sleeping habits, especially over the first and last week of the month. Despite petty squabbles, January can be a time of personal production. Everything you touch will come to life. At the same time, due to jealousy or competition, collaboration with others may be difficult. Keep planning to a minimum as you near the end of the Horse year. Look forward to the start of the mellower Goat year on January 31, when dissension will first dissipate, then disappear.

An event involving family will affect you emotionally in the final week of January. This incident will drastically change your schedule and may even wear you out. Time to start exercising again. At first, you can expect some soreness and muscle aches. The discomfort should only last a day or two. If you maintain your exercise program, by the end of the month, you will find your energy fully renewed and your nerves considerably soothed.

# TAURUS 2014
## OVERVIEW FOR THE WOOD HORSE YEAR

*Trusty Taurus,*

*If you are the kind of bull who likes to mosey through a field lazily munching grasses, then the Year of the Wood Horse may prove hard going. That patch of clover you find so delectable could deliver a bee sting or two. On the other hand, if are prone to charging ahead, you will find plenty of use for your bullish vigor. But I must warn you - it will be up to you to channel that energy selectively. Thought rather than instinct must guide you. I mention the year's possible bee stings only to suggest you remain on the alert for scrapes, pickles and predicaments. In this kind of year, Taureans who stodge out and stay put, will not be prepared to deal cannily with the odd entanglement with the law or even with the tax man. You must be especially active and thorough in this Wood Horse year.*

*2014 is also scheduled to bring you rewards for your diligence and labor - interludes of the kind of sensory delights that you adore. The intervals between life's goodies and its travails may be longer than you are used to. Any occasions where you loll about may be rudely interrupted by explosive surprises—one or two of which may come from within. These thunderbolts of awareness will come unannounced. They are not a threat to your health or well being. Long run, these eye-openers will help you understand what has been motivating you to occasionally serve as your own worst enemy. sw*

————————

## THE CHINESE YEAR AHEAD
## TAURUS 2014

### TAURUS February 2014

Technology snafus may interfere with your plans starting on the 6th. If someone does not reply to an e-mail, a friendly follow-up message may be in order. That e-mail may have ended up in the receiver's spam box or even in some undefined internet black hole. Be especially careful that you don't hit "reply all" on any private messages this month. Remember to back up all of your work so you don't lose any critical documents.

You've probably guessed that these warnings stem from this month's Mercury retrograde. These testy periods require a bit of extra patience. Since that's one of your virtues, you're usually less fussed about these times than more high-strung types. Just be aware of what's happening and try to work around it. Think of it this way - the universe is doing some road construction on part of your life. But apart from the annoying mechanical breakdowns and miscommunications Mercury retrograde is usually not a major upheaval. Until it's over on the 28th don't sign any binding documents or make commitments you cannot renege on gracefully.

If you are a parent with young children at home, be particularly alert to their social interactions around the 16th-21st. There's a possibility your son or daughter could be the target of bullying. Take the time to find out why and reassure your child of your love and support. Let them know your love is unconditional. Remind your offspring that you are always there, available to listen and to help without interfering.

Toward month's end, you may hear from an old friend. Although the reunion starts out happily enough, you'll soon discover your old pal has become bad news. He or she may even try to inveigle you into doing something reprehensibly dishonest. I don't think their request will involve anything as dire as holding up a convenience store or robbing a gas station. It's more likely he/she will ask that you betray your integrity in some way - launder some money, hide their illegal drugs or lie to their spouse regarding your whereabouts on a certain key evening. The wise Taurus would let this long-lost friendship recede once again into the past.

## TAURUS March 2014

You're likely to experience some concerns with your mouth around March 2nd. Make an appointment with your dentist. At least schedule least a thorough cleaning and quick check-up for cavities or incipient gum problems. If you do not have the funds for a dental visit, find a dental school or dental hygienist school near you. Often these kind of educational facilities offer low-cost treatments by students under the careful supervision of their instructors. Better to receive this kind of dental care than none at all. Dental visits are anything but pleasant. But the consequences of neglect are far worse.

Once you have attended to your dental health in early March, you can start using your mouth in more pleasant ways. The planets will line up to favor you with a sensual interlude during the second week of the month. Try to plan a special evening with your partner for that night. If you are single, then stop hesitating—call, text or e-mail that cutie who has been making regular appearances in your fantasies. Indulge in the kind of multi-sensory experience that feeds your sybaritic side. Start the evening with a gourmet meal. After dinner, cue up your favorite romantic music. Give each other massages with scented oils and indulge in the follow-up with gusto.

Make sure you emerge from romantic daydream mode before the end of the month. There's trouble brewing at your workplace. You may pick up the first hints of it during the period from the 22nd to the 26th. Pay attention to subtle cues. Observe body language as well. Notice who is lunching with whom. Who is being left out of the loop? I don't think this problem will affect you directly. But take care. You do not want to become part of the collateral damage of the approaching fall-out. Too risky.

## TAURUS April 2014

You're likely to have an embarrassing moment early this month. Perhaps you will unwittingly smear chocolate on your cheek whilst sneaking in half a chocolate bar between meals. Until later when someone mentions that gash of brown on your face, you will be wearing it and attracting no little ridicule. Or you'll arrive at work only to discover you left the house wearing mismatched socks. Or maybe you will be blithely peeing in the bushes and along will come a group of curious hikers. Don't get upset. No need to sulk or hide. Life sends us these moments to keep us up to speed on laughing at ourselves.

You could find yourself feeling bored around the 12th. You might need a new outlet for your imagination. Treat yourself to a creative shopping expedition. Visit an artists' supply outlet. Or look over the wares at a store which sells colorful yarns or glittering beads. Let yourself be inspired by the materials you see. Buy some supplies. Then come home and play with your new toys. Let go of judgment. What you fabricate or craft doesn't have to be perfect. What's important is the fun you have while creating it.

You may meet a mightily charismatic person around the 22$^{nd}$. He or she will seem warm, witty, full of interesting anecdotes and genuinely interested in you. This individual will extend some kind of invitation. Be wary. Don't share too much information about yourself with him/her. This character's charm is like bait on a bear trap. They may indeed be a con artist or a charlatan. Could also be a garden-variety narcissist, trying to recruit you for their fan club. Not to worry. Forewarned is forearmed. You will recognize this trickster by the amount of probing questions they pepper you with. If they persist and you cannot escape, make things up. Even if you are a mechanical engineer or an accountant, say you are a nuclear physicist or a ballerina. That's called "blinding them with science". Works like a charm.

## TAURUS May 2014

A long-delayed realization may suddenly click for you sometime around the 3$^{rd}$. You come to the conclusion that you have deluded yourself about a particular subject for years. You will wake up one morning in the knowledge that the ex you always thought of as the love of your life was a chronic moocher. Or after decades of looking up to a teacher or religious leader, you suddenly see that said person is a rank phony. At first, you may feel a bit disoriented by this awareness. Don't let your fear of acknowledging the real truth prevent you from absorbing your newly acquired insight.

You may have let yourself slide into slothful habits of late. If so, the third week of May brings a wonderful opportunity to re-charge your batteries. Be sure to choose some kind of exercise that won't bore you. If you hate gyms and weight machines, then don't waste your money there. Instead, look into movement classes you will enjoy---yoga, dance, martial arts? Or hang up your car keys, find a bike and a helmet, and start pedaling.

Your partner may surprise you with an unusual suggestion sometime after the 21$^{st}$. He or she may suggest an outing of some sort. It will be a different kind of excursion than what the two of you generally go on together. He or she may propose going to some type of gathering or function you never considered before - a sci-fi convention or a class on how to see auras. Your initial reaction might be to reject your sweetie's idea as too weird and not really your "thing". But do go ahead. Give their proposition a try. It's always healthy for Taureans to shake things up a bit. Your acquiescence will not only strengthen your relationship, it will teach you something brand-new in the bargain. You bulls have a tendency to enjoy your own ruts. Being jolted out of one often makes you cranky. Lighten up.

## TAURUS June 2014

Another of those pesky Mercury retrograde periods starts on the 7$^{th}$ of this month. It will last until July 1. This one may be a bit more difficult for Taureans than the previous retrograde phase. You are likely to feel its effects in relation to income and property. Be especially careful to keep records of payments you make this month. Do not leave any belongings lying on your car seat where they may attract thieves. Change the PIN codes on your debit and credit cards. Keep a cash reserve on hand in case any payments to you are delayed. Try not to sign any contracts or make any major purchases until after the retrograde period ends.

You may have to stand up for your beliefs sometime the 11$^{th}$ of this month. Your usual long-suffering patience will be pushed to the brink by someone's offensive remarks. The source of these comments is likely to be someone you care about. Perhaps a close family member or longtime friend will unthinkingly denigrate your religion, your politics or malign some cherished ideal. The comment will feel enough like an insult that you can't let it slide. Resist the urge to lower your head and charge with your all horns forward. If you make that mistake, people will take note only of your rage, not of the content of your remarks. Take a few breaths before speaking or shooting off an angry e-mail retort. Gather your thoughts so that you express your opinions clearly and eloquently. Defend yourself gently.

Guard against an inclination to excess toward the end of June. You may feel tempted to overindulge in either food or drink. Bulls do tend to have a keen appreciation for culinary pleasures. But you could face negative consequences if you overdo it now. This isn't a matter of weight but of health. You could harm your heart, your liver or your pancreas.

## TAURUS July 2014

A close friend who aided you in a time of need may try to abuse your gratitude the first week of this month. He or she did generously help you in the past. Now this person will come to you asking for something entirely unreasonable. In fact, it may be less of a request than an imperious command. Just because they gave you a leg up some years ago, do not feel beholden and let this individual take advantage of you. Make it clear that you deeply appreciate the assistance he or she provided previously. At the same time, let her or him know that it is highly inappropriate to behave as though they owned you. He or she cannot summarily demand your first-born or the loan of your kidney. If he or she does not accept a more reasonable form of re-payment that you may propose, sever ties.

It may be a good idea to burglar-proof your home this month. There is a definite possibility you could be the victim of a break-in around the 15th. Replace any non-functioning locks on doors or windows. If any doors have only a flimsy lock, augment it with a secure deadbolt. Pay close attention especially to any means of entry to your basement, attic or back door. If you can afford it, it may be worthwhile to invest in a home security system.

At month's end, you may have to deal with that unreasonable friend's badmouthing of you. Out of nowhere, people will begin to shun you. Of course they are misguided or confused in some way. It is most likely because you refused to cave in to the demands of your high-handed former friend and they went and complained to all your mutual acquaintances of your miserliness. You can tell your side of the story to most of the people and be believed. But there will be some who will prefer to believe the other guy. Don't insist. The more you do, the more it sounds as though you might be guilty as charged. Time will show that bully up for who they really are and you will recover most of your temporarily lost friendships.

## TAURUS August 2014

A so-called friend has been verbally sniping at you for months. They make their barbed comments under the guise of "jokes." You have tried to give this person the benefit of the doubt. But lately, you have become certain this rank nastiness is deliberate. The other people in the group fail to see through this individual's charming facade of geniality. At a gathering sometime between the 6th and the 11th, the elephant works loose his tether in the drawing room and matters come to a head. You know you cannot put up with this behavior any longer. You may explode. Probably do you a lot of good to, once and for all, just evict this sagging "friendship" from your life.

But how? Usually your instinct to address problems honestly and openly serves you well. But this time the person in question will no doubt lie and maintain that the problem is in your head. Bringing in a third party peacemaker/mediator may only aggravate the situation. Instead of either of these approaches, try another tack. Next time this individual deals out a snarky remark, widen your eyes in surprise and say something along the lines of, "It takes one to know one." or "Sticks and stones..." and leave it at that. Unless you are forced by circumstance to tolerate this person's presence in your life, ditch them. If it's a relative or friend's significant other or workmate, you will want to keep your distance and feign indifference. Indifference is your best weapon here.

A celebration with friends—perhaps a birthday party for a Leo pal—could get out of hand around the 18th of this month. The negative consequences of too much of a good thing could come in a variety of forms. You and your group might be ejected from a restaurant or bar for being too boisterous. If you celebrate at someone's home, a neighbor might summon the police complaining of loud music. One or more of your friends may end up on their knees puking in the toilet. Or... after hours of imbibing, the bar bill could be higher than anticipated, necessitating a scramble for funds. Make every effort to be the responsible one - the designated driver. Stick to just one drink. Then switch to juice or soda. Bring some extra cash to cover any unanticipated expense. Most importantly, offer rides home to those too inebriated to take the wheel.

**TAURUS September 2014**

For a while now, you have been stalking an ex-lover on Facebook. Almost every day, you read the updates he or she posts. You check out the articles, music, TV shows and movies your former lover recommends to their Facebook friends. You also regularly check out the Facebook page of this person's current partner. You don't necessarily want to get back with them. But you enjoy the sense of power that comes from knowing what they're up to. There's a strong chance your behavior will be exposed sometime around September 6th. This might relate to a change in Facebook policies. Or you could run into your ex in person who will know (through a mutual acquaintance perhaps?) what you have been up to. Make your apologies sound sincere. And cease the secret harassment as well.

A flirtation around the 15th of this month could take you by surprise. You may fail at first to detect the amorous intentions of someone who strikes up a conversation with you. Your slowness to put two and two together could stem from the fact that this new love interest lies outside your usual sexual hunting grounds. Moreover, he or she may be significantly older or younger than you. Or this guy or woman could be of a different gender than you normally date. Beyond your initial astonishment, gauge what your visible reaction should be. If you are really not interested and they are not unduly aggressive, turn them down gently. No need to explain your reasons for rejecting their overtures. That might only hurt feelings.

Toward the end of this month, you may have to comfort a friend for the loss of a beloved animal companion. Do not underestimate the depth of your pal's grief. If you live with animals yourself, you realize how strong this bond can be. Offer sympathy. Give your chum some time to talk about the deceased furry or feathered friend. Share any of your own positive memories of this animal as you would at the funeral of person. After this drama, at month's end you may experience some weather-related property damage. If you hear that a storm is on the way, batten the hatches. Stay home. If requested to evacuate, take only the most precious small items with you.

**TAURUS October 2014**

The third and last Mercury retrograde period of 2014 starts on the 4th of this month. For Taureans, this particular retrograde is likely to affect communications related to health. If you have an appointment with your doctor or dentist between October 4th and the 25th, call to confirm before heading to the clinic. Allow extra time to travel to the clinic. Delays are likely. Go over any health instructions, such as prescription directions, very carefully. Unless there is an emergency, avoid scheduling surgery or other procedures until next month.

Around the 16th of October, you could find yourself in an awkward situation. You might catch one of your co-workers engaged in some highly inappropriate behavior at the office. Maybe you discover this person using company property for job-hunting purposes. Or you walk into the co-worker's office while they are away from their desk, only to glimpse a vivid porno image on their computer screen. For the moment, I suggest keeping mum about any such incidents. The indiscretion may have been a one time lapse on this person's part. If not, then - soon enough - you will notice something else a bit devious or about this character. Will his or her misbehavior eventually come to your boss's attention? Let's hope so. Tattletale is not a flattering role to play.

Your partner may make an announcement which startles or even shocks you. This declaration will have an impact on the future of your relationship. It could be that he or she wants to move across country to seek another job or further an education. Or the news could be related in some way to reproductive plans. If the two of you were formerly on the same page about whether to have kids and now they have had a change of heart, you could be devastated. Unfortunately, there is also a slight possibility your sweetie's news involves an interloping third party.

Stunning news aside, the month of October for you personally will be positive. You can make progress with any negotiations you are engaged in. You will hatch many a new idea and become enthused and excited about potential new projects. You will definitely receive good news regarding a property or legacy which has long been pending.

**TAURUS November 2014**

Between the 2nd and the 8th, the penny drops. You finally put your finger on the thing that has been bothering you. All of a sudden you realize that a friend or family member has developed an unusual addiction. This is not about substance abuse but rather it involves some form of odd behavior. It may be compulsive shopping. Or perhaps this person is plotting a 3rd or 4th nose job. Although you will clearly see the pitfalls of this type of dependency, your friend or relative may not be ready to see it the same way. Trying to force someone to let go of addictive behavior before that person is ready usually backfires. For now, say nothing. Wait until your friend offers an opening. Avoid indulging your friend's addiction. Change the subject when they drag out recent purchases to show off or boast of their many visits to a newer, more trendy plastic surgeon. When next your friend mentions feeling depressed or anxious, encourage them to see a therapist. The doctor knows best and has seen many addictions like this one before. They can help. As you are not a professional, you probably cannot.

An offhand comment someone makes about your appearance may hurt your feelings at first. Try not to become resentful. There may be a kernel of truth in that person's tactless remark. It could be time to re-think the way you present yourself to the world. Venus, the ancient goddess of beauty, gives her name to the ruling planet of your sign. Many Taureans have a rather unbalanced relationship with Venus, veering to one extreme or the other. Make a resolution. Ditch the flip flops for some more attractive footwear. Lose weight if you should. Get fit. Then wear jeans that hug where they should and don't display holes and tears. Have your hair styled. Your soggy morale will soon boost itself.

Accidents do happen. Someone in your immediate entourage will be involved in a mishap of some sort. Whatever kind of accident it is, it won't be fatal. But the fact it happened will put you on alert. Is the person too old or too inebriated or too deranged to be driving? Should this or that chap or woman be put on notice because he/she can no longer follow the directives necessary to do their job right? Watch them closely and monitor progress. If they are prone to accidents, reveal your fears and see if you can help them to alter their behavior to suit their state of mind.

### TAURUS December 2014

Years of hard work finally pay off for you as December begins. Your professional accomplishments receive some sort of public recognition. A magazine or journal may feature an article about you. Or you could receive some sort of award. Enjoy the compliments and praise that are being showered upon you now. Take some time to bask in the glow of the spotlight.

It is especially important to demonstrate your generosity at times like these. Do not pinch pennies when selecting holiday gifts for family and friends. Let them associate your half hour of fame with you displaying largesse. You have a talent for gift-giving when you put your mind to it. Draw on this skill now. Do not buy the same item in bulk and present it to everyone. Choose gifts which suit the unique interests and needs of each individual in your circle.

A holiday celebration around the 17$^{th}$ may be marred by a minor injury. It is more likely to be one of your friends or family members experiencing a cut or bruise than you or your partner. Make sure you have a well-stocked first aid kit both at home and in your car. If there's a lot of bleeding, chuck the person in the car and hie them to the ER.

Try to take some time off from work toward the end of the month. You and your partner need to have some crucial discussions. It will be easier to have these talks when you both feel relaxed. Ideally, you should not have to squeeze these colloquies in between office meetings. Your relationship may reach a turning point as a result of these talks. It may be a breakthrough into deeper intimacy. Or there is a distinct possibility that your relationship has run its course. Either way, your life enters a phase of alteration as 2014 ends. Take it in stride. There are better times ahead.

### TAURUS January 2015

You and your partner may be managing the logistics of a major life change in early January. Whether you are preparing for a happy event, or fine-tuning the specifics of some type of ending, the two of you will have to confer and agree on many details. Even if this is a positive transition, you may find managing all the minutiae rather stressful.

Maintain your sense of equilibrium through physical movement classes (yoga, Pilates, tai chi) as well as meditation. Watch what you eat. Taureans often have a damaging tendency to graze throughout the day. This habit can wreak havoc with your digestion. It can also disturb your sleep patterns. Especially avoid late-night snacking. Nobody can sleep well while digesting. It is also wise to put away your work at least an hour before bedtime. Otherwise your mind will remain in overdrive and won't quiet down when you need it to be rested in order to fall asleep. Treat yourself to massages as frequently as your budget permits.

If you are not careful at a social event around the 18th, you may find yourself in ridicule mode. You Taureans tend to have a strong penchant for blatant honesty. Please remember that, in some circumstances, this usually admirable trait can cause you to appear rude and out of line. Failure to weigh your words at this gathering could have a negative effect on several of your relationships. Unless you want your toes to tickle your tonsils, avoid making quick, off-the-cuff, snarky comments. Any attempts at biting humor are likely to fall flat at this time as well. Instead of being perceived as witty, your words may be seen as boorish and crude.

The end of the Year of the Horse may bring you an excellent opportunity for investment. Move with your usual slow deliberation. Do your due diligence. Research the companies and individuals involved carefully. Hold your Horses. Invest wisely. There is an excellent chance of your placement paying off handsomely in May of 2015.

# GEMINI 2014

## OVERVIEW FOR THE WOOD HORSE YEAR

*Gregarious Gemini,*

*You Geminis thrive on communication. Connecting with others is what you are about. The Wood Horse year will certainly feature an abundance of rich messages. Make sure you don't run out of coffee or Red Bull because this is bound to be a high-energy year requiring your most scintillating, witty remarks be filtered through your highest intelligence. In this Horse year, you will make at least two new acquaintances who will become key figures in your life - both on a personal and a professional level. 2014 will also offer you several opportunities for growth and expansion. Some of this process will involve the sort of changes which advance you in the world's eye. If you play your cards right and use subtle strategy, you should emerge from the shadow of other's misconceptions about you.*

*However some of your development this year will be of the less comfortable inner sort as you arrive at new realizations about who you really are. Rather than resenting these unfamiliar (and rather uncomfortable) perceptions, think of yourself as a diamond being polished by the cosmos. You will come out improved and more independent. Less concerned about the impression you make than about how you feel inside. Major opportunities for change may come disguised as love affairs or investment opportunities or even as illness (not necessarily your own). Maintain your balance by shifting flexibly in and out of events beyond your control. The ease and sang froid with which you endure these changes will draw more caring people into your circle and enrich your effect on the world at large. sw*

—————— *ᴇ ᴄＥ ᴄＥ* ——————

## THE CHINESE YEAR AHEAD

### GEMINI 2014

### GEMINI February 2014

The beginning of this month is a good time to reveal that deep, dark secret which has been causing you to smile mysteriously - like the Mona Lisa. Everyone will be surprised to discover that as much as you love to jabber, you are capable of keeping a tight lock on certain crucial facts. Just because you excel at casual conversation doesn't mean you lack hidden depth. Silly isn't it how others always underestimate you? Enjoy the admiration and possible envy you will excite after the big revelation.

A new partner may enter your life shortly after Valentine's Day. This person will have the confidence and style necessary to capture your attention. You may find yourself in a whirlwind romance. Flirtation (your forte) could escalate very quickly into physical passion. Drama and excitement will characterize your romance. All eyes will be drawn to the two of you. To onlookers, the two of you will seem like a pair of eagles mating in flight. Although he or she provides the intensity you crave, this new partner also complements you in many ways. Despite your respective psychological and physical baggage, the two of you will fit neatly into each other's lives. The one drawback may be that you sometimes quarrel over small matters such as whose turn it is to tidy up the kitchen or take out the trash.

There may also be thorny issues if either of you began the Year of the Horse with loose ends from a previous relationship.

The former lover or spouse may pepper you with a barrage of hang-up phone calls, enigmatic e-mails, searingly nasty texts and even visits! This individual may also send unpleasant messages through mutual friends. If you and your previous significant other still share some financial assets, there could be some sinuous hassles about money. If you share parenting responsibilities, prepare to face battles related to custody or support. It's even possible this clingy (read jealous) person might engage in some stalker-like behavior. If possible, park your car indoors at night and lock your gates. There is evidence of possible vandalism.

One extra note of caution: Mercury goes retrograde from the 6th through the 28th of this month. Expect delays, missed as well as mixed messages and minor glitches of all sorts related to travel and communications. When electronics break down during this Mercury retrograde, don't be surprised.

## GEMINI March 2014

At work, you could gain a powerful new ally around the 5th of the month. This person truly admires your versatility and hard work. Other supervisors may feel uneasy around your obvious superiority. Some of them may even characterize you as insubordinate. Your new mentor especially appreciates your sense of humor. They realize it is your way of alleviating workplace tension. Under his or her protection, you gain more freedom to handle projects in your own unique manner.

Complications with that former partner of yours are likely to persist or even intensify in March. You may need to bring in a third party to mediate. Maintain strong boundaries. Be fair, but do protect your interests. Don't feel guilty about being happier now than when you were with the former lover. At times, you may feel tempted to use the surgical steel side of your tongue. Try to resist this inclination. Above all, remain courteous. Any show of ire on your part will be like throwing gasoline on embers. Steer clear of bringing in the authorities by handling this whole matter with velvet gloves.

Your new partner wants you to participate in a group related to her/his interests. Could be anything from tango to line dancing to bungee jumping. Although you find your partner irresistible, you do not share the same enthusiasm for their hobby. You may also find the people he/she mingles with related to this interest to be boring or even irritating. Quarreling about it will only create tension in your romance. Try to compromise with your partner. Agree to accompany them to occasional group events. But suggest also that the two of you do not have to be joined at the hip at all times. If your new lover is the clingy type, you will have to make quite clear that you require alone time in order to re-stoke your inner furnaces and regain stability. In the long run, your relationship will remain healthier if the two of you spend some time apart.

## GEMINI April 2014

With the protection of your new mentor at work, your productivity increases dramatically. You turn in stellar assignments because you know they will receive the praise they deserve. Your detractors at the office are silenced for the moment. Between the excellence of your work and your powerful ally, they have been rendered mute. Avoid however any hint of gloating about this triumph. Instead, seize this opportunity to mend fences. Try now to create pleasant or at least functional workplace relationships. A calm and forgiving demeanor on your part speaks well of your ability to successfully manage your newfound pride.

You and your partner continue to revel in each other's company. Around the 12th, you attend a party together. Your friends comment that the two of you can't seem to keep your hands off each other. You sometimes finish each other's sentences. You may decide around the 3rd week of the month to celebrate your romance in some way. Possibly you purchase jewelry symbolic of your union or get matching tattoos. If choosing a tattoo, select something you will want your kids to admire and that you will still want to see on your wrinkly skin when you are 80.

An old family drama rears its head in some way around the 24th. Perhaps you receive a phone call from one of your parents or a sibling. Or you may simply be reminded of this past situation by looking through old photo albums. Maybe someone connected with that period of time is briefly in the news. At any rate, this unfortunate episode haunts you and occupies too great a place in your thoughts.

You may hesitate at first to share this concern with your lover. You like to appear bright and sparkling. None the less you are anxious about the past. If you want the relationship to deepen and last, confide in him/her. If you cannot each reveal your vulnerability to the other, the relationship may not survive. Intimacy means just that. No secrets. No holds barred.

## GEMINI May 2014

You receive an unexpected opportunity to draw on an untapped talent sometime around May 6th. Perhaps a friend asks you to use your photography talents to make them look lovely for a dating site profile. Or they choose you to write them a letter or an ad for that dating site. Or someone sees the cute cap you knitted for a friend's baby and asks if you want to sell your creations at their store. Maybe your dance teacher asks you to substitute teach a class when she goes out of town. This opportunity provides an opening to use another one of your many diverse skills to create a sideline job. Go ahead and pursue this line of thinking. Geminis tend to be happiest when they have a finger in many moneymaking pies.

You and your partner still feel a strong current of attraction. However you also bicker more frequently about those minor matters. Try having a wordless day together to decrease these little quarrels. This may seem like a foreign idea at first to someone as verbal as you. But often words can serve as kindling for the fires of anger. Spend some silent time, communicating solely through eye contact and touch. This unusual method may really help you and your honey create a more peaceful ambience between you.

Toward the end of the month, your attention scatters. You run the risk of making errors at work. You could even get into an accident while driving. Use the same approach you used to soothe matters with your partner. Reduce words to a minimum. Words are the fuel of Gemini's energy. Yet, at the same, an excess of words can find them in a tangle of anxiety. In your office or car, listen to music without lyrics, perhaps classical or jazz. If you have not already learned the rudiments of meditation, try an introductory class now. Breathe deeply. Take some time to disconnect from that discombobulated internal monologue of opinions, plans and memories you carry around. Instead, focus on the simple rhythm of inhalation and exhalation. Once you have learned how to soothe the savage flood of thoughts streaming through your mind, you will own the perfect tool for maintaining mental harmony.

## GEMINI June 2014

On the 7th of this month, Mercury goes retrograde. Since Mercury rules your sign, Gemini mine, these periods tend to be especially trying for you. Try to exercise patience (not your favorite toy. I know). Don't sign any contracts. And wait until after Mercury goes direct on July 1 to undergo any medical procedures which can wait.

The sun is in your sign for most of the month. You will feel supercharged. You and your partner spend hours discussing ideas for the future. You may take a couple of small trips during this period. On these excursions, you acquire any number of small souvenirs, gifts for each other as well as for friends. Try to stick to items with more than comical value. Souvenirs should serve as reminders of your travels which bring more than a smile to the countenances of your friends whom you gift with these remembrances.

There's a possibility you'll put your foot in your mouth around the 10th of this month. You may express a tactless opinion on your Facebook page. Or one of your joking remarks at the office sounds like a personal insult to one or your co-workers. Please recall that not everyone forgives and forgets easily. A quick off-the-cuff comment could cause someone (a sensitive Pisces or a vengeful Scorpio) to hold a grudge longer than an elephant's lifetime. Not everyone shares your jaunty sense of humor. Take additional care in your choice of words around this time. Keep in mind the importance of timing. Some biting comments are best spoken in private to just one close confidant.

Put more energy into that sideline project or business of yours. Laying the groundwork now could lead to hefty profits later on in the year. Build a savvy network of connections who can help you with this project. And don't spend all your time just talking about it. Sometimes Gemini has more hat than horse. Create something which will showcase your talent and improve your image.

Around the 18th-24th, something small has the potential to cause you pain. Perhaps you get a spider bite. Or you might step on a tack while walking barefoot. You might chip a tooth by biting down too hard on a popcorn kernel. Nothing to become alarmed about. This accident shouldn't turn into a major health event. But do exercise a little extra care. Make sure you have a well-stocked first aid kit both at home and in your car. Make sure your health insurance policy is up-to-date. Read that annoying fine print.

## GEMINI July 2014

Some element of either your past or your partner's may come back and cause trouble for the two of you as July begins. It may be that the obnoxious ex has been spreading gossip. Or if one of you has unpaid debts, you may find your household getting a call from a collection agent. If either of you ever did anything illegal, you may discover there's a tired old warrant out for your arrest. This matter will take some time to sort out. You may have to seek the help of an attorney or some other expert. Rash or shady actions could have serious consequences for you right now. Behave soberly and honestly in the face of this new wrinkle.

If you and your partner have been living in each other's pockets, spend some time apart. Connect with an old friend, making plans to get together at a favorite restaurant or pub. Visit him/her without your partner. Also if you have ignored interests of yours that your partner does not share, re-discover these with old pals or cronies. The symbol for your sign is the twins. You sometimes have a tendency to become conjoined as twins when you fall in love. Then your differences can become grating. Keep the romance blazing in your love life by vowing to pursue certain activities separately.

Around the 24th, someone unexpectedly decides to play fairy godmother to you. Result? An unexpected influx of cash makes more luxury feasible. You won't have enough to trade in your cozy abode for a McMansion. But it may be enough to plan a special trip or major purchase for you and your sweetie. Plan the big getaway for next month. The stars will be in perfect position to smile on any journey you take in September. Try to visit a place neither of you has ever been before. Exploring a new place together creates a special bond.

## GEMINI August 2014

You might have a disturbing dream - more like a nightmare - in early August. The zany events and symbols in this dream will seem to hint at disturbing future events. Do not let this upset you. Write the dream down, including as many details as you can remember. Don't try to interpret it right away. Wait at least two weeks. Then go back and review what you wrote down. Perhaps the images that seemed to relate to death or upheaval were only pointing to approaching changes? Those two weeks you let go by- without all the emotional turmoil brought on by the dream itself - will allow you to see the whole event objectively.

Two co-workers or friends seek to draw you into their conflict sometime around the 16th and the 20th. Although you may have a strong opinion about this tussle, you had better remain disengaged. You believe one person is right. Of course you are biased. You like one of the people more than the other. There are, however, aspects of this contentious situation you cannot see. Avoid playing the role of second in their duel. If the conflict persists, the two antagonists might seriously harm each other. If you are perceived as taking a side, you too could become a target. No use trying to play peacemaker. Stay your hand. Butt out.

If you take that trip this month, it will go swimmingly. You and your partner feel as if you are visiting a place of enchantment. Because of this harmonious experience, the two of you fall even more deeply in love. You may even be inspired by this journey to work together on a creative project. Perhaps you will document your trip in words and photos. Or you could sell your lovely story to a travel magazine. You might conceive an idea for a children's book which one of you writes and the other illustrates. If you want to experience the full magic of this trip, I have one warning for you. You may have multiple opportunities to flirt with people while on vacation. No matter how attractive they are, keep your eyes solely on your partner.

## GEMINI September 2014

A neighbor, friend or sibling comes to you with a an irksome complaint the first week of the month. Apparently, some habitual action of yours offends them. Perhaps you park your car too close to theirs. You forget to hold the door for your elders. You eat too fast, smack your lips loudly and crush your napkin into a messy ball after a meal. Rather than dismissing these criticisms out of hand, listen up. If you do, you will hear between the lines. All the plaintiff really wants is for you to acknowledge their concerns. Or maybe they want your undivided attention focused on them. Once you understand that their real need is for your company, you can readily accommodate them.

The middle of September sees you tempted to overindulge in some way. It may seem innocent and harmless at the time. However, your luck is a bit precarious right now. One more drink before heading home could lead to a ticket for drunk driving or even cause a stupid accident. A rich dessert may trigger a previously unsuspected health problem. If you take a puff of something illegal, you may encounter a most inconvenient police officer. Best to live somewhat abstemiously for now.

Sometime around the 20th, you feel a strong urge to change your appearance. Perhaps you notice that the baggy pants or bright yellow handbag which looked so chic last year has become passé. The accessory itself may be outdated. Or you observe that some of your clothes have acquired visible indelible stains. Go shopping with your partner or a close friend. Find something new and trendy to accent your appearance.

Toward the end of the month, your mentor may offer you an exciting new project. This honor may, however, come at a cost. You will have to sacrifice a big chunk of free time to take it on. This will mean spending fewer hours with your significant other and giving up leisure time spent on hobbies or other part-time activities. If you accept this offer, you will have to commit to long work hours for several months. Saying "no" may mean your influential ally thinks you no longer want their help. If you say "yes" you will necessarily put a damper on everything from romance to your woodworking and book club activities. Ponder your decision carefully. But be aware that September is a favorable for enhancing your career possibilities. My advice? Go for the gold.

## GEMINI October 2014

Another (thankfully the last for the this year) Mercury retrograde period begins on the 4th of this month and lasts until the 25th. You know the drill: postpone contracts, major decisions, big purchases and surgery. Back up your computer files. Prepare to experience a few extra delays and hassles.

If you said yes to that big project, you could find yourself neck deep in work as October begins. Since most Geminis prefer multiple short sprints of work to marathon sessions of toil, the long hours may try your patience. Your partner is adjusting, in his or her own way, to your increased office hours. She/he may be spending more time with that group of friends you dislike. In fact, there's a strong possibility your sweetie will plunge zealously into a project with this group. This seems like competition and could make you a tad jealous. Particularly since there is that one individual in the group who is far too covetous of your partner's charms.

Unexpectedly, your jealousy takes another direction. There is a new person in your office. Your mentor appears to be taking this individual under his/her wing as a protégée. Now you not only need worry about your lover being kidnapped; you are wondering if this newcomer is slated to receive more of your mentor's favors than you are. Redouble your efforts on the big project. Whenever you see your benefactor, take extra care to be charming. Resist the temptation to say anything derogatory about the junior staff member. In fact, do quite the opposite. You will see by month's end. It's likely you will have been fretting over nothing.

You may run into some trouble with your vehicle in mid-October. It's very possible this is something serious (read expensive). Weigh your options. It may be wiser, in the long run, to invest in a new vehicle rather than pouring money into your current car. Consider a more environmentally-friendly vehicle. A hybrid car does carry a somewhat higher initial price-tag. But you will save money on gas.

Steer clear of people and situations which usually lead to gossip this month. Even if you don't think the people you're talking know those you are mocking, you may face consequences down the line. There are invisible connections between people in different spheres of your life. If you seem to cast aspersions on someone, your own reputation may suffer.

## GEMINI November 2014

You could find yourself caught between a rock and a hard place as November begins. None of your options will be too attractive. You want to get a dog, but your apartment complex forbids pets. Your work is so engrossing you don't have enough time to get your hair cut or coiffed. Your parents need attention, but one of your kids is going through a bad spell. You don't know which foot to dance on first. Do the best you can by explaining to one and all. You may, however, be without persuasive powers in this situation and have to use a bit of judicious misdirection to protect yourself. This dilemma will definitely prove to be a case of choosing between the lesser of two evils. Read a few trickster folktales such as that of Br'er Rabbit and the Briar Patch for inspiration on how to deal with such tricky problems.

Someone very close to you faces a serious health challenge around November 12th. You may be obliged to drive this person to the hospital for a series of tests. The results of those tests may be inconclusive. Then, the doctors could block or summarily dismiss your well-founded concerns about this person's health. They may refuse to discuss the situation with you. Stand your ground with both the patient and their doctors. If necessary and financially tenable, demand a second opinion.

You and your partner may lose some harmony around 21$^{st}$ of the month. An outside event reveals that what seemed like minor differences of opinion are actually gaping chasms between your ideals and his/hers. You will both feel shaken. You may be tempted to minimize and/or even deny this problem. Whatever you do, there is a thorny discussion in the making. The longer you postpone it, the bigger the potential blow-up. If you can't talk to each other without exploding, try couples therapy. One or two sessions may clear up years of misapprehension.

Toward the end of the month, an overheard conversation surprises you. You learn that someone you thought was among your detractors actually admires you. This casts an entirely new light on their words and behavior. You realize you made some hasty and inaccurate assumptions. Between this new information and the major alterations going on between you and your partner, you will become painfully aware that your emotional tectonic plates are shifting.

## GEMINI December 2014

You're not usually known for your forbearance. But this month the universe decides to give you a crash course in that virtue. Family members of different generations, some older and some younger, will test you with their needs. You realize they are not being deliberately selfish or demanding. Their situations simply have different priorities from yours. You may also have to help people several decades apart from each other in age to understand each other better. You can use humor to do this. So long as you remain sensitive to people's different needs, you can guide a potentially explosive situation to a positive conclusion. Be specific and clear about the solutions. Do not be tempted to fall back into glib generalizations.

A newly-revealed admirer may surprise you with an invitation or even a gift around the 17$^{th}$ of the month. Although you love flirtation and intrigue, consider the ramifications. If you want to end things with your current partner, do so before beginning the new relationship. Avoid the temptation to test drive the new person before the separation. Handle the break-up with compassion and dignity. On the other hand, if you want to continue with your present sweetie, gently discourage the new suitor.

With the holidays right around the corner, you could discover that some home repairs and decorating improvements are essential. No way to postpone them. You may have to downsize your plans for celebrating. A leaky roof won't wait. Nor will dingy walls or buckling floorboards. Tighten your belt. Prepare to forgo a few luxuries. Shop at the right stores for quality merchandise at lower than low prices.

At a New Year's party, you may meet someone who can help you with that sideline project. This person's talents may aid your potential new business become highly profitable. However, you will have to exercise keen powers of observation to spot this potential associate. He or she is a bit shy and retiring. Make sure you mingle with everyone at the gathering - even the apparent wallflowers. This quiet character is a treasure well worth seeking out.

## GEMINI January 2015

Your life may feel like it's on a slippery slope as 2015 commences. Change is the only constant. Unfortunately, many of these changes do not seem to be of your choosing. Step back and look at the situation in a detached manner. Perceive the ways in which your past actions could have set these unwanted changes in motion. In a way, you have been unconsciously emulating a speed demon - your personal version of the Road Runner. Slow the pace. Then make haste to observe your own input where the major shifts are taking place. No matter the schisms, you are (unwittingly perhaps) partially responsible.

The obstacles you encounter this month arrive accompanied by hidden opportunities. If you only focus on the slamming doors, you will miss the open windows of opportunity. Those windows, by the way, may be on an entirely different wall than the one you're staring at. Chat up the new acquaintance you made at the New Year's party. They may be able to assist you in spotting those hitherto invisible open windows.

Once you crawl through the right window (and it may be a tight fit), everything changes for the better. This is likely to occur just before the end of the Year of the Horse on February 18th. Suddenly, opportunities and invitations abound. Friends whom you thought had dumped you call and invite you to dinner. Colleagues who failed to return your calls or e-mails suddenly want your input on new projects. There is a long list of people wanting to friend you on Facebook. Most of them are friends of friends, distant acquaintances and even total strangers who have heard the growing buzz about your breakthrough project.

The one fly in the ointment is that you could experience an embarrassing health problem around this time. This is something you will want to keep confidential. Share the information only with one or two close confidants whom you absolutely trust. This ailment may take a while to resolve, but it won't be anything too serious.

# CANCER 2014

## OVERVIEW FOR THE WOOD HORSE YEAR

*Comfy Cancer,*

*Take a deep breath, Cancer. The Year of the Wood Horse is riding in to both challenge and reward you. Unless you dare venture beyond your comfort zone, 2014 could prove to be a disappointment for your kind. Crabs, the animals which symbolize your sign periodically molt and renew their shells. During this process of shedding and re-growing their shells, there is a period when Crabs go all soft and naked. Cancer people do likewise. They encourage growth by disappearing for a time into either to a depression, a long silence or a period of melancholy. The beginning of the year will be one of retreat and vulnerability. Until you get your new shell built and are ready to take on the labor necessary to survive in the work-crazed Horse environment, I advise you to sit tight.*

*Stay home and pickle beets or grow pot, embroider patchwork quilts and complete all the handyman/woman projects you have been neglecting. Consider the first half this year a period of growth. A time to plot your future and eliminate the pain of the past. This year will demand that you learn how to value adventure over security. Timidity and playing it safe will deprive you of the best that this year has to offer you. So after July, to best reap the benefits of this Horse year, become more adept at taking creative risks, forming new friendships and acting spontaneously instead of stodgily waiting for the safe moment to pounce. sw*

———— ❦ ❦ ❦ ————

## THE CHINESE YEAR AHEAD

## CANCER 2014

### CANCER February 2014

The beginning of the Year of the Horse offers an opening for frank discussion. Broach that relationship issue that has been nagging at you. Choose your timing carefully—not when either of you is driving or chopping vegetables! Eye contact is important in this kind of conversation. State your concerns calmly and unemotionally. No recriminations or accusations. Allow an opening for him/her to speak. Listen attentively to their words. Don't rehearse what you're going to say next while pretending to pay attention to them. Remember the goal is to work things out, not to "win" or prove that you're "right." These kind of serious, re-thinking things discussions are perfect for Mercury retrograde periods like the one taking place this month from the 6th until the 28th. However, Mercury retrograde is a dicey time to make any new commitments or undergo elective surgery. Electronics too are affected by Mercury when that planet decides to appear to go backwards.

Around the 17th someone may approach you with a business proposition. Be more cautious then enthusiastic. There's a good chance their proposal is a pyramid scheme or some other dressed-up scam. The person who comes to you may be a victim rather than a con artist though. Don't condemn them. Don't even make negative comments on the venture. They may be in too deep to want to see the truth. Denial is a powerful state of mind and a fearsome hedge against reality. Even your kindly-meant advice may be viewed as meddlesome interference.

You sense change is in the air at work. No one has made any official announcements yet but something is definitely shifting. Don't slack off now. Even if higher-ups appear to be preoccupied, notes are being taken of who handles things well and who doesn't. Quietly, on your own time (and your own computer), brush off your résumé. Just in case.

A small windfall comes your way toward the end of the month. You may want to apply it to updating your appearance. Reinvent yourself. Get a new haircut from someone other than your usual stylist. Buy some clothes with a bit more flair than the rest of your wardrobe. Nothing *outré* —you're not trying to look like Lady Gaga. Be careful to make sure your new appearance doesn't age you. Highlight your best points. Legs? Show them off. Slouching shoulders? Find jackets which improve the shape. Don't wear running shoes with silk shirts. Avoid sporting flip flops at elegant dinner parties.

## CANCER March 2014

Travel beckons you and you may feel the urge to be uncharacteristically impulsive. Go ahead. This is a great time for a whirlwind trip. A romantic weekend away with your partner will help dispel any stress you may feel. If you're currently between partners, a trip to a lively destination either solo or with a couple of pals may yield an intriguing encounter.

Unattached Cancers who can't find the time or funds for a mini-vacation will want to accept every social opportunity that comes their way. The first three weeks of March offer a potential gold mine of romantic possibilities for you! But staying at home alone reading a book will limit your opportunities. Your new sweetie is unlikely to fall through your roof carrying a pizza and a DVD. Go out and meet her/him! This is where that new haircut or outfit from last month helps out. The confidence it gives you helps attract more admirers.

If you retreat into your shell this month, Cancer, you also run the risk of being seen as selfish and ungrateful. Make the phrase "thank you" your March mantra. Use it as often as possible. Let everyone from the grocery store "bagger" to your sister-in-law hear these words from you. Elaborating on your thanks with compliments ensures others see you for the sensitive and kind soul you really are. You often mean to be more cheerful. But you tend to forget the smile imperative.

Someone who has been especially helpful to you needs more than just a thank-you. Plan a fun outing for this person or purchase a thoughtful gift for them. The week of 22nd offers a magnificent opportunity for telling someone how much you value them. During this period, any generous or kind actions of yours resonates more strongly. If you want to undo any misconceptions others have about you, this is the time to show your real worth.

## CANCER April 2014

Around the 4th-8th, you may discover you have uninvited visitors of the non-human variety milling about in your home. Probably not poltergeists, vampires or zombies. I am guessing some kind of wildlife decides to make its abode in your attic or basement. Unless you want to provide housing for squirrels, bats, raccoons or snakes, call in an expert to evict them.

Nature may affect you in another way this month as well. Either your home or your vehicle may bear the brunt of a weather event. It could be a tree branch crashing onto your car during a big storm. Or if you live near a body of water, a torrential rainfall could cause it to overflow into your basement and even to invade your ground floor. Make sure your home and auto insurance policies are up-to-date and will cover any and all damage.

These homeowner headaches can contribute to a lot of stress. After taking care of practical matters, steal some time to nurture yourself. Schedule a massage. Treat yourself to a fabulously decadent gourmet chocolate treat (just one!). Get together with your closest confidant for a long heart-to-heart talk. Watch your favorite old movie again. Maybe buy yourself some elegant new sheets and pillowcases to make bedtime feel more luxurious.

Toward the end of the month, your health needs attention. It may be that you are just out of balance. Unless the symptoms seem urgent, I advise looking into natural remedies. Read up on herbal treatments. You may even want to think about medicinal herbs you can plant in your garden. You can also benefit from a visit to a holistic health practitioner such as a chiropractor, acupuncturist or specialist in Ayurvedic medicine. If you haven't already tried a movement practice such as yoga or tai chi, this is a propitious time to begin. Even if you already do strenuous exercise, yoga, martial arts and tai chi offer something deeper which will quiet the mind and balance your body's energies.

### CANCER May 2014

You make a new friend sometime in the first half of May. I know how special old friends and family are to you, Cancer. But do take the time to develop this new friendship. Look past surface differences to see the potential for a deep and warm, although platonic, connection of two hearts here. This individual may be able to offer you helpful advice, enabling you to see your way clear of a situation which has been troubling and even hindering your progress for some time. Listen to and heed the advice of your unfamiliar new crony.

This is also a red-hot month for you romantically speaking. If you bought those new sheets and pillows last month, you and your partner will get a lot of use out of them now. Don't over-schedule yourself for weekends as you and your honey will want to have long, lingering sessions in bed. You'll intersperse bouts of passionate lovemaking with long, soul-to-soul conversations— followed perhaps by a playful session in the shower. (I know how you Cancers adore water!) If you have young children living with you, see if a relative or close family friend can take care of them for a weekend mid-month. It's important that you and your partner re-connect with each other intimately right now.

The outward effects of that workplace change you first picked up back in February become evident. You will probably come through this shake-up unscathed. A work friend of yours may not be as fortunate as you. You may have to offer them tea and sympathy - plus a box of special-for-tears Kleenex. This person is also likely to ask you to be a reference when they interview for a new position. Try to steer clear of any continuing venting sessions this person may want to initiate, though.

Things are still unstable at the office. Engaging in further gossip could prove perilous to your own position now. Also be extra cautious if this person wants to borrow money. As they certainly will not be able to re-pay it for a while, hand over a minimum as a gesture of friendship. A sum you can afford to lose. Consider it a gift. If they repay you, it will be a nice surprise. If they don't, you won't be disappointed.

### CANCER June 2014

The month of June carries a new Mercury retrograde alert. Between June 7 and 30, be prepared to contend with more delays and confusion than usual in regard to communication and transportation. It's nothing worth becoming anxious about, but Mercury retrograde often creates confusion and obviates the use of our best reason when signing documents or making long term commitments.

Security is usually your byword so you feel surprised to learn in the wake of last month's office shake-up that chaos actually feeds you creatively. Suddenly you have ideas for new projects at work and for your own imaginative outlets. You choreograph a new dance routine; develop a great idea for a screenplay; begin plans for a backyard greenhouse or start painting a summery mural on the dining room wall. It's like you're running on liquid lightening. You feel so charged that it alternately excites and frightens you. Stay grounded and in fine physical nick to handle this energy. Exercise of all kinds, as well as sex and massage all help you remain centered. Even simple things like hugging your child or petting your dog keep you in touch with your core self.

That new friendship you began last month could be valuable here. She/he may become a creative collaborator. It's also possible this new pal can connect you with a gallery to display your artwork. Or this person may simply help you stay balanced through this dicey period by accompanying you on becalming nature walks. At any rate, this new individual's value becomes more apparent as you immerse yourself in your creative project. You become closer and start to trust this person more. Around the 19th, the two of you have a talk together that forms a turning point in your relationship. Go over this conversation in your head for a day or two so that its full significance registers and you can make some changes in your original strategy.

Toward the end of the month, a young person in your life needs your advice on a ticklish situation. Your keen listening skills along with your gift for empathy can enable you to help this child or teen through a challenging period. It may, however, be necessary for you to relinquish some old prejudices in order to see your way clear to actually lending assistance to this troubled kid. If parents are in the picture, be sure to clear your plan with them before proceeding to dole out so much as a syllable of your inimitably cozy, Cancerian wisdom.

## CANCER July 2014

Feed your new creative outlet as July commences. Scan your local paper for events that will excite your imagination. Could be a glassblowing demonstration or an African dance performance. Something unusual and, to you, exciting. Right now it's important to think of your artistic side as a fast-growing child in need of regular nourishment. You will want to supply that through frequent excursions and exposure to cultural events. Give your artist-self healthy doses of the novel and unusual. Steer clear of a junk food diet of stultifying television shows or trite, same-old-thing books. Behave toward yourself as you would if caring for a tot.

Steer clear of negative influences. Banish (at least temporarily) people who disparage or ridicule your creative efforts. Also avoid people who seem stuck in a rut. Find yourself a "play group" of likeminded folks who will encourage your imaginative output. You may locate these people by participating in a workshop or seminar geared to your creative discipline.

What fun! Your new friendship continues to grow. Around the 13th, the two of you may decide on a day-trip to a nearby city to take in a play or festival. You will find this getaway most invigorating. Although you'll enjoy this trip, some type of confusion may scotch things a bit. Carefully check on details such as dates, times and driving routes before you leave. Avoid carelessly leaving your belongings lying around visible in the car. Look carefully when picking up your bag, mobile phone or sunglasses to make sure you haven't accidentally appropriated a look-alike belonging to someone else.

Your body's need for balance become even more important as you pour more energy into your creative endeavors. Do not forget to continue to exercise regularly. Eschew boring gym classes in favor of something novel which thrills you as well as helps you stay fit. Too much routine can destroy one's enthusiasm. Go horseback riding. Try a circus trapeze class. Learn to kick and chop at a martial arts course. The energy spurt you are benefiting from now will not always be there. Use it.

## CANCER August 2014

As August begins, a challenging new assignment is likely to come your way at work. It will require extra meetings, longer hours and perhaps more business travel. But this added responsibility can also mean more money down the line, if not immediately. You may have to re-organize household arrangements with your partner, shifting some of the areas of responsibility. Lighten the load on everyone by hiring childcare, a dog-walker and/or someone to help out with laundry and other chores. Older children may also be able to assume some of the drudgery. Pitching in and participating now will stand them in good stead later on.

If possible, between business trips, try to be in town for a social occasion around the 16th. Your involvement is crucial to making this event a success. The host/ess will be grateful you found the time to attend. Also, this party will give you the opportunity to mend fences with someone with whom you have too long been on the outs. You quarreled and you are sorry. Just say so and see what happens. If you sincerely apologize now, you will clear the air. If not, you face negative karmic repercussions later on. I know that you find it difficult not to hold grudges. But this time, be the bigger person. Drop your pique in the umbrella stand as you leave the party.

Make time around the 23rd for private time with your partner. He or she needs to feel reassured. You have been very busy these past months. First came your creative project. Then along bounced your new work assignment. Both have been taking you away more often. Make plans to go out to that chic French restaurant you both love so much. Or cook a favorite meal together. Then curl up on the couch and talk. Conversation is restorative - even curative. Of course you also want to make sure the communication goes beyond the verbal level. Renew your physical connection.

You may fall prey to anxiety toward the end of the month. Even as the plane takes off, you feel sure you forgot to pack your best underwear. Practice yogic breathing techniques to release stress and control the tachycardia. Breathe in through your nose. Expand the abdomen with that air. Hold that breath for 12 counts. Then let it out slowly to the count of 12. Do this ten times. Your worries will evaporate.

## CANCER September 2014

Your own words seem to betray you the first few days of September. Everyone misinterprets you now. You ask your partner to buy some olive oil at the store and they come home with crankcase or peanut oil. You plan a meeting at work and a simple typo has everyone arriving at 9 rather than 8am. For this period of time, everything you say or write will somehow seem obscure to everyone else. It is frustrating. But it is not anyone's fault. Blame it on the planets. Don't let yourself become angry with others. Try to see the humor in any and all situations.

Your nurturing instinct swells to epic proportions around the 11th-26th this month. If you have children at home or grandkids nearby, indulge yourself and them in some bonding time. Raid the local crafts store and come home with clay, finger-paints and other supplies for an intergenerational arts and crafts day. Or make special gifts for your loved ones according to your own skills—cooking, carpentry, or whatever else allows you to give of yourself. Critter-loving Cancers will want to spend extra time playing with their dogs, cats, house rabbits, or ferrets. If you don't have a furry friend at home, this is the perfect time to visit the local shelter and bring home someone who will repay your love with unswerving devotion. For some reason, I see you with a black-furred companion - a beautiful, affectionate mutt or feline friend whose enthusiasm for munching on or clawing at your furniture should cheer you right up.

Your partner dislikes the new friend you made this spring (not the mutt or the cat). Try to keep the two of them in separate spheres of your life. But don't give up your nascent friendship. Help your partner understand that your love for him/her is not diminished by your attachment to the new wrinkle. Remind them that jealousy is a wasted emotion. You simply need to develop all sides of yourself. Chances are he/she isn't all that eager anyhow to attend the type of events you and your new pal frequent together.

**CANCER October 2014**

The third and final Mercury retrograde period of the year takes place from October 4th until the 25th. If people seem especially scattered or unreliable this month, chalk it up to Mercury retrograde and cut them some slack. While you're at it, cut some slack for the electronic devices and household appliances which go on the blink during this time. Best bet? During Mercury's backward run, take a philosophical view of everything. Make plans. But don't buy the tickets or pop the question till Mercury has relented on October 25.

The changes at your workplace could evolve into all-out drama in early October. Don't get sucked into the vortex of office politics. Keep your head low. Disengage from gossipy conversations. Maintain your usual high level of efficiency. If it looks as if the people who stir up drama aren't leaving, it may be time for you to prepare your exit. Go back to that résumé you polished earlier in the year. Start sending it out discreetly. Your new friend may turn out to have some contacts in your field. It's also possible that the creativity play group you found this summer contains one or two people who can pull some strings to help you.

A sad event in your circle mid-month means you have to extend your nurturing to someone beyond your immediate family. Proffer support in whatever way matches your personal gifts. Provide a listening ear. Drop off a casserole for someone too busy and/or too sad to cook. Offer to drive your friend to the hospital or hospice. Take your friend's dog for a walk when she/he is occupied with funeral plans. Your excellent natural instincts about how to take care of people will guide you as to what is best to do in each case.

Although you continue being a rock of support for your grieving friend or relative, the end of the month finds you again craving excitement and creative stimulation. Plan another of those mini-getaways with your new friend. Maybe lunch in a nearby city followed by an art exhibit or performance. Go for the unusual. Dine on something you usually don't eat—frog legs or Ethiopian stews. Watch a performance that's a bit daring, something that challenges your newly awakened sensitivities. You might also want to buy something you can wear - a souvenir T-shirt or a pair of colorful socks, some tie-dyed underwear or even a symbolic tattoo.

**CANCER November 2014**

Early November promises to give you a bit of a jolt. You hear some shocking news about somebody else's plans which may include you. Don't overreact. Avoid letting your emotions run wild. If you allow them to, they can drag you too far from the here and now. Remain focused on the present and not on a future-*maybe.* Tempting though it may be, avoid spreading the stunning tidbit of news you have just received. The source is less reliable than you think. Could even be a sick joke.

The past also tries to interfere with your current life. An old lover or ex-spouse returns, seeking a way back into your life. He/she may try to lure you into a flirtation or more. You'd be wise to sidestep these romantic overtures. Although your ex may speak words of cloying, delicious sweetness, I sense they are aiming to make trouble. If you don't respond to her/his advances, this individual may try to find another way to gain your attention. He or she may pursue a relative or friend of yours, suddenly turning up at a social event on the arm of someone you know. Warning people about this person will only make you look bitter. You might be better off briefly staying clear of the friend or relative who becomes involved with your ex. Let them decide for themselves about the ex's true nature. That way you may elude entanglement altogether.

It may be best to stick close to home from the 15th through the 21st. You could very well become afflicted temporarily by both verbal and physical clumsiness. You may find yourself accomplishing startling feats like tripping down a flight of stairs with both feet lodged firmly between your incisors. Speak less often, offering nods and smiles instead. Better to seem quiet and reserved than to accidentally insult someone. Take baby steps when walking on wet or icy pavement. No slippery shoes please. It's preferable to move slowly than to take a sudden tumble onto your tailbone. As far as possible, postpone activities requiring social or physical grace until the 22nd or later. A dance recital or tango contest could prove disastrous until after the 21st.

**CANCER December 2014**

You make an unfortunate discovery early this month. Someone in your extended family suffers from severe loneliness. The person's state of mind has gotten so bad that it endangers their physical and emotional health. This person needs love and attention. Naturally you want to help. But don't go taking this project on alone. This individual is more than needy right now. She or he could become like emotional quicksand, swallowing up huge chunks of your time and causing you to get stuck in a depressive state as well.

Why not arrange for two or three people at a time to visit the lonely family member? Make it feel like a small party. Perhaps get some younger members of the family involved. This can help teach them about caring for others. Have the group meet regularly at the lonely person's house for tea or lunch. This will cheer up the victim, giving them regular socializing to look forward to. Organizing this as a group project means you will still have time for your partner, your job and your own well-being.

Although you are looking forward to holiday celebrations later this month, finances may be tight right now. Do not rely on credit cards to purchase gifts. This shortage of funds may continue for at least another two or three months. You do not want to build up debt. Instead, use your creativity to deal with this challenge. You can apply your many talents to make your own gifts for loved ones. You can also fashion rather than buy decorations. And you can cook all the food for any entertaining you plan to do. Barter with other creative friends, swapping your services for someone else's so you can each give a wider variety of presents. Cancers are good at stretching money when necessary. You may even want to share some of your creative DIY projects by writing about them for a website or newspaper. Do not worry or grow melancholy. This money shortage is temporary and will sort itself out in time.

## CANCER January 2015

The financial strain is likely to continue into the first month of the western New Year. But with the holidays past, you have fewer expenses. Continue to exercise your creative gifts to cope with this temporary lack of funds. If you crave new clothes, invite some friends over for a clothing swap meet. A jacket one friend no longer wears may be the perfect new addition to your own wardrobe. Surely you too have gobs of garments you have cast aside. Even other peoples' once-worn clothes can make you feel brand new. Or look into offering a class in one of your skill areas. Teach a language, invite people to study woodworking with you or take on some handyman chores for extra cash. Use your imagination to add a new stream of income. Coming up with novel ideas to augment your revenue is both fun and confidence-building.

Your significant other has big plans for 2015. Resolutions to fulfill or items on a Bucket List to check off. Rein him/her in a bit. The resolutions in question could prove costly. Help your sweetie re-focus on whatever on the list can be accomplished with little or no money. Putting more energy into your romantic life will ease the tension you're both feeling. The recent holiday frenzy combined with the crimp in your spending may have put a damper on your passions. Rekindle those flames. Remember to be seductive and affectionate. Perhaps add some fresh, playful elements to your lovemaking. You are likely to make fireworks together right around the 12th of January. Have fun!

Tending to so many different people and projects may leave you feeling tired and depressed mid-month. Let the people close to you know nurturing is a two-way street. It's time for Cancer-Appreciation Day.

The new friend you made last year could help you make a breakthrough of some sort as the Year of the Horse draws to a close. Some surprising advice from this person points you toward a lucrative new business venture. Don't rush in too quickly. Take your time to examine all the details before you leap. As long as you prepare carefully and ask the right questions, this new idea can yield strong profits.

# LEO 2014

## OVERVIEW FOR THE WOOD HORSE YEAR

*Lofty Leo,*

*From the very start of the Horse year, you will appear more splendid than ever. In this year of the Wood Horse, you Leos will receive the accolades and admirers you so long have desired. The Horse - of course - requires that you avoid roaring or growling at anyone or thing. Expressions of leonine anger or spite could bring you costly consequences. Instead, you will have to walk the tricky tightrope of tact. No loud noises. Not booming voice. No outspoken remarks. Keep your mane firmly attached and well-groomed. Forego any and all temptation to proclaim yourself king or queen of your own neck of the jungle. We know you are the best, the cleverest, the most magnanimous and special.*

*Now come down off that rock and join us plain folk so your magnificence can be more closely appreciated by the meek and mild among us. This year, mix with the lowly multitudes. We will aid you in unexpected ways. Not to worry. Your gifts and skills should be recognized this year. But any expression of excessive pride could interfere with your well-deserved moments of glory. Temptations may arise this year to behave without integrity. Try not to let impulse or basest desires lead you down a path which will tarnish your reputation. Work harder than ever and put everything you have behind producing a stunning performance. Horses smile on achievers. sw*

————— ℯ ℯℭ ℯℯ —————

## THE CHINESE YEAR AHEAD

## LEO 2014

### LEO February 2014

I hope you're up for a challenge, Leo. You have to purr rather than roar for a few weeks. This month begins with a tricky social situation. Your sweetie may get a bit testy with someone in your circle. The ripple effects of this minor tiff have the potential to affect your career and/or reputation. Stay out of the line of fire. Avoid taking sides. Try to lift the mood with your usual *joie de vivre*. Keep the conversation as light as a soufflé. Your flair for social gaiety can save the day. Dealing with this problem may require a larger expenditure of your charm than usual because of this month's Mercury retrograde. Between the 4th and the 28th, communications are unreliable. Hold off on matters pertaining to the signing of binding documents. And don't go too crazy when transportation snafus arise. It's part and parcel of Mercury retrograde's influence on your life.

Around the middle of the month, someone might share a bit of shocking gossip with you. The person who spread the rumor doesn't realize how well you know some of the people involved. It will be up to you to be discreet. Don't create a social oil slick where everyone gets stuck in the muck. If there is news you must share, avoid doing so in public. Exercise surgical precision in your choice of words and choose your confidants wisely.

Your skill to inspire may be required to motivate someone at your workplace. You possess so much inner fire you are sometimes surprised when others lack confidence. For now, be satisfied with knowing you helped someone. Asking a favor in return can make you appear calculating. Your gesture of aiding this individual will pay off down the line in some amazing and unexpected ways.

A minor windfall will come your way toward the end of the month. Use it for some special treat to reward yourself for a month of outstanding social efforts. Maybe a stunning accessory—a gold watch, a pair of designer shoes? The very fact that you take the time to look fabulous feeds your social super powers.

## LEO March 2014

Another influx of cash this month contributes to your ability to shine even more brightly than usual. Buy yourself a few snazzy household items suitable for your lair. With your usual generosity, you may also spread the wealth around. Find little baubles and trinkets for your friends.

You experience a bit of a sexual renaissance early this month. Things are sizzling between you and your special someone throughout the early part of the month. The 4th through the 8th and the 11th through 13th will be most strongly characterized by this sense of passion. Lavish some of those new funds on your red-hot love life. Perhaps use it for those little details which add extra romance or playfulness to lovemaking. Any Leos currently in between partners will find themselves attracting even more potential admirers than usual on those days. Make sure to look your best - even if it's only to take out the trash or run to the store. You never know around which corner the next lover will appear to sweep you off your sneakers.

Opportunities for romance still abound after the 15th, but you'll also want to exercise caution. You could become accident-prone around this time. The slip-up may be something as small as an insignificant cut while slicing vegetables. Be careful not just with sharp objects, but in other circumstances. Look both ways while crossing the street. And for heaven's sake, don't text while driving. Avoid shortcutting through alleys at night. Careless actions carry penalties for you at this time. Remain alert. Don't count on your charm to secure you a pass on a single rule.

Toward the end of the month, you learn in an oblique way that you may have been wrong about a relationship issue in the past. You may have placed your trust in someone untrustworthy or mistrusted someone who turned out to be innocent after all. The upshot will probably not be life-altering. But you will want to re-consider some of your previous remarks and actions around this subject. If necessary, make amends. Particularly if you have spoken unfairly of someone and jeopardized their reputation as a result.

## LEO April 2014

Leo, you occupy one of your favorite spaces this month: center stage. Everyone displays appreciation for your many talents and innate gifts. Your partner is suitably amorous, showering you with attention. He or she may take the time to arrange special romantic interludes or getaways for the two of you. If you are single, you might well find yourself beset with admirers. A secret admirer who has nursed a crush on you for a while may rather clumsily reveal their attraction to you. Be kind. If you are not interested, at least be diplomatic.

Your family finally expresses gratitude for past generous actions on your part. If someone borrowed money from you some time ago, it may be repaid now. Your friends, even those normally prone to jealousy, compliment you. Someone may offer to do you a favor in some small but very helpful way. Since you will have a whirlwind trip in the offing this month, perhaps they drive you to the airport or offer to take care of your animals or plants while you are out of town.

Social invitations flow in, providing a veritable feast of celebrations. Naturally, you shine at these gatherings, everything from your impeccable style to your *bon mots* eliciting favorable reactions. The peak of all this partying may arrive around the 10th of the month. At that time, you will make a connection that can open new vistas for you both socially and professionally. This is especially true for Leos who work in the arts or perform in some way. Even if you only have a sideline in this area, it may expand as a result of this new opportunity.

Relationships with your colleagues at work also flow smoothly. Someone may become your mentor or ally in some way, smoothing the way for you to achieve new promotions and honors. Even that iffy project you completed months ago, earns some overdue recognition.

### LEO May 2014

After a couple months' season of stellar romance, suddenly your partner seems aloof. You are puzzled. After all, you know you remain the same dazzling sex deity you always were. (You do so enjoy being worshipped.) But your native generosity shows us that you always give as much passion as you take in the bedroom. Why this sudden emotional shift?

A bit of time spent discussing the source of the sudden inexplicable chilliness with your main squeeze, combined with some astute observation on your part reveals the issue. A sense of inequality and consequent issues of control have sneaked into the relationship. The significant other's lack of self-confidence could simply be misdirected energy. Your partner may be projecting issues from his/her workplace or from an earlier family construct. Use empathy rather than impatience or disdain to overcome this obstacle to your couple's harmony.

In the workplace, too, you encounter resistance. People fail to appreciate the genius of your ideas. You have the power to change this. But it may require tact and patience. Adjust your attitude a bit. See if you have dismissed someone else's proposals too loftily in the past. Try to become a gold-medalist at the art of open-mindedness. Listen carefully and thoughtfully to each individual's point of view. Try becoming more pliant and flexible. Remember that the need to prove that you are always right can be a liability. If you try to force your point of view on others, you will end up feeling stressed. Ironic though it may seem, your leadership qualities shine brighter through compromise. Showing some vulnerability reassures others about your basic humanity.

Your health, vitality and beauty should shine especially brightly this month. You may decide to undertake a new physical challenge. Why not start training for a triathlon? Or try out a new sport. Even if you have recently veered dangerously close to becoming a couch potato, you will experience this sea change. Staying in shape can be as simple as deciding to walk half an hour a day or take the stairs more often. Others notice the effects of your renewed energy, garnering you even more than your usual share of admiration. Make tracks while your energy level is at its peak.

### LEO June 2014

The time is ripe early this month for you to display your outstanding talent for hosting the perfect get-together. Keep the guest list fairly small. This isn't the time for a major shindig. Invite only those who share your ability for scintillating conversation. Invite no dead wood negatives who may drag the event into moping or sourness. Mix things up a bit, perhaps inviting people from different spheres of your social set. Imbue the occasion with casual elegance. You know how to do this standing on your head. Entertaining is a snap for you.

This event will serve as a magnet for good luck for you throughout the coming season. And it may help solve a problem for someone else. Perhaps two of your single friends make a romantic connection? Or maybe your unemployed pal finds a job lead. At any rate, some good karma comes to you from creating an opening for this new development.

If possible, try to schedule this gathering before the 7th of this month. That's the date when Mercury goes on one of its fictitious backwards journeys. These retrograde phases of the planet of communication and travel can be trying. There's a chance this one can zap your circle of friends. So play it safe with all relationship issues until after July 1 when Mercury turns direct.

Later this month, an older person you know requires a bit of your charm and dazzle to relieve their melancholy. It may be time to pay more frequent visits to that elderly relative or kindly neighbor. Loneliness is obviously affecting their health. They need someone to talk to. Your natural sparkle provides the perfect medicine. Lend encouragement. Leo's planet is not the Sun for nothing. When you wish to, you can shower sunshine all over someone's life.

You may discover that you have outgrown some facet of your existence. A hobby which used to enchant you suddenly seems dull. This may of course affect your social life to some degree. The people who shared that interest with you also begin to bore you a bit. Don't go burning any bridges. But do let the connections draw gracefully to a close. Slowly inch toward making an opening - a time slot - for something brand-new which will enter your life later this year.

Toward the end of the month, one of your siblings or perhaps a close friend needs you to lend a strong shoulder. This person experiences a loss of some sort. Your strength helps them move through a painful change. No need to play Jolly Pollyanna. Just be there to listen and comfort.

## LEO July 2014

At the beginning of the month, you may well feel stressed. Your family starts making demands on you which conflict with your job. Friends may expect too much of you as well, cutting into your time with your partner. Meanwhile, office colleagues seem stuck on minor, petty issues. You always try to offer warmth, strength and motivation. All these obligations and generous giving of your light can take a toll on your equilibrium. Even your seemingly boundless inner fire can deplete at times. You should take a break mid-month. Have a massage. Take long solitary walks in nature. Read trashy novels or play dumb video games. Tend more to your own needs. The others will survive without you for a bit.

If possible, schedule a vacation before the end of July. Don't break the bank on this trip as another expense else could arise later this month. At least take a weekend away. Or plan a "staycation" with your sweetie where you both steal some time from all external obligations. Make the entire weekend about play and relaxation. Turn off your phones. Don't even check your e-mail. Massage treatments can have a marvelous effect on you, restoring you to your usual sunny cheerful self.

Late in the month, when you return from your rejuvenating trip, re-consider your boundaries. If others have been expecting you to cover the tab for every celebratory dinner, casually suggest sharing the bill instead. Don't feel you have to provide the largest, most impressive gift for every relative's birthday. If you attend a potluck supper, it's fine to bring one dish. You don't have to supply the entire buffet. Life is not a competition for being the good guy. Sometimes your well-known generosity can be your downfall. Setting limits (on yourself and others) will prevent you from feeling tense and resentful in the future. You needn't roar or show your teeth and claws to get your points across. Use the velvet paw. That's what it's for.

Toward the end of July, you encounter an unexpected expense related to your home. This is the reason you didn't splash out too much on that vacation. Take care of the problem as thoroughly as possible. No halfway measures. Failing to repair things completely now will only mean headaches later in the year.

## LEO August 2014

Ideas you have mentally gestated for some time are ready to be born early in August. With the Sun moving through your sign, your creative flame burns even brighter and hotter. Motivation and confidence crackle through your veins like lightening. Old obstacles such as writer's block or lack of confidence in your performance will collapse. You are ready now to seize the moment, and make that brilliant notion a reality. Even if others do not react at first with enthusiasm, you must not feel deterred. You realize that rejection does not signal failure. It merely provides a form of feedback. Use any and all criticism as a tool to hone and polish your creation. Thank the critic for zeroing in on what was missing.

Your enthusiasm is so strong mid-month that you seem magically to draw support to yourself. Perhaps, after searching fruitlessly for months, you finally find a writers' group or a surfing club or a band of folks to go hiking with. Could be as well you re-connect with an old friend on Facebook. Amazingly, you will learn that she/he is now an important liaison for the kind of work projects you need to have placed under the noses of the right people. Remain alert so that you perceive this source of aid when it arrives. It may come under an unusual guise. Marty Littlefield who, back in the day, was the class dunce may well be that perfect liaison you so desperately need today. People do change.

The one fly in the ointment may be that a sneaky temptation of some sort beckons you. Hold on tightly to your principles. Doing anything underhanded right now could have dramatic repercussions for you down the line. You might even undo your own potential for success with this new creative endeavor. Avoid manipulating or taking advantage of anyone. Malicious gossip about someone seemingly unimportant could come back and bite you in the posterior. Look at it this way: the price of your new muse is unswerving compassion and honesty. Humility is less expensive than fighting a court case for committing some unsavory act you will regret.

Someone at your office makes a stealthy bid for power around the end of August. You may be the only one who recognizes their secret agenda. Take steps to protect yourself. But remain silent for now about what you see. Otherwise, you may be dubbed "The Snitch". Nobody needs such a disparaging nickname.

## LEO September 2014

You usually prefer the company of others like yourself. People who also adore the spotlight. But in early September, you will reap benefits if you get to know a few of those you folks you see as outsiders or hermits. In their own quiet way, this tribe of mushroom people who live in outside the mainstream may guide you toward a crucial turning point in your life. They may casually suggest a revolutionary new ending for that screenplay you're working on. Or one of them might help you make a lucrative career move. They may indeed hold the solution to a tricky relationship issue you've been puzzling over. You will have to learn to speak their language, however, to gain their trust and aid. Remember that, among this tribe, humility is seen as a virtue. It's possible you'll encounter your quiet new allies at a volunteer event. So if you feel a new impulse to dispense some altruism, go ahead and follow it. Your new efforts will not only further the cause you believe in, they will introduce you to a source of aid and personal growth you formerly overlooked.

In fact, it's certain people whom you formerly trusted that may try to undo you this month. An old friend may have designs on your sweetie. Their jealousy could take the form of trying to seduce your honey sexually. But since everyone knows you're nearly invincible on that front, they may try to plant the seeds of discord in your partnership with idle gossip. Take preventive action. Heal any minor rifts between you and your spouse or lover. Gently remind him/her of the infinite power of your leonine love.

Subtly convey to that person trying to maneuver behind the scenes at work that you're on to them. No need for confrontation. A wink and nod from your stern countenance will more than suffice. You're letting them know you are not blind and that he/she would do well to cool it. No need for a declaration of war. Better to use muted tactics than to bandy harsh comments. Sarcasm will get you nowhere with this devious type of troublemaker.

## LEO October 2014

Around the 5th of October, you get some good news about a family member. Someone's life is about to undergo a dramatic improvement. Take some time to share in the familial happiness and renew your ties. This may be a fortuitous time to mend fences with someone in the family with whom you had a quarrel. Also, it may be wise to postpone sharing your own good news at this time. Wait until events reach fruition. In the meantime, remain out of the limelight. Let others in the family revel in their newfound felicity.

Your partner experiences some emotional turbulence around the middle of the month. It could be that events trigger memories of old pain. That relationship-wrecker from last month may still be lurking in the background. Do not let your partner's emotional neediness become an opportunity for an interloper. Be patient and supportive. Remind your honey of all the positive things you share together now. Reassurance rather than passion will have to be the keynote of your time together for a while. Bolster your partner's ego until he/she regains more emotional buoyancy.

You may find yourself experiencing unusual bouts of indecision now. Life could be offering you more opportunities. You may feel torn about which direction to take. This indecisiveness may also show up even in seemingly insignificant ways. You can't decide whether you want to order Chinese food or pizza. You're not sure if you want to watch a documentary or a comedy while unwinding after work. Do not feel concerned. This spate of ambivalence is only a temporary change from your usual decisive confidence. Use it to better understand those with less fire than you.

There is one aspect of this transitory shift in your mental gears where you must use caution. You may find you not only have a hard time making up your mind, you also have difficulty remembering things. Mark important occasions, both personal and professional, indelibly on your calendar. Make lists. Keeps them close at hand. Enter them on your computer. Consult them regularly. You don't want to miss an important business meeting or forget to attend your child's school play.

What feels like a memory loss phase is connected to the fact that Mercury retrogrades again between the 4th and the 25th of this month. Expect the usual delays, setbacks and hassles related to these periods. Don't panic if you meet someone you know in the supermarket and can't recall their name. Laugh it off and blame it on Mercury retrograde.

## LEO November 2014

Last month's uncharacteristic absentmindedness and wishy-washiness ends early in November. You roar back to your usual self full throttle. You know exactly what you want and how to get it. The lion is a-hunting. And you are ready to pounce. Anyone who tried to take advantage of your temporary confusion quickly discovers this month that you have razor sharp claws and are unafraid to use them. No more playing pussycat.

The efforts you initiated earlier this year start to pay off on all fronts. So long as you stuck to the spring regime you started, you glow with health now - a sleek wild cat of the jungle. I hope you didn't permit last month's uncertainty halt your creative flow. You should find yourself earning acclaim for your efforts. Your astute handling of the interplay of different tensions at work has landed you in the catbird seat.

Your only dangers now are complacency and a hint of misplaced arrogance. Don't think that events going your way are an invitation slack off. If you take a victory lap now, others will use the opportunity to sneak away with your laurels. Continue the same efforts that gained you these rewards. Keep the rewards themselves somewhat under wraps. Avoid boasting. It tarnishes your sterling image.

People you count on to handle details for you will seem error-prone toward the end of November. Your assistant forgets to send an important document. A cab-driver takes you to the wrong gate at the airport. The waiter mixes up your dinner order. Be patient. Make allowances for others' mistakes. Otherwise you will be seen as both egotistical and insensitive. Should the opportunity arise, the peasants, whom you would lord things over may rebel against your royal wishes. Never forget that they can stick a gigantic spoke in your master wheel and ruin a lot more than your day.

Avoid making jokes at others' expense now. Your attempts at levity will not go over well. Even your sweetie won't find your jokes entertaining. Miscalculated humor could cost you some of those precious gains you so recently achieved. For now, keep any sarcasm or caustic remarks to yourself.

## LEO December 2014

Take that postponed victory lap now. But if possible, do it far from home. Avoid exciting others' envy or resentment. A trip with your partner would be just the thing. Excite your senses with a new destination rather than revisiting some place you have already been. Perhaps a country you've never toured in. Maybe one where you do not even speak the language. I advise changing your traveling style—go camping rather than to a spa or vice versa. The sense of being immersed in an unfamiliar environment will challenge you. You will find out about how clever you aren't when you try to use the lift in a country where the lifts are operated by voice recognition instead of the familiar buttons. New sights, new foods, new scents, new sounds—all of these feed something inside of you now. You may also discover a new passion or new subject of study while abroad.

A young person you don't know all that well comes to you for guidance. Give generously of your time. Resist the temptation to see this young man or woman as a mirror. He or she may exhibit some traits in common with you. But they are decidedly not merely a younger version of you. Instead, see this youthful person as a unique individual, possessing gifts and flaws entirely different from your own. Provide support and encouragement tailored to this young person's unusual gifts. This will take some deep thinking on your part. If in doubt, consult a therapist.

Make plans to expand your volunteer efforts during the New Year. Look into ways you can contribute more of your talents. Those quiet, soft-spoken friends you made this fall can help you with this project. They will have a plethora of unexpected insights about how your project can benefit even more people. Restrain your instinct to assume the leadership role, and instead form a team with your new friends.

Although invitations to parties abound this month, be careful of what you consume. Too much of a good thing can lead to health consequences next year. Partake of what is offered only in moderation.

## LEO January 2015

The first month of the western New Year is also the last month of the Chinese year. Take the time to wrap up loose ends. This is a good time to get your financial house in order. Review your insurance policies, bringing them up-to-date if necessary. If you carry any credit card debt, see if it is possible to transfer it and garner a lower interest rate. Also banish chaos and clutter from your house. Re-organize your closets, chests of drawers and bookcases. Throw out what you do not use. Or give old clothes, etc. to a charity thrift shop. Make sure you know where belongings are stored so you can access what you need when you need it.

Organization may sound like a boring project. But in order for you to continue to reap the benefits of the new projects you set in motion in 2014, you want to avoid losing time to unnecessary muddle.

Around the middle of January, you may have to see a doctor for a minor health problem. Attend to this soon after it flares up to stem the problem at its inception. Your partner's health may also cause some concern. His/her problem may have deeper roots and require more attention. Do not let your sweetie ignore this health issue. Gently nag if you must to ensure this gets attention from an expert. Sooner rather than later is always best.

Someone at the office or on a work junket starts a flirtation with you. As a Leo, you naturally enjoy the attention. But stay within the boundaries of what is appropriate. A gathering of those in your line of work toward the end of the month may tempt you to go too far. A detour from fidelity just now will only lead to problems both at home and in your career. This lady or gentleman may be wildly attractive. But he/she is far less scrupulous than you think. Don't compromise yourself, even electronically through texts, emails or photos. Nothing is private anymore.

# VIRGO 2014
## OVERVIEW FOR THE WOOD HORSE YEAR

*Virtuous Virgo,*

*The Year of the Horse will take you on an unexpected ride around the zodiac. You will become acquainted with less familiar astrological venues. At times this year, you could even find yourself behaving less like the perfectionist we are used to and more like a dreamy Pisces or a babbling Gemini. In any case, the zodiac itself whirls you around in an attempt to first befuddle you. Then it will loosen any bolts that have been too tightly wound. For example, if you can't stand your opposite sign of Pisces, you might find yourself displaying Pisces' tendency to daydream. This carousel of astrological experience is designed to teach you to view other signs from a new angle. If you've always written Sagittarians off as unreliable, one of them will probably surprise you and come through in a pinch. Or if you think of Taurus as stodgy, a Bull might tell you a joke which will tickle your funny bone for weeks.*

*It's time in this Wood Horse Year, for Virgos to shake themselves out of their characteristic picky meticulousness and let go and let God. In any case, be prepared. As this Year of the Wood Horse gallops forward, you will notice your former prejudices and preconceptions have been stood on their respective heads. Don't hang up on this book just yet. There is plenty of love and passion ahead. You may fall plumb in love with a magnificent messy Leo or a disorganized loony-tunes Aquarian. My advice? Work your fingers to the bone to keep the Horse happy. Then after work, take a few joy rides into untrammeled territory where you'll find a slew of racy new chums to hang with. sw*

―――――― ❧❧❧ ――――――

## THE CHINESE YEAR AHEAD
## VIRGO 2014

**VIRGO February 2014**

The landscape of your past may appear to alter as the Year of the Horse begins. An old grudge, previously as large as a boulder, suddenly shrinks or even disappears. You see things from another perspective. Perhaps you were as much at fault as that individual you formerly blamed. At the same time, your rose-colored glasses fall off in regard to an old friend or teacher whom you used to idealize. You find this shifting of the past both disorienting and oddly liberating.

Housework could become a bone of contention between you and someone else living in your home. The other person claims his/her disinterest in domesticity justifies ignoring workaday tasks. What he or she views as carefree disregard for convention you perceive as slovenliness. Avoid either nagging or sulking. Simply have a firm yet polite talk with this individual. Establish a household minimum level of cleanliness. Create a schedule for handling chores equitably. Mercury, the planet of communication, goes retrograde on February 6th and doesn't go direct again until the 28th. You and your roommate's wires may be crossed until the beginning of March. Give the person till March 2-3 to come around. If they simply refuse to take responsibility for chores, it's probably time to think about getting a different roommate.

Don't accept flattery at face value this month. People may use honeyed words to trick you or make you appear ridiculous in front of others. Your assistant tells you that you look terrific before you go into a big meeting. Check the mirror. You may have spinach on your teeth or toilet paper on your shoe. Your so-called friend encourages you to sing at karaoke night at the bar, claiming to love your voice. She/he plans to mock your performance while you are onstage. Be especially aware of such machinations this month.

Avoid tense discussions or tricky negotiations toward the end of the month. In fact, choose silent smiles and nods over words as often as possible. Your tact and diplomacy will likely be at an all-time low. You ask after the health of a friend's deceased spouse. You misread other people's signals. You try to smooth the way with compliments only to find yourself choking on all ten of your toes.

## VIRGO March 2014

Focus on your career this month. If you feel unfulfilled at your current job, why not do some deep thinking about what you really want to do? What are your true priorities? What do you feel passionate about? What kind of work will feed and nourish your soul? What steps might lead you to a sense of genuine fulfillment? Don't be afraid of change. Look into educational opportunities that will support your dream. Start to attend events where you can meet others who share your passion. Can you begin to do some version of your ideal job now? Perhaps you can do targeted volunteer work in your area of interest or start a creative side business. Do some research to discover the paths other people took to achieve success in the career you hope to pursue. How did they get to that place? Don't expect to go from caterpillar to butterfly overnight. But at least begin to envision the weaving of a cocoon and start the incubation process

The feng shui of your home may require some adjustment around mid-March. Maybe you should re-arrange the furniture to attract more harmony and good fortune. Adding a few green plants will contribute more *chi* to a room which has become dull and stagnant. Or it may be time to raise the energy level by increasing the size of your household with an animal companion. If you're not a pet person, or if your home already has its quota of feathered or four-footed friends, purchase an animal sculpture. Elephants with their trunks raised traditionally symbolize protection, strength and good luck in feng shui.

It may be time to act upon last month's realizations about the past. Send a message of reconciliation to the person you mentally demonized for so long. If forgiveness doesn't seem feasible to you, write an actual handwritten letter to the person, acknowledging that you forgive them. Read the letter out loud, then burn it. The kindly thoughts expressed in the letter could be the beginning of the actual process of pardoning the person in question. Remember what Gandhi said: "The weak can never forgive. Forgiveness is the attribute of the strong." Be strong.

## VIRGO April 2014

April may find you in a dreamy mood. You struggle with concentration. Focusing on any task seems impossible. You find yourself daydreaming at work. You may become inattentive to your partner and friends, slipping into escapist fantasies during conversation. Even while driving or standing on line at the supermarket, you find yourself drifting off into space. Part of this is normal and healthy for you right now. Creating a sense of hope and new possibilities is a positive activity. You are planting mental and emotional seeds for the future. This brief head-in-the-clouds phase will help you move toward those career ideals you began to define last month.

At times this month, you may find yourself tugged into the past, haunted by sad memories, lost in the nebulous grayness of regret. When this occurs, release all versions of the past, both what happened and what only might have been. Pull up your bootstraps. Bring yourself back into the present. Using deep breathing, anchor yourself to each moment. Observe the flowing rhythm of inhalation and exhalation. Breathe in for ten counts. Hold it for ten counts. Breathe out for ten counts. Do that ten times until you are once again grounded in the present.

Changing your diet may also help. Virgos tend to thrive best when they eschew junk foods. Eating a preponderance of animal-based foods can make you soporific. Try eating more fruits, vegetables, seeds and nuts. Google it. Find out which foods are especially good for increasing mental alertness. Keep a stash of walnuts and sunflower seeds in your desk to snack on when you find yourself drifting off. Never eat chips or ice cream. Add foods like sweet potatoes and greens to the menu at home.

Spend some time with an older relative around the 22$^{nd}$. He or she is ailing - perhaps only emotionally. They need some cheering up. Tell him/her some funny anecdotes about your life. Reminisce together about happier times in the past. Watch a funny movie together. Lifting his or her mood will help dispel the last vestiges of your own April moodiness.

**VIRGO May 2014**

Last month's daydreams disperse like morning fog. Your mental acuity level rises precipitously. You regain your normal efficiency at work. You multitask with ease. Churning on the high-octane fuel of that new diet, you achieve keen new insights into problems which formerly stumped you. You accomplish tasks in a fraction of the time they used to require. The only danger now is that your brain is so sharp you may cut someone to the quick. Snarkiness becomes your default mode of communication. Without even intending to, you cut directly to the heart of the matter in conversation, using as few words as possible. Some people revel in this dry wit. But some more sensitive souls may shrink from you now, seeing you as verbally ruthless.

Use part of the new, heightened mental power to find a balance between two extremes. Temper your sharp observations with sensitivity to others. Choose the targets of your incisive wit carefully. Don't be too hasty when speaking about the problems that you perceive. Try carrying a bottle of water or juice with you and take a sip before you speak. Drink slowly and as you do, weigh the possible effects of your words. Consider a way to convey the essential information without demonstrating your black-belt level insult skill. If you come up with a devastatingly witty criticism of a co-worker, save it to tell your best friend or partner when no one else is present. Or start collecting your best verbal slams as part of a humorous book. You do want to enter the next half of 2014 with your reputation for kindness and goodwill intact.

Toward the end of the month, your sexual allure increases. If you are in a relationship, you may discover that even a previously inattentive partner can't keep his/her hands off you. If you are single, you will be beset by intriguing invitations and dubious innuendoes. Some of these may surprise you. Someone you think of as a platonic friend may begin out of the blue to flirt with you. Either way, there's strong chance that spontaneous romance overtakes you in a novel place —perhaps the changing room at a department store or the ladies' room at your favorite restaurant. Be prepared.

**VIRGO June 2014**

You become somewhat inattentive at the office again as June begins. But what you experience now does not resemble April's sometimes weepy daydreams. Back then you occasionally channeled Ophelia from Hamlet. Now you're more like Shakespeare's Mark Antony, so wrapped up in sexual passion that he tells a messenger "Let Rome in Tiber sink." You don't care about much that happens outside of the bedroom (or wherever else you and your sweetie find pleasure.) Fortunately, you exude a golden glow now that prevents anyone from thinking ill of you. Your boss is so dazzled by your beatific smile and that she/he doesn't stop to wonder why you were late to work two times this week.

In this torpor, you could find yourself tempted to skip social engagements in favor of intimate interludes with your partner. There is one invitation this month you must accept. It takes place sometime between the 1st and the 4th. At this gathering, the planets align for you to meet someone who will be very helpful to you. She or he may be in a position to assist you with those long-range dream career plans you developed earlier this spring. Arrive at this party prepared to mingle rather than nuzzling and giggling with your sweetie. Follow up with this new contact before June 7—that's when Mercury will go retrograde for the rest of the month. Hard to make any real solid connections when Mercury is in a snit.

Don't permit erotic focus to make you depart from that new dietary plan you began earlier this year. If you and your sweetie have a post-coital snack, make it grapes, not pizza. Toast your partner with a single glass of wine. Your passion is strong enough not to require an entire bottle as fuel. Moreover, right now, your health is more fragile than you realize. Over-indulgence of any kind could have serious consequences - and not just to your waistline. Continue to enjoy your romantic idyll, but keep in mind that for the next few months, you have to protect yourself by making wise lifestyle choices.

## VIRGO July 2014

Opportunity knocked at your door last month. Then it walked right in and handed you an assignment. That helpful contact from the party has given you an opening to demonstrate your talents. Don't ignore this lucky chance. You may not be given a shot like this again. In July, you will want to direct most of your energy on seizing this moment. Let go of last month's sexually-induced lassitude. Focus on your future with laser-like intensity. You will have to make the most of your time-management skills right now. It may sometimes feel like there are not enough hours in the day for your job, plus this project, plus your home, your family and your partner. Some area will have to be sacrificed, and it should not be your new career direction.

This of course means that your relationship with your sweetie will enter a new phase. If he or she seems unwilling to support your goals, then you must re-consider the nature of the relationship. Perhaps it would be better to find someone more accommodating for your future endeavors. Or you may simply have to classify the person with whom you currently share your bed as a friend-with-benefits rather than a long-term relationship partner. Sometimes our domestic associates find relinquishing our undivided attention makes them hideously jealous. That is their problem to grapple with. If they want to be with you, they must accept every part of you - even the ambitious, go-getter part.

You will also have to rein in expenses this month. Perhaps you have been a bit profligate with your funds over the last few months. You may have bought a few luxuries for you and your honey to enjoy together. Or if you have offspring, they may have taken advantage of your good mood to tap you for additional funds. At any rate, when you look at your bank balance this month, you are surprised to find it much less hardy than expected. Reconcile your records with the bank's as there may be discrepancies. Cut back on expenses. No more take-out coffee or restaurant lunches. Bring your own from home. Cancel any unnecessary subscriptions. No more shopping online. Hide your credit cards on a top shelf you can't reach or - better still - freeze the Visas and Master Cards in an ice tray. Then hide the tray under a ton of frozen foods.

## VIRGO August 2014

August opens with a bit of a shock. Someone close to you experiences a health crisis. It is most likely to be someone you think is brimming with wellness. It's possible this person is middle-aged or younger - not one of the seniors you know. Everyone around this person will be shaken by this event. Some people may, in the heat of the moment, grow irritable or try to start an argument about why your mutual friend is ill. Don't take it personally. This sudden edginess helps them avoid dealing with the sadness and fear they are experiencing. Remain patient and supportive. Let their harsh words roll off you like water off a duck's back. Whatever you do, don't draw on your well-stocked verbal armament to retort. If someone speaks rashly in tense circumstances, it's actually quite normal.

Keep a low profile with regard to your big project and the opportunity it represents. No point counting your chicks before they hatch. Also, well-meaning friends and relatives may make clumsy attempts to advise and assist you. Say "Thanks but no thanks." Remember. You are building your new self now. You have a golden opportunity. Only your own efforts can transform your life into what you want it to become. Avoid cutting any corners in handling the details of this assignment. Any deviation from integrity will spell doom for your ambitions. Carefully check and re-check your work to avoid embarrassing errors.

Tension may put your own health in danger around the 26th. Avoid letting this problem take root. Take a yoga class. Get a massage. And don't forget the best form of stress-reduction. Schedule some passion time with your partner or that friend-with-benefits. If need be, fly solo. Get your favorite toy and/or erotic DVD from that box in the closet. Whatever you do, don't resort to overeating or any other vapid vices as a means of escaping your stress. Remember. Virgos are going through an especially vulnerable phase when it comes to health matters. Make tracks to have a medical checkup and increase your intake of iron and B vitamins.

## VIRGO September 2014

Dedicate some time to neglected friends as September begins. Between your steamy romance earlier this year and your current big project, you have probably not paid enough attention to your pals. Keep in mind that friends are your emotional support team. They have helped you through difficult times in the past. Most likely you will need their comfort again. Reconnect for a fun social outing or two between the 2nd and the 11th of this month. At those gatherings, you will probably realize how much you missed these people. Let them know how much you care.

Still suffering from last month's excessive tension? You probably need more satisfactory sex. If you have a full time lover and things are not moving along smoothly in the passion department, you need to have a talk. If you don't have someone you can count on for good sex at the moment, I suggest you go hunting. Online? Maybe. Clubs? Definitely. Bars? Not your style.

Your period of financial strain ends around this same time. You may want to use some of the funds that come in to host a party for your closest cronies. Make it a birthday celebration. (If you were born in August rather than September, it can be a belated birthday party). Tell your friends not to bring any presents this year. Remind them that their very presence is present enough.

Someone you barely know invites you to an unusual social event around the 21$^{st}$. You may feel tempted to go, particularly if you are on the lookout for a new sweetie. The event sounds like the kind of thing you might have enjoyed when you were much younger. Resist the temptation to re-visit the worst aspects of those days. Politely decline this invitation. You'll be glad you sat this one out. Attending would only open the door to some rather dubious connections you can well do without.

You start to yearn for travel toward the end of September. Why not plan a trip for December? Start sketching out now where you want to go. You usually enjoy vacations most when you have outlined the details in advance. Research airfares, accommodations and interesting and amusing things to do. If you're between partners, why not go on this journey with a close friend? Ask around. See which of your buddies has itchy feet and the necessary spare cash for sharing expenses.

## VIRGO October 2014

You may learn that you made an enemy earlier this year. One of those snarky remarks you made last spring wedged itself right under someone's skin. You wounded this individual's pride. Ever since, he or she has been simmering with resentment. The funny thing is, you can't even remember what you said. Unfortunately, you have to see this person all the time. It might be the parent of one of your child's classmates you run into while picking up your kids. It could be that insecure co-worker in the next cubicle or that creepy neighbor who has been giving you odd looks when you venture out to pick up your mail.

As far as possible, try to de-escalate the tensions. It may be difficult. You could have to swallow your pride. Ignoring the problem won't make it go away. This enemy has long experience in despising his or her peers and is very skilled at it. They won't hesitate to attack your reputation or cause trouble for your family. Even if you think he/she is making a mountain out of a molehill, apologize sweetly. Send them flowers or give them a box of candy from a very special shop. Offer no excuses. Append no "ifs" or "buts" to your admission. Just say you know you were in the wrong. Best to make these peaceful overtures either before October 4 or after the 25$^{th}$. During those three weeks in the middle of the month, Mercury is retrograde. Mercury in a bad mood always increases the likelihood of miscommunication.

During the three weeks when Mercury goes into apparent backward motion, you may face issues related to debt or shared property. If you have creditors, be prepared to deal with collection calls this month. If you own any property jointly with anyone—an ex-spouse, a business partner, a sibling—you will be involved in meetings about how to handle that property. Any assets you acquired through inheritance may also be the subject of discussion. At this time, do not sign anything which compromises you for a long time. No major legal decisions or documents should be concretized during Mercury retrograde. (Oct 4 thru 25).

## VIRGO November 2014

Some kind of refresher learning experience is needed to make that big project of yours succeed. You may want to sign up for a seminar or workshop to polish your skills. If the course takes place around mid-November, there's a distinct possibility you'll meet an attractive stranger at the class. Could be another student. Or perhaps the instructor will catch your eye. This person may hail from a foreign country or just have a very different background to yours. Her/his exotic accent piques your fancy. You'll experience exceptional magnetism and chemistry. You and this person will turn out to have much in common. Oddly, this individual may have a vague connection to your past. Perhaps he or she once dated your ex's ex. Or maybe they were once married to your distant cousin or aunt. Or they knew you current lover in rather intimate circumstances well before you two were together. Whatever the connection, it will serve to draw you two closer.

You will want to wrap up your pet project before the end of November. The most auspicious time for that helpful person to review your work is from the 17th-29th of this month. He or she may offer some constructive criticism along with a few words of praise. Do not become defensive about the criticism. It's all part of the refining the project until it's perfect. Although you pride yourself on your ability to critique the work of others, you are not always gracious about being on the receiving end of criticism.

Don't be too impatient about this person's help. Cinderella didn't tap her foot whilst her fairy godmother was busy transforming the pumpkin into a coach. You may not receive the full benefit of knowing your patron until sometime next year.

A young person in your life makes a surprising announcement before the end of the month. Perhaps he or she decides on an entirely different career path than anticipated. Or a whirlwind romance may have led to a hasty engagement. Could be he or she will come out of the closet and be openly gay. Even if you feel hesitant about this youngster's new direction, be careful not to alienate the them by showing disapproval. Instead, express your support and offer to give them a hand.

**VIRGO December 2014**

The first week of December is the ideal time to take that trip you and your friend have been planning. Going with a friend leaves you open to romantic dalliances with one or two of the intriguing people you're likely to stumble on at random. Something about being in unfamiliar territory makes you more open to adventure. A gorgeous local you meet may suggest something a bit more daring or kinkier than what is on your usual sexual menu. Go ahead and experiment a bit. But save some time to hang out with your travel buddy. The two of you are likely to have a blast exploring. Take lots of pictures - just make sure no photos will embarrass you if someone posts them on Facebook.

Upon your return, you may have to deal with a minor problem at home. In some small way, things went awry while you were gone. It's possible your absence triggered a kind of resentment for feeling left behind. Your cat may have peed on the carpet behind the couch or clawed down the drapes in your living room. Or your child had a tantrum when the babysitter wouldn't let him or her have ice cream for dinner. Your house sitter may have neglected to feed your fish or water your plants. Take this unpleasantness in stride. Fun such as you just experienced usually has a price.

Take extra precaution with regard to your health during the month of December. I know it's difficult with the holidays approaching, but try not to overindulge or lose the pace of your exercise routine. If you attend any potluck parties, bring a healthy veggie dish that you can enjoy. That way you won't have to watch hungrily while everyone else munches cookies and crunches chips. Resist the temptation to nag other people about their dietary choices. Let your visible good health and vitality speak for themselves.

## VIRGO January 2015

Someone whom you dislike has moved into your neighborhood. You don't yet know this individual very well. But he or she still manages to get on your nerves. You were able to be polite to this person for a short time, while still maintaining your distance. Now this character is ringing you almost every day. You worry that he or she will start dropping by unannounced, expecting to sit and gossip over coffee. This person is both determined and needy. Could be a Dog who needs your company or a Goat person in need of reassurance. But you don't have any comfort or companionship to spare. Set clear boundaries. Say NO. Explain, if you must, that you're writing a book or teaching someone a foreign language on Skype or practicing a musical instrument for 6 hours a day. Make very clear that your activities cannot be disturbed. Say you can't concentrate if anyone else is in the vicinity. If you set them politely and firmly, he or she will eventually get your drift and begin to perceive you as their "off limits" neighbor.

Inspiration strikes around the 16th of the month. You feel charged with enthusiasm for an adjunct project. You may want to find someone to collaborate with on this one. This is an especially fruitful time for you to begin creative partnerships. That unusual person you met at the class you took back in November might offer some intriguing perspectives.

You are financially flush right now, but avoid any major new purchases or investments. Major expenditures during this time are likely to fail you in some way. A car you purchase during this period turns out to be a lemon. The apartment building you buy as an income property turns out to have hidden structural problems. If you take a major trip right now, the weather is likely to sabotage your fun. The expensive oil painting you acquire now could turn out to be a forgery. Sew your pockets shut.

You will have to resist the temptation to say "I told you so" to a good friend later this month. Someone ignored your good advice a while back. Now, as a result, that pal is going through a difficult time   Avoid even the slightest hint of judgment. Instead, be encouraging, supportive and useful. Lend an ear and a shoulder to cry on. But don't lend money.

# LIBRA 2014
## OVERVIEW FOR THE WOOD HORSE YEAR

*Lovely Libra,*

*Horse years rarely deliver the balance of peace and harmony you Librans all live for. This Horse year demands only that we work harder than usual. Librans are not afraid of putting in time in the workplace. But the Horse is an unrelenting taskmaster and Librans do like to be granted time off for fun and frolic. You may feel cranky and out of sorts some of the time. You wish for more luxury and less drudgery. Do not despair. The wood Horse is generous with those who live up to his draconian standards. So brace yourself Libra, for a year of slog and toil, peppered intermittently with periods of productive creativity and dedication to causes. Whatever hobby horse you jump on this year, it is likely to prove to be a bucking bronco.*

*You will ride in style if you devote your energies to something close to your heart. Avoid trivial pastimes in favor of political and social groups you believe in. Don't torture yourself over aesthetic decisions - the perfect placement of your art collection or where to stash the family jewels. Instead, reflect. Choose a purpose and decide to make a difference. Permit your fiery, passionate side to emerge. Let social standing take a back seat to social justice this year. Engage your diplomatic skills on behalf of something that benefits others and gives you the kind of satisfaction you so richly deserve. Embracing rather than seeking to avoid the servitudes of the Horse year can make this a very rewarding year indeed. sw*

---

## THE CHINESE YEAR AHEAD
## LIBRA 2014

**LIBRA February 2014**

Education occupies much of your thoughts as the Year of the Horse begins. You or your partner may be contemplating returning to a learning environment. Or it may be that you are helping your children prepare for university studies, perhaps taking them to visit different institutions. Maybe someone close to you is preparing to enter a graduate program, law school or medical college.

You and your partner have been at odds for a while. You seem to irritate each other more frequently. Little irksome things. But they do mount up. You disagree about which direction the toilet paper roll should hang. You snap at each other over how best to load the dishwasher. The two of you carp at each other in the morning over coffee. You haven't confided this bickering to any of your friends. Deep down you still feel love for your sweetie. Your sex life is still OK, but only in that "Sex is like pizza, it's kind of good even when it's bad" sort of way. Try discussing the tension openly, candidly. Ask your sweetheart how he or she feels about the strained ambiance between you. Never do this in the heat of a protracted bicker. Wait till evening before dinner when you are sharing a glass of port or having a tipple of wine or beer. Just come right out with it. In relationships, communication is king!

Be especially careful with your personal information. Mercury is in one of its retrograde periods from the 6th through the 28th of this month. This particular retrograde brings Librans the danger of identity theft. A store, an online company or restaurant employee may abscond with your credit card details. When and if you charge something, do so with utmost discretion - or better still, pay cash. At this time as well, someone may access your passwords and personal particulars online. Take precautions in advance to protect yourself. Change your passwords often. Make them unique and as long as possible. Vary the letters with figures. Do some research on the latest methods of foiling attempts at identity theft. Remember technology changes all the time. And hackers become more adept at filching one's precious data.

## LIBRA March 2014

Someone you've previously overlooked or taken for granted, perhaps a quiet co-worker, suddenly reveals hidden depths. A casual conversation with this person takes a surprising turn. You discover he/she is extremely well-informed on a certain topic of interest to you. As a result of this talk, you re-evaluate some of your opinions and beliefs. Following this discussion, you may be moved to take action in some new way. Perhaps you will sign a petition or post a link to a controversial article on your Facebook page. You may even delve deeper into the subject by volunteering or participating in a workshop. Whatever you are inspired to do. Go ahead with it. There is much wisdom to be taken away from this encounter.

A part-time job or volunteer project opens doors for you. In any case, this new position offers the opportunity to expand the scope of your current duties. Initially, this project provides little or no financial reward. Accept it anyway. This line of work has the potential to introduce you to some important and influential contacts. Be alert to the opportunities as they come along. Agree to work longer hours. This is a good time to show your true mettle.

There is some mysterious *malaise* in your home. It's not affecting you or your family directly. But maybe one of your beloved pets becomes ill. Or perhaps your formerly flourishing houseplants start dying. Change your pet's diet from dry to wet food. Make sure the air in your home hasn't become bone dry. You may want to switch to using non-toxic cleaning products such as white vinegar and baking soda. Try organic detergents or use old-fashioned soaps. You should think about installing a filter to remove unhealthy chemicals from your tap water. Eliminate the sources of poisonous substances and the household unpleasantness will disappear.

The latter half the month ushers in a period of hidden opportunity. This is not the month to crack jokes or act silly. Dress to impress. Put your best foot forward everywhere you go. Display every last ounce of your charm all day in all your encounters. Some important people are watching you, weighing your words and actions as well as your appearance. Based on how you present yourself, you could land a plum assignment. Or you could ruin your chances without even knowing about it.

## LIBRA April 2014

A person you have admired for a long time exhibits feet of clay early in April. Those heavy feet may step on your toes as well. Besides dealing with your disappointment, you'll have to fend off the ill-effects of this individual's disreputable behavior. This person may be unaware of how much damage they have done and how far they have fallen in your estimation. And you may be one of the few to see through their facade. They will behave as if nothing has changed. Remain your most polite self in their presence. But gradually distance yourself. A more public downfall awaits this person. You don't want your own reputation to be collateral damage.

You could have difficulty sleeping this month. Cut down on caffeine, limiting yourself to just one cup in the morning. Also attempt to get some exercise each day, even if it just a half hour of walking. No need to rush. Just walk for thirty minutes. Too little physical activity can leave you restless at night. Turn off the television and computer at least an hour before bedtime to let your brain quiet down. Listen to soothing music, read pleasurable books and/or meditate during that hour. You might try drinking a glass of tart cherry juice. Cherry juice contains melatonin which promotes regular sleep. Make sure you are getting enough vitamin B. Complexes of B vitamins serve to settle the nerves. Get the organic kind without additives.

An e-mail from a former lover has you contemplating a renewed romance. Even married Librans may find themselves tempted. This is a person who once played an important role in your life. He/she is newly single and wants to see you. This beguiling ex of yours may even propose flying you to a distant city so the two of you can meet up again. Weigh your decision carefully. Does this individual want a fling? Or for you two to become a couple again? Review the reasons why the original relationship with him/her ended. Think about the direction your life will take if you accept this person's advances. A single heartbreak over the same person might just be enough for one lifetime.

## LIBRA May 2014

You overbooked yourself this month. Your life feels supercharged and chaotic. You have far too many meetings and commitments. You made too many promises to too many people. In a funny way, you are a bit miffed at all of them. How dare they impose on you? But you know full well the blame belongs to you. It is not they who are greedy. The culprit is your burning desire to polish your self-image. You love to appear to be the gracious host/ess, the helpful and charming source of favors, aid and bounty. So you tend to overdo it. Don't be cross with the people who have merely accepted your generous offers. Work through each obligation with good cheer. Then begin setting better boundaries for yourself. Start with self-discipline, limiting your future obligations. State your limits to your entourage. Explain that you need to cut back on social engagements and curb your altruism. Make sure people know it's your problem. Not theirs.

That ex-lover who turned up last month continues to seek a place in your life. He/she offers much that you value. As a Libra, you esteem beauty and culture. This person can make your life shimmer with those qualities. But there are other considerations. This person could uproot your current life in so many ways. You can't ask any of your friends for advice. They are invested in you continuing the life you already have. Perhaps you can turn to someone impartial. Seek counsel from a trusted therapist, rabbi or minister. Or... spill the beans about your current romantic problems to a wise astrologer who can not only reveal where your basest desires want you to go, but can see where you ought to be going.

Around the 20th, you achieve excellence in some small but satisfying way. It could happen at work, but I sense it's more likely to be in a hobby or small sideline job. Perhaps you beat your personal best game at golf or tennis. Or maybe you turn out a smashing gourmet meal which leaves your family raving and suggesting you open a restaurant. If you teach something like tai chi or dance or spinning, students may start flocking to your class in larger numbers than ever before. Whatever it is, your skills dazzle everyone.

## LIBRA June 2014

Your path through June may involve a few detours or even a pothole or two. This is because Mercury goes retrograde on the 7th. Take the usual Mercury retro precautions about backing up data, putting off signing any contracts, etc. If surgery is advised, see if you can schedule it for after Mercury goes direct again on July 1st.

You have somehow gained an unsolicited admirer. This person sticks to you like a tick. It may not even be sex or romance they want - just unlimited quantities of your time and attention. Your usual gentle diplomacy won't work for this Velcro-like individual. To discourage this person you will have to become a veritable cactus. Tell him or her (in no uncertain terms) that your social life is already full to the brim. Do not yield to any requests or invitations from them. If he/she is present at group events you attend, drop a pleasant "hello" without stopping to chat. Your new fan will misinterpret anything beyond "hi" and "bye" as encouragement. Keep your distance. Display a grim countenance which implies "No Trespassing".

Your creative energy increases dramatically around the 16th of June. Ideas come to you fast and thick. You may feel as if somebody just plugged you into a power outlet. Whatever form your imagination takes, you may be up late at night producing new works and unavailable for fun and frolic with your buddies. For now, share your artistic output with just a few trusted friends. Choose people who are similarly creative as your confidants. Some non-artistic people in your life may actually be jealous or resentful of your talents right now. When the products of your artistic endeavors are finally being exhibited or published, they will change their collective tune. Meanwhile, let them talk.

Toward the end of the month, you hear from an old friend. You and this person may have quarreled in the past. He/she has spent some time out of the country. Now they have returned temporarily and want to renew the friendship. You are intrigued by their glamorous tales of living abroad. You recall you used to have fun with this person. However you also feel hesitant. Last time you were together, this friend reacted unreasonably to almost everything you said and did. Feel things out with a phone call to see if they still seem volatile and too full of their own self-importance. Perhaps this person has matured. Or perhaps not. Up to you to judge the risks involved in renewing this acquaintance.

**LIBRA July 2014**

You have cause to re-consider your ill treatment of someone a year or more ago. You learn that this individual whom you held in disdain has quietly performed several selfless acts of generosity. This person is rather plain in appearance. You realize now that you permitted your Libran preference for physical beauty to blind you to his/her inner qualities. See if you can contact this person through Facebook or get in touch through mutual acquaintances. Express your regret for any unkind words that passed your lips. Do not offer any excuses. Avoid using the words "but" or "if" as these render an apology meaningless. Express admiration for the individual's good works. Invite them out for lunch or to come to your house for tea.

Meanwhile, that part-time job or volunteer project you began earlier this year begins to blossom. The project is gaining momentum. Your talents are being recognized. Suddenly, important people are seeking you out. They praise your good work and seem to value your opinion. It is also very likely they will ask you to join forces with them in another venture. Choose carefully from the plethora of opportunities that come your way now. It won't do you any good to over-commit yourself again. On the other hand, these people can help you in some significant ways.

Your creative projects can continue to supply you with a regular source of joy. Do not let yourself become so busy that you neglect the soulful side of yourself. If you do, you will grow frustrated and anxious. You are a rather nervous person by nature and require major periods of down time to chill and find your own direction. Decisions are not easy for you. Any kind of artistic involvement is advised as it will take your mind of fretting about what's next.

You're still having a hard time discerning that old lover's intentions. He or she seems to flirt and encourage you, and then dance out of reach. Perhaps you'd be better off deciding what you want than trying to read your ex's desires. Decision is not an easy task for a Libra. But you must take the lead in this dance—whether you decide to tango with your former sweetheart or shimmy away from her/him for good. Time's a-wasting.

## LIBRA August 2014

I don't know who it's with—that mysterious ex, your current partner, someone new? But your love life becomes mighty steamy around the beginning of August. Make sure you don't leave any scorch marks on the sheets in the heat of passion. Carnal pleasures consume you now. You become uncharacteristically nonverbal, wrapped up in physical sensation. You'd rather moan with delight than chit-chat about art or the gossip about the neighbors' suspicious comings and goings. You and your partner feed each other in bed. You only go out to the store to stock up on wine, food and massage oil. When you return you shed a path of clothing from the front door to the bed. You're unlikely to be answering any phones for awhile.

When you can't be entangled in your lover's limbs, you move languidly. This slowness affects your perceptions a bit. Absent-mindedness is never a good state to be in for an already ambivalent Libran. So fuzz-brained will you be that you might miss the first signs of a political upheaval at work. Fortunately, you're not the target of this planned coup. However, you will want to take steps to protect yourself from subversive entanglements. Step back from your wooziness. Assess the situation carefully. You can be very astute about office politics when you're paying attention. Things are about to get seriously tricky. Think of this upheaval as a small inter office war. Determine which players in the game are loose cannons. Avoid these people. Decide who is likely to come out on top. Mend fences with these individuals. Stay as aloof as you can without appearing snooty.

All eyes are on you at a big gathering around the 25th. Perhaps everyone senses the sexual heat wafting off you and your lover? At any rate, you attract a great deal of attention. Although you're not wearing anything new and haven't changed your hairstyle, everyone comments on your spiffy appearance. It's as if your Clark Kent disguise fell off when you weren't looking and now everyone can see that big red S on your chest. Sexual release does wonders for our image.

## LIBRA September 2014

After your August feast of love, the mood shifts at home. Your partner becomes overly busy at work. Putting in long hours. Business travel is suddenly a necessity, taking him/her away for days at a time. When you talk on the phone, your partner seems distracted, perhaps tired.

The political intrigue deepens at your own job. You have to play the game and you do so very adeptly. It can be exhausting some days. You have to produce your usual flawless work. Plus you have to keep track of the various plots and players. Best bet is to find excuses to avoid water cooler gossip and steer clear of coffee klatsches. Folks who are directly involved will want your opinion. Keep that strictly to yourself.

You continue to earn acclaim for that volunteer project. In fact, you are becoming quite prominent in some circles now. One of the influential friends you've made as a result of this work has hinted about offering you a job. You decide this be a great way out of the nest of vipers your workplace has become. Why not amp up your friendship a bit with this individual? Share a meal and a bottle of wine. Come right out and say you are looking for radically different employment. Likely they will use the chance to mention that plum assignment they have been keeping rolled up in their sleeve. Don't force the issue. But do gain some clarity around what might be on offer.

Maybe as a result of expending all this energy on maneuvering, you revert to being indecisive in most other parts of your life. When you go out to eat, you agonize for a quarter of an hour over what to order. You buy five shirts at the store because you couldn't decide on just one. Then you return all of them the next day. You also become extremely anxious. A friend who lives in your favorite city invites you to visit for the weekend. You almost miss your flight, paralyzed by worry that you will forget to pack something important. As soon as your plane lands, you call your neighbor to check and see if you left the oven on. Prepare in advance to maintain your sense of humor during a muddled final week of September.

## LIBRA October 2014

Your creative surge returns, dispersing the anxiety and indecisiveness of last month. You realize that the more energy you put into your artistic project, the happier and more well-balanced you feel. You should soon be restored to a state of utter calm.

Regaining your equilibrium will come in handy later this month when you are called on to help someone in an emergency. You may get an urgent 4:00 am call from a friend who needs your assistance. It has something to do with a vehicle. Perhaps this pal of yours has been in a minor fender-bender. Or were they pulled over and stopped by the police for driving while under the influence. At any rate, you will have to play the responsible big brother or sister role and do your level best to dig your friend out of this scrape.

You'll be spending some time with a teenager around the middle of this month. It may be your own offspring suddenly demands more parental attention. Or it could be that you hire a neighbor's child to do some chores for you. At any rate, this teen will look to you for guidance. Being a teenager, he/she may not come right out and seek your advice. Rather, they will ask searching questions of you as they try to understand something they have no experience with. Could be sex or love or money or parents or drugs etc. Do not be squeamish. The child is not prying, just grappling with new issues. Remember, Libra, your symbol is the scales. The balance you must strike here is between modeling maturity for this young person while not appearing stodgy or old-fashioned. Best bet? Let the kid do the talking. Just nod and agree and answer questions candidly without too much added adult blather.

Your workplace's internecine war continues to acquire new plot twists. Your charm and diplomacy enable you to remain on good terms with opposing camps. You really ought to remind that well-connected friend about your work-related conversation last month. Don't think it's pushy of you to insist with this character who offered to help you in September. Busy people often forget promises unless prodded to remember. This potential benefactor of yours, along with most other people, is more likely to be forgetful this month due to the Mercury retrograde period which starts on October 4 and ends October 25. Patience as well as gentle persistence is advised at these times.

## LIBRA November 2014

Minor health problems are likely to plague you throughout this month. None of these is really serious. But they will appear in a wide range of costumes. You may get over a head cold only to sprain your wrist lifting weights at the gym. Or you may need extensive dental work, then have an allergic reaction to the antibiotics the dentist prescribed. It's possible you'll develop plantar fasciitis the same week as you get strep throat. When it rains...

All of this may just be a message from the universe telling you to slow down. As far as possible, try to re-create the kind of relaxing, home-sick-from-school days you enjoyed as a child. Wear your pajamas all day. Read in bed, choosing something light and escapist rather than a serious book. Watch a trashy movie while drinking fresh fruit juice to boost your immune system.

Unfortunately, you may have to emerge limping or coughing from your own sick bed to help take care of an elderly person mid-month. It may be one of your own relatives. Or it could be an older neighbor or friend. Summon your most charming smile and offer concrete aid to this person. Meals. Treats. Read to them. Chat and comfort. Above all, don't give them your germs. Wear a mask for close contact and wash your hands twice as often as usual. Their health issue is complicated. Part of it is physical. But some form of mental anguish contributes as well. The emotional issues are taking a toll. You don't have to solve their every problem or offer a cure. Your caring presence will be sufficient to improve the situation.

A financial windfall around the 22nd is likely to brighten the end of November for you. Buy something beautiful for your home. Then use some of the funds to treat a bunch of your friends to a special evening. Dinner and a play? A fancy supper party at home. Perhaps a day at the spa with massages for everyone. If the windfall is considerable, why not splurge on a dinner at your town's most fabulous restaurant? Be sure to conserve some of that surplus cash for the mad gift rush in December.

**LIBRA December 2014**

Your social life sparkles throughout December. In particular, a party around the 13th of the month gives you grounds to look for spectacular positive change in 2015. You and your partner host your own small, intimate event. All your guests have a wonderful time and they sing praises of your hospitality far and wide. You may make a change from your usual holiday pattern this year. Perhaps you forgo the customary visit to your in-laws. Instead you may spend some time with old friends who have a beautiful home in the mountains. Or maybe you and your adult children spend the holiday on a beach rather than hosting everyone in the universe.

This is a wonderful time for travel for you. The positions of the planets this month will help promote all sorts of lucky events when you journey away from home. Air travel should go smoothly. You enjoy sumptuous meals at scrumptious restaurants. You might make a spectacular find, bringing home an unusual souvenir that will impress your friends. Any unattached Librans will enjoy a wonderful window of opportunity for holiday romance while traveling abroad.

Make sure your partner does not throw caution to the winds on New Year's Eve. There is a small but definite possibility he or she could meet with a minor mishap that night related to over-indulgence. Advise him/her against too much rich food or too many glasses of champagne. Take steps to ensure that whoever is behind the wheel that night remains stone-cold sober. Also, use your well-honed diplomacy skills to ensure that minor tiffs between party-goers do not escalate.

You may receive a surprising e-mail or text message while on vacation. Someone at your office will share a late-breaking development in the ongoing machinations there. Don't let this distract you from your holiday fun. But keep in mind you must maintain silence on the subject of the discord at work. Despite your persistent efforts to stay out of the fray, certain people will continue to attempt to drag you into it. Zip that lip and keep it that way.

## LIBRA January 2015

There's an excellent chance you'll get that real job offer in early January. This will come as a result of those connections you fostered during the past year. Eager though you may feel to leave your present employment, take the time to size up this new position. As far as possible, ascertain that the new workplace is not as chockablock with political intrigue as the old one. Try diplomatically to negotiate the best possible salary and benefit package. Make sure you get ample vacation time so you can spend more time with your family. Weigh the two jobs against each other. Then talk them over with someone older and more experienced whose judgment you trust.

The new position will have you in the public eye more often. You will probably earn more money too. But some of that will have to go to a wardrobe upgrade. A shopping expedition is in order. Take your most style-savvy friend along to help you select a few classic-yet-chic additions to your closet.

Word of your new career assignment may attract the attention of some less than scrupulous acquaintances. Be wary of anyone who comes to you with propositions for investment now. Don't co-sign any loans. Overall, keep a low profile in regard to your increased wealth.

You will have more authority at your new workplace too. Make clear to those who report to you that you are a down-to-earth, willing to get your own coffee guy. But do avoid appearing indecisive or vague. Let people at your new workplace see that you are a relaxed person, yet you can also be firm and assertive. They will soon understand that you are neither a bully or a pushover. Your talent for maintaining balance in chaos will be much appreciated and will help you to establish your position.

Someone in your family, perhaps a sibling, may reveal an addiction of some sort as the Year of the Horse draws toward a close. Show that you support this person's efforts to overcome this health challenge. Express respect for his or her decision to go into rehab or start attending AA. Encourage others in the family to be supportive as well.

# SCORPIO 2014
## OVERVIEW FOR THE WOOD HORSE YEAR

*Sassy Scorpio,*

*Think of this Year of the Horse as twelve-month self-improvement seminar. Life will offer you temptations aplenty to behave like the negative stereotype of a Scorpio: suspicious, angry and lascivious - incessantly plotting vengeance and/or seduction. A successful wood Horse year will alter your outlook and soften your hard heart. Horse years demand application and nose to the grindstone. But they also want to effect changes in the lives of the people they co-habit with on this planet. Relying on your old standby weapons of sass and sarcasm in order to deal with the Horse year's challenges could result in you having to spend next year in extended detention. Some of the keywords for you to consider this year include: forgiveness, generosity, reconciliation and forbearance.*

*You will find that the more you integrate these qualities, the more confident and empowered you will be. If you can develop a sense of altruism and social consciousness, the universe will shower you with the rewards of unconditional love, the return of old friends and better mental and physical health. Just remember that in order to make room for these new gifts, you must let go of sour attitudes that you have outgrown. Your creativity can reach a high-water mark this year. Abilities and talents you formerly felt unable to access become more available to you. You may learn to sing or play the ukulele or dance the tango. This Horse year could mean a serious artistic breakthrough for you. Be patient as you slowly gain mastery of these valuable new skills. sw*

―――――― ❡❡❡ ――――――

## THE CHINESE YEAR AHEAD
## SCORPIO 2014

### SCORPIO February 2014

Shortly after the Year of the Horse gallops in on January 31, Mercury will snap into retrograde again. This period of potential miscommunication, electronic snafu and travel problems will run from February 6 until the 28th. For you Scorpios, the effects of this retrograde are likely to be felt primarily in the areas of creativity, home, family and the past. If possible, do not make any agreements relating to purchasing or renting a home until March. Choose your words with care when conversing with family members to avoid misunderstandings. Resist purchasing new electronic equipment and take extra care with the machines you do own. If you must have work done on your home during these weeks, expect delays and reversals.

Curiously, retrograde periods also offer opportunities. If there is a creative project you shelved months or even years ago, this would be a good time to go back to it. Review any old songs or stories you wrote and stashed in a carton somewhere. Why not polish and revive them? If you began a painting or a sculpture and abandoned it a while back, drag it out and finish it now. There is also a strong possibility you will hear from someone from your past this month, perhaps an old lover or a relative you had almost forgotten you had. Welcome this person's renewed presence in your life. They care deeply about your general welfare and are eager to be of service to you.

During this retrograde period, acts of kindness you perform will resonate powerfully. Be alert to others' needs. Could a friend with an illness or injury use some cheering up? Perhaps you can walk their dog or clean out their garage or take them on an excursion to a museum or to the theater. Is there someone in your life, who feels bullied or insecure? Take the time to bolster this individual's confidence. Compliment them and encourage them to be brave and face their opposition squarely. The ripple effect from your generosity will be especially forceful if you offer aid to someone a member of your family from whom you have been estranged. This is a wonderful time for you vengeful Scorpios to heal old wounds and release old grudges.

### SCORPIO March 2014

The first week of March may bring arguments and power struggles related to money. This could manifest in several different ways. There could be an issue related to an unpaid debt—either one you owe or one owed to you. If you recently came into an inheritance, there could be legal struggles related to the apportioning of the legacy. Could be as simple as you quarreling with your live-in sweetie about how to allocate household funds. Watch out. Someone close to you may tap you for a loan and then react angrily when you tell them your resources are already stretched. Be kind. But frank. Right now you cannot loan any money.

Try not to let your testy Scorpio temper show in these money matters. Decide what to say beforehand. Then state your boundaries - gently. No need to initiate an argument. Or come on too strong. In general, because you appear so capable when handling your own funds, people feel they can approach you for handouts. Whether this financial issue pertains to your family's money or your own, you must maintain a certain impenetrable façade so as to avoid being pillaged at this time. You are vulnerable now. Street clear of any and all potential thieves.

Your keen intuition helps you detect a health problem with someone close to you around the 14th of this month. You may pick up on this matter even before your friend perceives it him/herself. Urge them to take care of this problem quickly. It is even worth nagging a bit. Again, use your charm rather than the forceful side of your personality to persuade this person to have a thorough checkup. If not treated soon, this health issue could become quite serious.

Toward the end of March, be especially watchful online. Someone could be trying to gain access to your private information. Don't open any e-mail attachments unless you know who they came from and what they contain. Change your privacy controls on Facebook and other social networks to safeguard the names and photos of your children and close friends. Don't accept friend requests from people you don't know. If you cannot resist the temptation to make new friends, drop the person a private message asking why they would like to befriend you. If they reply, they are more likely to be sincere. If you don't receive an answer, there is probably something shady going on.

### SCORPIO April 2014

Between April 1st and the 5th, expect an important and influential person to enter your life. Your suspicion meter may be set to "high" after recent events, causing you to question this new connection's motives. In this case, your hunch is only your imagination working overtime. This person does not have ulterior motives. He or she is not seeking any advantage over you. Go ahead and accept invitations or offers of assistance without harboring reservations. The way things turn out sometimes is surprising. There is a remarkable co-incidence behind why this person has come along just now. Either it turns out they knew someone you knew in another country or they may have graduated from the same high school you did in different year or they used to work with your Dad or your Uncle Louie. Expect the happenstance to increase the likelihood of this chance meeting bringing good fortune to your current existence.

On April 10th, you may have a splendid opportunity to shine. Your new acquaintance could have something to do with helping you attain this moment in the spotlight. Make sure you are ready. Do not let this be the day you go out wearing grotty sweatpants and torn sneakers. Avoid making sarcastic comments about co-workers. Do not behave in a surly way to inefficient restaurant servers. Don't snarl or turn up your nose. So long as you are prepared to maintain a cheery countenance, your lucky day will yield many benefits.

The latter half of the month brings mixed blessings. Your creative powers may be at their zenith. However, your capacity for observation will be less acute than usual. Try to use this period for tasks requiring imagination rather than lucidity. You are going through a creative renaissance. But remember that "renaissance" means "re-birth." You are a bit like a newborn puppy now. Since you are more vulnerable during this last week, avoid the company of unstable or angry persons. Spend time instead with reliable people who possess good common sense. You are frequently seen as the fierce mother or father wolf defending those who are not as strong as you. At this time, instead of you playing hero, you may need someone to protect your interests.

### SCORPIO May 2014

Around May 3rd, you should recover from the pleasant haze that characterized your mood for the last two weeks of April. You feel the need to shore up your sense of organization by going through a period of intense cleaning. Go ahead and ruthlessly edit the contents of your closets. Throw out whatever you have not worn or used for more than two years. No sense being accused of hoarding. Bags upon bags of discarded belongings can go either to a charity shop or, if it's in a really sorry state, into the trash bin. Knowing your proclivity for throwing yourself into any task with almost frightening intensity, you may find yourself staying up into the wee hours to accomplish this closet purging. Beware, loss of sleep makes you cranky.

I foresee two probable results from this cleaning period. One is that your single-minded enthusiasm for tidying up may cause a negative reaction in someone who lives with or at least near you. Could be your late-night cleaning sprees irritate your roommate or a neighbor in your building. Or your partner or one of your children may complain about the phase in which your fervent re-organization results in temporary chaos. Do not snap if someone gripes about your activities. Instead, take their remarks as a signal to slow down. Scorpio so often overdoes it. You need to relax. Sip at a cup of tea whilst pondering the rights and concerns of the others in your personal entourage.

The other possible consequence of your intense tidying up is that you will recover something of value. A precious item (jewelry, a first edition, a painting) you thought you had lost suddenly reappears. If you have been experiencing tight financial straits, consider selling your treasure on E-Bay.

That VIP who befriended you last month may ask for your input on a project. Even if you already feel over-committed, do not reject this request. Consider whether you can shift some other tasks to the back-burner. Remember. You stand to see considerable gain from your affiliation with this individual. They have no other motivation than to see you succeed at what you want to succeed at. Grant them your opinions and assist them generously.

## SCORPIO June 2014

Try to wrap up important discussions related to travel, inheritance, taxes or shared property before June 7 when the second Mercury retrograde phase of this year begins. As this retrograde lasts through July 1 it's advisable to avoid signing any contracts or going to court until after that date. That is especially true for Scorpios during these June weeks of the retrograde. You (or your attorney) could miss some crucial detail. Or else everything may need to be re-done at a later date. Abstain as well from buying new appliances or electronic equipment till at least July 2nd.

However, this wonky period does offer an opportunity for planning and research about future foreign travel, business decisions and/or higher education. If you are considering returning to school, begin to collect information comparing different programs now. Or spend an evening or two drooling over some colorful vacation brochures for an exciting trip you might take later in the year.

Romance is in the air in June. And with it comes the usual sexual preoccupation for which you Scorpios are so famous. You can do with better sex at this time in your life. But you are not quite sure where to go looking for it. My advice? If you are itching to stray, do so outside of your own entourage of friends and/or family. The guy or woman who takes up with a sister or brother-in-law ALWAYS get found out. If you would rather avoid a messy breakup in your future... steer clear of flings with people you know.

You may awaken on the morning of the 21$^{st}$, give or take a day, to the realization that your nighttime dreams included a surprising sexual situation. Maybe, in your dream, you were passionately kissing someone you actively dislike. Or your dream saw you intimately caressing a platonic friend you never seriously considered as a lover. Could be the sexual activity you were engaged in your dream is something you would never dare do in real life. Knowing you, you will probably keep this nocturnal fantasy a deep, dark secret. Just make sure you don't hide its meaning from yourself. Examine the events in the dream and attempt to understand its meaning. It could point to a facet of your sexuality that you have not yet explored. Or... as it involves affection as well as sex, the dream may indicate that your subconscious mind has forgiven someone whom you still resent in your waking thoughts.

## SCORPIO July 2014

You could receive a health alert this month. Perhaps a routine test from a doctor visit comes back positive, requiring more complex tests. Or you may discover a suspicious mole or lump on your body. You might experience chest pains after climbing a set of stairs. Avoid taking the ostrich approach. No hiding your head in the sand. But don't panic either. It's never useful to assume the worst. Especially avoid internet-based self-diagnosis. Many health websites are designed to awaken the users' latent hypochondriac tendencies and excite alarm. Deal only with reliable health professionals. If you don't trust your current doctor, ask for references from friends. Physicians, like every other type of professional from car mechanics to lawyers, come in a range of styles and competence. Choose someone you like who likes you back.

Toward mid-month, you may get a sneaking suspicion that someone has been moving your belongings. Perhaps your car keys are on the kitchen table when you feel sure you left them on the mantle. Or when you return to your office after a coffee break, your laptop seems to have shifted a few inches. Relax. You know how you are. Scorpios are born detectives and can be hypersensitive to subtle cues and overreact to less than nothing. Perhaps someone in your family used your keys to fetch something from the trunk of your car. Or maybe your assistant or a roommate moved your laptop while looking for a document you asked him/her to look for. This hunch or qualm of yours doesn't appear to be anything more than the result of a moment of forgetfulness on your part. Keep your antennae raised for the rest of July. You could be right. Maybe someone is rifling through your personal belongings. But from a planetary standpoint, it doesn't seem likely.

A friend of yours may take a controversial stand this summer. As a result, around the 25$^{th}$, you could have to stand up to some mean-spirited gossipers on your friend's behalf. You might say how much you disapprove of people who spread rumors. But avoid sinking your claws too deeply into those who engage in this idle slander. Stay on point. Defend your pal by remarking on how ugly you deem gossip to be, without implicating those particular gossipers. Don't descend to their level of negativity.

## SCORPIO August 2014

You may find yourself dealing with gossip mongers again around the 5$^{th}$ of the month. This time, the nasty rumors could focus on you. Perhaps some snobs resent your ability to be stylish without relying on labels. They can't stand it that you look better in resurrected thrift store duds than they do in expensive designer apparel. No need to deploy your inner Navy SEAL team to perform a verbal assassination on these pathetic individuals. Let them hang themselves with their own tongues. Their catty language will serve to reveal their envy. The reactions other people have to this backbiting will help you separate the social wheat from the chaff and sort your true allies from the pretenders.

An elderly relative is likely to make demands on you around the 13$^{th}$ of this month. This person may call you frequently. He or she will ask you for rides to health care appointments, help with grocery shopping, assistance with personal grooming tasks like clipping their toenails and minor technology challenges like operating the television remote. You may suspect a deeper problem underlying these requests for help. This individual could be suffering from the beginning stages of dementia. Alert his or her primary physician to this possibility. Try to recruit other relatives to help you cope with this older person's needs. Also look into community resources such as volunteers from a social service agency. Find out if the older person's place of worship offers some kind of home visit services. It may be time to look into a senior housing facility whose personnel possess the skills to deal with this person's decline. This maneuver will take all the diplomacy you can muster. Perhaps you should be meditating or at least doing yoga - if only to manage the stress levels this delicate situation has imposed on you.

If you made sincere efforts to reconcile with that estranged family member as I recommended earlier this year, you will be rewarded in some way toward the end of the month. Perhaps that person wins the lottery and shares some of the wealth with you. Or you discover that relative has precisely the wherewithal to assist you right now. And they even offer you their services free of charge.

## SCORPIO September 2014

As this month begins, you should find yourself with more disposable income. Buy yourself one or two personal treats. But save most of the funds for presents. From a karmic point of view, this is a perfect time for you to give gifts. If you have children, choose unusual presents that will delight them. Show a loyal close friend how much you appreciate their support with a well-chosen offering. Whatever you give anyone around the 5<sup>th</sup>-12<sup>th</sup> of this month has the power to enhance warmth and connection.

Around mid-September a flirtation of yours may grow into something more significant. Perhaps a waiter, a waitress or a coffee crew member has been slipping you notes of admiration on the saucer under the coffee cup he or she hands you each morning. You and an attractive co-worker may have been exchanging lingering looks in the elevator. Or maybe one of your neighbors has been deliberately walking the dog at the same time you go running in order to exchange a few casual words with you. Whoever this person is, they are ready to move things to the next level, to deepen your acquaintance. Consider your response carefully. Do you see yourself in a long-term relationship with such a person? If the flirtation does evolve into something beyond teasing words and glances, what consequences might result from a casual fling? Could it be a "just for fun" dalliance. Or... it could break your little black heart?

A friend confides something intimate and a little bit horrifying to you toward the end of September. This conversation may confirm a suspicion that you have had for a while. Resist the temptation to share this confirmation of your intuition with others. Whatever you do, hold your tongue. Guard the story your friend has shared with you as closely as you do your own secrets. Stash it in the vault. Throw away the key. Scorpios are the best keepers of secrets. They know how to stand guard over other peoples private information because they are so secretive to begin with.

## SCORPIO October 2014

As a result of this month's Mercury retrograde (October 4th through the 25th) you may feel you have lost your secret super-powers. Scorpios in long-term relationships could notice a mysterious coolness emanating from a previously devoted partner. Single Scorpios are likely to observe a drop-off in the number of admirers. That cute receptionist or wait person who used to flirt with you, suddenly doesn't seem to notice you at all. Wondering what happened to your exquisite allure? Are your friends less interested in you, interrupting your anecdotes and failing to laugh at your acerbic, witty observations. Your bosses or teachers don't appreciate your work. You may begin to doubt yourself during this Mercury retrograde.

Don't be alarmed. This is a temporary phase. To regain your sensual powers and native charisma, recharge your batteries. Retreat for a while. Take long walks alone. Meditate. Check a pile of books out of the library. Curl up and read them. Write in your journal. Or write poetry. Or grab your guitar and strum your heart out. When you are surrounded with people, keep still. Listen sympathetically when others speak. Look into their eyes when they talk. Nod in empathy but say little. A more tranquil you will attract a new kind of attention. You will appear more mysterious. Once again people will consider you with respect and curiosity. Try it. Kick back. Slow down both body and tongue. Your charisma will gradually return.

After the end of the Mercury retrograde period on the 25<sup>th</sup>, communications should begin to improve. Why not celebrate this return to normalcy with a party? Perhaps a birthday celebration, a masquerade ball or Halloween bash. You might even consider combining the two. If you don't yet feel up to hosting an event, make sure to attend a reception or social event or two. Not up to cooking and receiving at home? Plan to give a small dinner party at a restaurant. The period from the 27<sup>th</sup>-31<sup>st</sup> offers an exceptional opportunity for social interaction. Take advantage of this window the universe is offering to indulge in moments of pure joy and playfulness. Dance. It's good for the soul.

## SCORPIO November 2014

Your jealous streak may get the better of you around the 8th of this month. You overreact to some minor incident between you and your love partner, triggering a transformation into your Mr. (or Ms.) Hyde persona. You may find yourself boiling with rage even while your more rational self stands back observing, in full knowledge there are no grounds for such outrageous behavior. Forewarned is forearmed. Take some advance precautionary measures. Go on a long solitary hike in nature to quiet your mind. This time alone will help you recognize just how responsible you are for your emotions. You cannot control your partner. However, you can choose your reactions to what he or she says or does. You can determine how best to interpret your partner's words and actions. Developing a deeper, more loving and trusting relationship with your partner may require that you learn to control your suspicious impulses. Improvement will require facing up to the less positive parts of your nature which, you have to admit, do need work.

You always get a hit of fresh energy during November. It's your birth month and allows for new beginnings as well as completions. This November brings a chance at some personal satisfaction you had only dreamed of till now. Maybe you finally finished that book you were writing or you put together enough art work for an exhibit. Perhaps you made a video or recorded your singing voice. Those personal projects you have been pondering are favored in the climate of November for Scorpios. Is it the influence of your birth month? Very likely.

That VIP you got to know earlier this year will provide you with an exciting new opportunity around the 14th. However, this once-in-a-lifetime chance could entail a hitch of sorts. Perhaps you will be offered a dream job offer with a fantastic salary and benefits. But taking said dream job would mean relocating, uprooting your family and altering your lifestyle. Or... you may get the chance to travel to some destination you've always wanted to visit. The drawback is that taking this trip means missing a major family event. There's no room for bargaining or compromise here. Your knack for dealing with rocks and hard places by wriggling between the two won't work this time. Your considerable persuasive skills can't make a dent in the necessity to choose either A or B. No options. You must make a decision. Black and white situations like these teach us about where our personal priorities really lie.

## SCORPIO December 2014

You may notice a dip in energy from the 2nd through the 7th of this month. Pushing yourself too hard? All that November speediness could have negative consequences on your general well-being. If you have a tendency to put in marathon hours at work or slave night and day on a creative project, you will have to impose some moderation and perhaps even discipline on your schedule. If you cope with stress by putting yourself through long, grueling workouts at the gym or dojo, maybe you should retreat a bit from excessive exercise. If you don't relieve the pressure by yourself, there's a strong possibility your body will rebel and cause you a fairly serious health setback.

After a slight slump in your romantic life during October, plus that jealous spate last month, your sexual magnetism returns full force around the 18th. Your partner becomes even more loving and attentive than usual. He or she strives to please you both in and out of the bedroom. Breakfasts in bed. Trips to fun places you love. Outings with good old friends he or she knows will delight you. If you are single, you will notice you can barely walk two blocks without attractive people sidling up and overtly flirting with you. An especially satisfying evening with your partner (or even someone new!) occurs on or around the 26th.

An ingenious deduction or creative notion of yours earns you kudos at work around the 16th. This praise is likely to carry with it at least some of the additional income and authority you have been craving. Do remember the famous saying by your fellow Scorpio, the French Enlightenment philosopher Voltaire, "With great power comes great responsibility." As a Scorpio, you may be tempted to abuse your new clout in order to get even with some of your co-workers who previously underestimated your talents. Resist any yearnings to avenge. Vindictiveness is beneath your dignity and would have a negative effect on your excellent reputation. Your astrological sign actually has three symbols. a) The Scorpion = poisonous stinger. Don't sting just anyone. b) The Eagle -you can soar above petty actions. c) The Phoenix - you can birth yourself anew like the phoenix who rises alive and healed from his own ashes. These symbols of strength are freighted with great responsibility. Never abuse power. Or it will bite back.

**SCORPIO January 2015**

Spending time around young people helps you maintain your emotional equilibrium though a tense early January. Problems seem to come at you fast and thick from all directions. Challenges arise on both the home and work fronts. If you are a parent, make time even at the end of the most difficult days to play, read to or talk with your children.

If you are not a parent, volunteer to take your grandchildren, nieces and nephews, the offspring of a friend or some underprivileged kids on an outing. Be both materially and emotionally generous with children now. Buy them treats, but also offer them to your best non-judgmental, non-condescending, undivided attention. Turn off your phone when you are with them. Listen and really hear what they say. The kids will benefit from this kind of respectful kindness from an adult. And you will gain stability from being more playful and letting go of the stressful mental attitudes most Scorpios impose on themselves.

Around the 20th, there will likely be enough of a break between minor crises for you to sneak away for a brief trip. Do not announce this journey in advance to anyone at work. Leave your secret trip itinerary with key people who must be able to reach you in case of emergency. Arrange for your e-mail box to send out an "away from office" message with your date of return to everyone who e-mails you.

Your trip is likely to be unpredictable in many ways but will yield many happy memories. Travel with your partner, or if you are single, go with the kind of friend flexible enough to help you find fun even if the weather is bad or your flight is cancelled. If you take your children on this trip, explain that changes in plan constitute an opportunity for adventure. If the weather is inclement or a train is late, make a joke of it. No use spoiling the fun with any cranky reactions to reality.

# SAGITTARIUS 2014
## OVERVIEW FOR THE WOOD HORSE YEAR

*Spunky Sagittarius,*

*Already part horse, part human you feel a sense of relief and comfort when a Horse year rolls around. Certainly this Wood Horse year is likely to prove less constricting for you than the preceding Snake year. 2014 will see you enjoying both professional respect and financial rewards. You will also experience a returning sense of personal magnetism which enables you to attract the sort of relationships you want. You will make valuable friends and connect with the type of serious business associates or co-workers you have long hoped for. If you seek new romantic involvement this year, you are likely to find an abundance of willing, worthwhile partners. But do remember to exercise prudence and discretion where words are concerned.*

*You can easily soil all this good karma buy speaking out of turn or being brash where brashness is not welcome. Turn your tongue seven times before put in your two cents lest you find one of your hooves firmly ensconced in your big mouth. If you are cautious about whose feelings you hurt, you should sail on through this year with flying colors. Pay heed to the best side of yourself. Work harder. Make tracks. Gamble less and labor more. There will ample travel in 2014 for restless Sagittarians. And there will most certainly be passion - in spades! sw*

―――― *e·℮·e* ――――

## THE CHINESE YEAR AHEAD
## SAGITTARIUS 2014

**SAGITTARIUS February 2014**

The universe offers another opportunity for you to practice patience this month. Mercury goes retrograde from the 6th to the end of February. Electronics get buggy. Messages go astray and local travel becomes more complicated during these periods. Steer clear of signing any binding documents until the beginning of March. And avoid commitment till the coast is clear after February 28.

As the Year of the Horse begins you will feel restless and at loose ends. Your alliance with your long-term partner has grown stale. Since you cannot tolerate boredom, you seek to change that situation. Some Sadges will look for novelty and excitement in discreet dalliances and flirtations. Others will choose to end the old relationship and begin a quest for a new partner. Still others will try to bring back excitement to an existing relationship, perhaps by spicing things up in the bedroom. A few of you may talk with your partner and decide to try an open relationship. Whatever you decide to do, it will constitute a major upheaval in your love life.

Your public reputation may rise this month. Important people, perhaps your boss and even his/her boss, grant you unexpected acclaim. You naturally enjoy the positive attention. However, you may learn that the praise you receive is not based entirely on your own accomplishments. Through some mix-up, people have given you credit for a project or achievement that is not rightfully yours. Doing the honest thing and correcting the mistake may be embarrassing. Too, you may lose some of the fans you have gained. If however the error is allowed to persist, you will be guilty of deception. You prize honesty in others and are often quick to criticize them when they fall short of your high standards. Now is the time to practice what you preach. 'Fess up. Tell all. Coming clean will wash your conscience and clean up your karma in the bargain.

You may have to intervene this month to help a sibling or give a boost to an old friend. This person has a problem which has begun to interfere with his/her previously harmonious existence. Perhaps he or she has become such a terminal hoarder that their home is no longer healthy to live in. Or they may have frightened others by engaging in erratic or perverse public behavior. You will be called upon to organize some sort of help for this person, perhaps hiring a therapist or getting your friend into a residential treatment program.

## SAGITTARIUS March 2014

Did you decide to act on that romantic restlessness last month? If so, this month finds your social calendar chockablock with coffee dates and lunches designed to audition possible new partners. You may have difficulty finding someone who meets your standards. You picture yourself with someone whose entrance into the coffeehouse fills the entire room with electricity. You seek someone whose wit, intelligence and life experience is equal to your own. Failing that, you're willing to take on a highly attractive younger person who finds you enthralling. Don't be disappointed when you meet people who need a therapist instead of a lover. Take your time.

You may have better luck finding someone with the charm and sparkle you seek offline. Try getting involved in an activity related to performance or music. Join a community theatre group. See if there's a drum circle or book club in your neighborhood. Sign up for a class in circus arts or tango. You will meet many lively and confident people in this sort of setting. Online dating sites are crawling with misfits and bitter divorcees.

The work front is freighted with small fires you have to put out. You wonder why so many colleagues are so resolutely irresponsible. They create disasters and go whistling home at closing time. Is your sense of duty too well-developed?

By the end of the month, you will not be your usual jolly self. You feel frustrated, irritated. At a social gathering around the 19th, you snap at someone who dominates the conversation with a TMI tale of his/her old traumas. You may spend the rest of the evening sniping at those who insist on repeating dull stories. Be wary of exhibiting this caustic side of yourself. Some of this sarcasm could actually serve as a secret mating call. You might attract a person who shares this tendency - possibly a gabby Gemini or sexy Scorpio with a gift for gibes. You and this person may have a slew of things in common. There may even be strong chemistry between you. Don't rush into a friendship or romance however. Test the waters. Take your time. The unknown quantities in love affairs can prove treacherous.

## SAGITTARIUS April 2014

In early April, someone you hire to work on your home may screw up royally. You will find yourself very angry at this person. That new crack in your ceiling or leak from your toilet won't repair itself. This person, an acquaintance or friend of a friend, represented him or herself as an expert. Yet they show up without the proper tools. Then they leave, ostensibly to fetch their equipment. Then they don't return until three days later. You explode, hurling insults. The other individual, perhaps a hyperactive Aries or a proud Leo, becomes angry in turn. Since you know each other socially, the argument becomes personal and nasty. Try to contain the situation. Fire this character right away quick. Then clean up the building site, take a loan from the bank and choose a reputable contractor to finish the job.

That Gemini with the wicked wit keeps calling, e-mailing or texting. This person's sharp observations about other people make you snort with laughter. If you decide to pursue an alliance of some sort with them, be wary. As a Sadge, you are ruled by Jupiter, the largest planet and the one named for the king of the gods. As a result, you sometimes fool yourself into thinking you are invulnerable. Remember that someone who talks behind the backs of friends may stab you in the back as well. If it's a roller coaster adventure you are after, this Gemini will deliver plenty. But if you are looking for long term partner, you might as well lose this person on the first turn.

A younger person in your theatre group or drum circle has developed a crush on you. He or she laughs longer and harder than anyone else when you tell a joke. They are in awe of your myriad accomplishments. They admire your vast experience and lofty professional standing. You feel a bit flattered by all the hero worship. Meanwhile, your talent is making you a more prominent member of this group. Perhaps you are asked to direct an upcoming play, or do a solo at a drum performance. If it's tango you are about, choose this admirer to be your partner.

**SAGITTARIUS May 2014**

You may receive an unusual and intriguing assignment at work around the 3$^{rd}$ of May. This project, although it does not carry any particular honors, piques your intellectual curiosity. You find yourself growing more enthusiastic about work than you have been in a long time.

Now of course you have become far too busy. You are juggling multiple lovers, enjoying newfound social popularity as well as the sexual variety. That fascinating new work project takes more of your time as well. Then pile on those new creative responsibilities which require more disciplined commitment than you bargained for. You are one busy camper.

Be wary about pursuing anything beyond a mild flirtation with that younger person. He or she may not yet have learned how to keep a relationship light and casual. Without meaning to, you could hurt someone too inexperienced to know what to expect. Instead of bedding this admiring youngster, assume the role of (non-sexual) mentor or teacher. Their fawning appreciation and esteem for your shared wisdom will largely compensate any time you spend giving him/her guidance.

You keep discovering intriguing new facets of that friend who excels at funny-bone tickling mockery. He or she has an advanced degree in ethnobotany or speaks five languages or lived with a forest tribe in Peru for two years. If you go ahead and become more deeply involved with this person, remember to step carefully. You are walking on a field of landmines - even if it is strewn with beautiful wildflowers.

That sibling or old friend you aided a couple months ago is doing better now. The program you got them into or therapist you arranged for has helped this person make steps toward recovery. He or she may call you and express their gratitude. Remember that is important to welcome their appreciation. Recovering people are fragile. If you cut them short when they say "thank you", they may relapse. You can continue to help this person by demonstrating respect and compassion for him or her. This approach is obviously much harder to pull off than simply staging a rescue.

**SAGITTARIUS June 2014**

Mercury does one of its backtracks this month (from the 7th of June until the 1st of July.) This shouldn't affect your travel plans since Mercury rules local rather than distance travel. But if you do face minor problems concerning electronic devices and household appliances going on the blink, remember to keep your sense of humor. And whatever you do, don't choose June 2014 for signing documents.

You are likely to receive a windfall of some sort this month. Perhaps an investment you made a while ago pays off with a handsome dividend. Or you receive an unanticipated bonus at work or a gift from a departed friend who lived far away. Whatever the source, use at least part of the funds to travel. I hope your passport is in order. This month the stars are perfectly aligned for you to attain a crescendo of enjoyment while in a foreign country.

You may want to take along one of your part-time bed partners. Or you may want to travel alone. Of course traveling solo will allow you more chances of rubbing shoulders (or other portions of your anatomy) with the locals. Your charm and allure are at their height around the 17th of June. People who meet you for the first time are instantly drawn to you. People around your own age whom you encounter instantly want to become your lover or your best friend. Older people act as if you were a long-lost son or daughter. Children smile and wave when they see you as if you were a favorite aunt or uncle. You are invited into the homes of several of the locals where they serve you exotic, delicious meals. You may be offered a private, behind-the-scenes tour of an important museum or historical site.

Be sure to take whatever prescriptions or remedies you usually rely on in your carry-on as one fly in the ointment could be a bout of severe indigestion while on this trip. Something you eat or drink disagrees with you. Whatever it is tries to exit your body at both ends simultaneously. Nothing life-threatening. But you will feel quite weak afterwards. You may have to rest for a day or two. Afterwards, your resistance will be quite low. Find some vitamins and build up your electrolytes. You will have to eat more carefully for a few days. Porridge and soups to start. Avoid pulpy fruits and other intestinal irritants.

**SAGITTARIUS July 2014**

When you arrive home from your recent trip, you will be somewhat bewildered. You'll have a hard time concentrating at work. You may even find yourself making excuses to play hooky. You'll call in sick, and then spend the day at a sporting event or taking a walk in a forest preserve. As long as you turn your projects in on time, your boss will probably let your increased absences slide. It's only travel hangover. Next week you will return to your feisty old self.

You may be surprised when one of your new friends from abroad contacts you online. He or she actually plans to visit your town later this month. And they hope to stay in your spare bedroom! You had great fun with this person and he or she introduced you to his/her circle, making your trip that much more festive. You agree to play host/ess. Unfortunately, this visit will probably not play out as a reprise of your fabulous vacation. One way or another, your houseguest could wreak havoc on your home life. They leave dirty dishes in the kitchen sink and/or strew wet towels across the bathroom floor. Or they expect you to stay up all night talking and drinking. Explain, if you can, that you are not on holiday now. You must get up at 6 am to go to work. You will no doubt heave a deep sigh of relief when this quirky guest leaves.

Is money is burning a hole in your pocket? It will be around the 22nd. You'll want to buy things which are unique and perhaps a bit eccentric. Maybe you'll acquire an exotic musical instrument: a didgeridoo, a dulcimer or an Egyptian Djembe drum. Or you might spend hours in antique and vintage clothing stores where you can turn up a fabulous old oil painting of a scene from classical mythology or unearth a 1940s fedora. Maybe you'll augment your collection of tacky souvenir plates from all 50 states. Or else you'll spend hours on E-bay shopping for Persian rugs. Might it be the influence of the quirky guest? Whatever it is... have fun. But watch that bottom line.

## SAGITTARIUS August 2014

You've been romantically footloose for a few months, playing the field. But that changes radically around the 1st-6th of August. Either you meet someone new or your relationship with one of those people crowding the revolving door on your bedroom shifts into higher gear. You and this creature discover you share everything from political viewpoints to a fondness for orange popsicles. You simply can't get enough of each other. When you're not making vigorous love with her/him, the two of you immerse yourselves in hours-long discussions. You cook meals together. You take long walks, holding hands the entire time. Whenever you have to be apart, you text each other voraciously. Some of your messages are funny; others sweetly loving and still others would shock and titillate the NSA snoopers.

That young person who looks up to you may come to you for advice around the 16th. She or he has gotten into a jam. You offer suggestions to help them extricate him or herself from this pickle. It turns out this character doesn't have a very strong support network. You may have to offer a small amount of financial aid or perhaps even a temporary place to stay. Make sure it's clear that the handout is a loan - and that the lodging is short term.

Between your hot romance and your expanded mentoring role, you may become inattentive at the office. For a few weeks, this probably won't matter. Your expert intelligence enables you to turn in excellent work even when your brain wanders a bit. However this is not the time to skip workplace socializing events. You may deem these both stuffy and unnecessary. But be sure to go to the one that occurs around the last week in August. Failing to attend could attract some raised eyebrows among the powers-that-be. Your boss may start casting a more critical eye on your currently rather sketchy production level.

I advise you to step up efforts to effect renovations on your home now. These improvements are not absolutely essential. But this is prime time for enhancing the home and garden part of your life. Maybe you will build a deck or add a new room, modernize your kitchen or replace that grungy bathroom tile. The time is now for such work to be undertaken.

## SAGITTARIUS September 2014

Your young protégé may make sexual overtures toward you in the first week of the month. This person is very physically attractive and seems to idolize you. I know this is a tempting combination. However, giving in to impulse could have a disastrous impact on your life. It could bring your affair with your new partner to a screeching halt. It could also create waves at the theatre group or drum circle where you met your young friend. Gently, yet firmly, turn down any sexual offers from this fledgling adult.

Your occasional predilection for excess could make you look foolish around mid-month. I know how you love parties, so I am not suggesting you stay home. But do avoid giving in to any reckless impulses. Too many drinks could make you pass out drooling on your host's favorite armchair. Too much rich food may send you to the bathroom for an embarrassingly extended and noisy interval.

In fact, this month is an excellent time to nip any bad health habits in the bud. The positions of the planets will give you added energy and motivation to kick start your health. This is a great time to start a new diet or exercise program. If the only exercise you get is in the bedroom, maybe you and your partner can take dance classes together. If you are already active, assess what needs improvement. Perhaps you are inflexible from frequent weightlifting and too little stretching. Sign up for a few weeks of yoga class. Most Sadges feel a strong connection to the equine world. Horseback riding provides excellent exercise. If you feel sluggish and tired, try eating more fruits and vegetables. Visit a farmer's market to find a delicious variety of produce. Cook more vegetables more often. Cut back on meat and dairy products.

The spiritual side of your life needs refurbishing now. I am not suggesting you suddenly wax religious. But you may want to think about undertaking some form or meditation or other spiritual practice. Generally speaking, you are a down-to-earth person who doesn't feel a particular calling to spirituality. You will be amazed how much lending time and energy to your inner self enhances your self -image.

## SAGITTARIUS October 2014

Early this month, you will have the opportunity to redress a wrong. A few years ago, you let your petty dislike of someone get in the way of your good judgment. Ultimately, you regretted being so harsh. This person did no harm to anyone. He or she simply grated on your touchy nerves. Your unkind comments resulted in this person being ostracized from your close-knit group of friends. Now the cosmic alignment of the planets grants you a chance to do some sort of favor for this person. Do not pass up this second chance. You can actually erase some of your bad karma now. Also, although they may come in an indirect way, you will reap spiritual rewards from this good deed.

This kind of redress and re-thinking project is a perfect example of how to make positive use of a Mercury retrograde phase. Yep. We have another of those this month, starting on the 4th and lasting until the 25th of October Rather than moaning about Mercury's backward shift bringing hassles and headaches, focus on what opportunities this period may bring.

Your group creative project gives you an opportunity to bask in the spotlight this month. Your drum ensemble may perform at a community event where your solo receives praise. Or the play you direct earns a rave review in the local paper. Offers for more creative projects may come your way as a result of this success. These new projects carry tantalizing incentives—perhaps some extra cash or maybe the opportunity to collaborate with artists whose work you admire. Even if this new project involves taking a minor role you will do well to participate.

An elderly person, perhaps your partner's relative or maybe one of your older neighbors may make an offensive remark to you around the 18th. Handle this diplomatically. Express your disapproval of their crass language. But refrain from using your Jupiterian strength to hurl lightning bolts at this senior citizen. He or she grew up in a very different era from yours. Provide an opening for this older person to learn about how easy it is to be civil. Instead of providing them with fuel for their ire, give them some of your time. Sit down and chat with them. Kill them (no don't) with kindness.

## SAGITTARIUS November 2014

You lose patience with an old friend of yours early this month. He or she says something which you misinterpret as a criticism of your new romance. Later when you review the situation, you realize you were too hasty and ought not to have taken offense. Contact your pal immediately. Admit that you have been feeling defensive lately. Acknowledge that the quarrel was your fault. Ask for forgiveness. Don't let pride stand in the way of continuing to enjoy the fruits of a long term friendship.

You will be glad later in the month that you did not let this situation fester. Another of your old friends faces a serious health crisis. Everyone gathers at the hospital, coming together as a group to support the friend and his or her family. There is a strong possibility that there will be a sad final farewell to someone you have loved as a friend for years.

Your love partner may want the two of you to move into a new relationship phase. Perhaps he or she wants you to merge your households. Or she/he may be talking about wedding locations and honeymoon destinations. You find the idea very attractive yet feel hesitant. Do have a serious discussion about finances. Your partner may harbor very different ideas about spending, saving and investing. Better to discuss things calmly now than to have a heated argument when you have merged a few of your assets and cannot extricate yourself.

That spiteful new friend whose humor you find so delightful may try to throw a wrench in the works around the 20th. He or she plays games with you and someone close to you. This character repeats your words out of context, giving them a nasty twist. She/he tries to undermine your happiness. You may also discover around this time that this person has lied to you. Best to gradually steer clear of him or her completely. Don't make a grand announcement about ending your association. That will only rouse this vicious person's anger. Let the friendship taper off. Don't answer every e-mail or text. Stop laughing at their jokes. Tamp down this character's enthusiasm little by little by ignoring their efforts at communicating with you. They will soon get the picture.

**SAGITTARIUS December 2014**

You find yourself contemplating a huge change in your life for 2015. You may decide to finally fulfill a long-postponed dream of moving to the country after decades of city life. You have always wanted to tend to a few chickens and goats. Or if you've always lived in a small town, you may decide it's high time to live downtown in a big city with easy access to culture. Could be you will contemplate becoming an ex-pat and hie yourself off to New Zealand or Fuji or France. The change may include higher education. You feel excited and stimulated by the prospect of making a fresh start. You are confident you have the skills you need to maintain your income while making this major transition. Begin to research and make long-range plans for this shift.

In the meantime, your new creative project offers exciting prospects for the near future. You're invited to an event where you will get to meet someone very influential. This won't be one of those huge group meet-and-greets where someone famous shakes hundreds of hands. You will actually get to trade ideas with this person who is highly respected within your creative field.

Make sure you have on hand whatever precautionary measures you use to ward off colds. Drink a lot of juice; take extra doses of vitamin C or an immune-boosting herb like Echinacea or astragalus. Several people around you will be getting sick, sneezing and coughing non-stop at the office. You don't want to meet that prominent person while you're snuffling into a tissue. So wash hands frequently. Take all your vitamins - especially between the 10th and the 16th of this month.

Some object you thought you lost long ago suddenly re-appears. It happens a bit mysteriously. You feel sure it wasn't on that shelf or in that closet when you looked there just last week. You almost wonder if someone is playing a trick on you. Or maybe you are hosting a poltergeist? Consider yourself lucky and stop right there. Ghosts are not in your future this year.

**SAGITTARIUS January 2015**

Shortly after January 1, you may experience some kind of health accident which limits your ability to move about. Northern hemisphere Sadges become more prone to slipping on the ice around this time. Southern hemisphere Sagittarians may step on a jelly fish on the beach. Or it may be a past physical problem reappearing. Perhaps the knee that never completely healed from that old soccer or field hockey injury goes out and you limp for a few days. Try to be patient and give yourself time to recover. Getting back on your feet too quickly now could result in a longer period of immobility later in the year. Kick back and be a good patient. Don't whine or snivel about the pain. Take your meds. Be kind to whomever is caring for you. Remember that you need their help more than they need to bring you that 30th glass of orange juice.

Being less active than usual could lead to an odd discovery. Maybe you spend more time online and track down some old friends on Facebook. To your surprise, you learn that two people who formerly hated each other are now married. Or you may see something unusual (even obscene) going on at your neighbor's home while you are convalescing on the couch. There are no steps to be taken in light of this revelation. Just enjoy and have a good giggle.

The last week of January may also bring you some unusual psychic experiences. You could have a premonition your co-worker is pregnant long before she makes the announcement. Or an old friend from high school appears in one of your dreams wearing ballet shoes and sporting a hole in her head. Puzzled, you Google her the next day. You find an article online from her local newspaper talking about a dance school she founded and mentioning that she had surgery last year for a brain tumor. Your neighbor tells you she can't find her cat. You immediately know that her feline friend was accidentally trapped in another neighbor's garage. Don't be afraid of this new talent. Instead, learn to develop it. Write down the psychic perceptions you receive, even if they seem eerie or inaccurate.

# CAPRICORN 2014
## OVERVIEW FOR THE WOOD HORSE YEAR

*Conscientious Capricorn,*

*To successfully meet the various challenges that 2014 brings, you Capricorns should try to become an expert Horse whisperer. First and foremost, understand that the Year of the Horse involves a few things you are not fond of: constant movement and abrupt change. As a stolid Capricorn with fixed notions of how to do things right, you tend not to imagine too many alternatives to your practiced lifestyle. You like routine and you cherish stasis. You are an earnest sort of person who climbs the mountain slowly but surely toward goal after goal every single day. This Horse year will oblige you to let go of your attachment to the status quo. It will impose flexibility on you and encourage you to become a more elastic thinker.*

*So rather than seeking to control the unexpected, and fend off the unpredictable as you always have, you will find it necessary to approach life in a more relaxed fashion. Reach out to those around you. Share their emotions and explore their doubts and fears. At the same time, generously instill some of your own grit into them. Give them hope. As you become more adept at this, you will observe that people are eager to pitch in and help you. I know that at first, some of this advice may go against the grain. But I have faith in your determination and native intelligence. By the end of the Year of the Horse, I expect you will have learned how, instead of announcing your demands, to effectively whisper your dreams to your fellow creatures. sw*

----------♈♈♈----------

## THE CHINESE YEAR AHEAD
### CAPRICORN 2014

**CAPRICORN February 2014**

Stoicism is high on the Capricorn list of virtues. You will get plenty of chance to utilize this talent of yours in February when Mercury goes retrograde from the 6th to the 28th, causing delays in communication and transportation snafus. Electronic devices may fritz out on you and household appliances break down mid cycle. Annoying? You bet.

The kick-off of the Year of the Horse may find you suffering from some kind of infection in your mouth or throat. Do not ignore this. You're prone to boast of the long hours you work. What others see as workaholism, you proudly view as a show of stamina and intelligence. But this time, back off the work a bit. Take a day or so to see to your health. Postpone that weighty project. See the doctor or dentist ASAP. Follow the instructions you are given to clear up the infection or inflammation you have contracted.

Your partner may seem easily miffed these days. You make what you think is a light-hearted suggestion. Your significant other snaps at you, reminding you that you're not the boss. Please remember that, as a Capricorn, you exert a great deal of natural authority. While this helps you succeed at work, this sense of command can act as a strain on your partner. Even when you don't intend to be pushy, you come off as "in charge". Make an extra effort to show your sweetie you can and will do things his/her way. Try not to insist that "your way" is more efficient - even if is. Each of us approaches life from a different angle. Sometimes cooperation and harmony require sacrificing your power for the benefit of all. Praise your partner more often. Do this the same way you might compliment an equal co-worker or even your boss. Weed out any words or vocal tones that sound patronizing. In your leisure time together, let your sweetie make more choices about the direction your couple is going.

You may find yourself intrigued by a new hobby toward the end of the month. The subject that piques your interest will be an unusual one for you. You might develop a passion for Thai cooking, fixed-gear bicycling or Middle Eastern-style drumming. Whatever it is, you feel drawn to devoting time to this activity. Go ahead and permit yourself to invest some time and money in this interest. It will help reduce your stress and give your partner a break in the bargain.

## CAPRICORN March 2014

Between the 4th and the 10th of this month, you may be surprised by flirtatious overtures coming from an associate or crony of your ex. If you are currently partnered, behave with scrupulous integrity in this matter. Steer clear of saying or doing anything that could be misconstrued as encouraging the person's come-ons. Even if you are single, mull this over carefully. If you and your ex are still involved in each other's lives in any way, this kind of fling could provide a reason for further bitterness to be born. Capricorn's symbol is the goat. Many of you Capricorns, beneath your strict business attire, yearn to embody not only the ambitious, mountain-climbing goat but the horny old (or not-so-old) goat. Don't permit your rambunctious Billy or Nanny Goat side to trip you up this time.

Flexibility and humor (not your strong points) become paramount around mid-March. Some project you have been planning will go awry. It may be that a major presentation fails because of technology snafu. Or possibly a dinner party where you hoped to showcase your culinary skill is somehow ruined. If you worry too much about being caught with egg on your face, you will appear pompous and stiff. Instead, be prepared with a Plan B (and even a Plan C and Plan D). If your soufflé falls, send out for pizza. Don't blame anyone else. Laugh the incident off gracefully. Demonstrate that you don't take yourself too seriously. Capricorns can be self-critical to a fault. Give yourself a break. Life is too short to let small failures be anything more important than a trampoline to jettison you to the next challenge.

Try to continue last month's efforts to make your partner feel valued. If possible, arrange for a romantic interlude for the two of you. If time and funds permit, take a short getaway together. At the very least schedule a "date night" at home where you focus on her or his interests, concerns and needs. The stars are positioned for a sizzling sex session between the two of you around the 22nd.

## CAPRICORN April 2014

Some saddening news about an elderly relative casts a pall around the beginning of April. More than the other two Earth signs, you Capricorns are often perceived as the rock to lean upon (Virgo by contrast is frequently the nagging pebble in someone's shoe and Taurus can sometimes be a bit of a mud puddle.) That strength of yours will be needed now. Someone closer than you to the ailing elder will require your aid. You may have to help out with the practical matters at which you excel. Be extra generous with your time and resources. Offer emotional support as well.

During the course of helping your relatives, you may come across a surprising bit of family information. You could discover an unexpected facet of your older relatives' early lives. Or... could be that you will learn something about your ancestors which casts a new light on your family history. Was Grandfather a philanderer? Was there a great uncle who drank? A zany aunt who flitted from lover to lover? You will be amused and surprised when you unroll this bit of shady linen.

Business may well have to be put on the back burner this month. A younger person in your circle needs your guidance. He or she lacks a sense of stability and confidence. You have these qualities in spades. I know you often prefer to display your perceptions through what you think of as constructive criticism. But right now, positive words and optimism are needed. The youngster in question is in a muddle and needs to be stroked and valued. Near the 16th, remain alert and observant. Don't let this kid slip through your fingers.

During the last week of the month, a favor you did for someone a year or more ago pays off. You may have assumed the individual you aided would never offer any form of recompense. You may even have thought this person deliberately took advantage of you. To your surprise, he or she gives you a leg up now - in unexpected ways. Permit yourself to dial back any cynical attitudes you may have developed along the lines of "no good deed goes unpunished."

## CAPRICORN May 2014

Your capacity for long hours and hard work will serve you well this month. The planets are aligned for you to land a new assignment or work project. It will consume a lot of extra time. However, the rewards you'll earn will make it worthwhile. The extra responsibility could lead to a hefty promotion or a large raise or bonus. Be careful whom you choose to help you with this assignment. Someone at your workplace envies you and, if given the chance, could attempt sabotage.

An accumulation of stuff you bought too much of is threatening to take over your digs. You have no more space in the basement, garage or attic. You will be tempted to rent a storage unit in a nearby facility. Better to plan a giant garage sale in the coming months; or get thee to the nearest charity shop with a couple of loads of your excess belongings. Clutter is the enemy of Capricorn peace of mind.

You will hear from an old friend this month - possibly a Pisces - around the 18th. Unfortunately, it's not a happy reunion. He or she seems not to have fared well over the years. This old pal hints at financial and health problems. You sense a request for a loan is just around the corner. Give this individual only as much money as you feel ready to kiss goodbye. He/she is unlikely to have the resources to re-pay you. Also consider offering some other form of aid. Research social services agencies that can assist this needy individual. Or hire the person to handle some small task for you either at the office or at home. Perhaps they can design a brochure for your company or do some garden work for you.

Minor money glitches may create a hassle for you toward the end of May. Perhaps a payment you make on your credit card or to a utility company does not get recorded. Or your bank may make an accounting error which results in an overdraft. You could receive a notice claiming you owe unpaid taxes. Make sure your financial records are in order. Have emergency cash on hand. You may temporarily lose access to some funds. This mess could take two weeks or more to sort out.

## CAPRICORN June 2014

Between June 7th and July 1st, you may experience a trickier-than-usual Mercury retrograde period. This time around, the missed messages and traffic tie-ups could affect you more strongly than they will other signs. No. Mercury isn't out to get you. But you are not a person who adores change or upheaval and Mercury retrograde manages to engineer much of both for Capricorns this month.

The likelihood of your being involved in a minor fender bender rises during the second two weeks of this month. Parking lots in particular become a potential trouble zone for you right now. Choose to park your car far from others. Make certain that nobody can pull in next to you and slam open their door to scratch your pristine finish. Steer clear of iffy neighborhoods where young drivers careen around looking for trouble. If you can, walk or take public transportation. If you must drive, exercise extra caution. Be on the lookout for light-headed or distracted drivers taking reckless chances. Don't get into any road rage face-offs. Let everybody else have the right of way. Do exercise caution. The odds are strong you might encounter problems with your insurance company over any traffic mishaps.

Your luck increases around the 17th of this month. Don't go overboard, but this is a good time to gamble. Purchase a few lottery tickets. Enter another raffle or drawing to benefit charity. Sign up for a free online sweepstakes. You stand to win at least a modest amount of cash in the gaming sector.

Whether or not the lottery comes through for you, do host a party this month. The last week of June is an auspicious period for you to play host or hostess to a group of friends. Invite people whom you trust and value. Put out a healthy buffet and a nice selection of beverages. Nothing too elaborate. But do be generous and provide hearty fresh food. This isn't a business networking event. Don't design your guest list based on success and influence. Use this time for bonding with a small group of friends. One of your friends has been out of sorts. Perhaps someone who recently went through a break-up or lost a good friend. This jolly occasion can help lift their spirits.

This party may also alert you to some social trouble. You notice that one of your guests indulges in bullying - and even spreads malicious gossip. Make clear to them discreetly that you don't engage in or tolerate this kind of cheap discourse.

## CAPRICORN July 2014

An unusual character enters your life around the 6th of this month. This person could be associated in some way with that new hobby you took up earlier this year. Your initial reaction may be to shun this person. Not the type you usually befriend. Perhaps this individual is a decade older or younger than your social set. Or she/he could appear slightly eccentric or weird. Cast aside prejudice. Permit yourself to get to know them. He or she could be a breath of fresh air, blowing away cobwebs you didn't know were there. Through this new acquaintance you will find yourself exposed to ideas which infuse your creativity with new energy.

Mid-July you may find yourself made the scapegoat for someone else's major *faux pas*. The guilty party has managed to persuade others of his/her innocence in this dicey matter. They may even play victim. Don't express overt anger over this. Calmly state your side of the story to friends and family. Then let the matter drop. You may have to bide your time before fully clearing your name. Pleading your case repeatedly now will only inculpate you more. Eventually others will perceive the truth through the sham the perpetrator has constructed.

Is the excess stuff gone yet? Have you begun to dig out from under your clutter glut? If not, take a weekend in July to do nothing else. Be ruthless. Throw away that garish ceramic kitten you won in the Girl Scout raffle when you were 12. Ditch those conga drums you never learned to play and for heaven's sake divest yourself of all that too small out-of- fashion clothing you haven't worn in the last ten years. Should the task seem beyond you, ask a tidier-than-thou friend to come help sort out the treasure from the trash.

Toward the end of this month, you shine brightest when you behave generously. Purchase a thoughtful gift for someone in your life who feels discouraged or is perpetually gloomy of late. Choose a present which supports and encourages an interest this individual wants to develop. Give without thought of future benefit or return. Think of the guidance found in this poem by Hafiz: "Even after all this time the Sun never says to the Earth, "You owe me." What happens with a love like that? It lights the entire sky."

## CAPRICORN August 2014

Northern hemisphere citizens usually take time off during August. It's summertime. Weather seduces you wintry Capricorns outdoors. Doffing clothing and soaking up sun rays becomes a veritable lifestyle. In the southern half of the planet, you may be just exiting a cruel, cold winter. You can almost smell spring. Either way, August is a month of hope and good humor. Take time to kick back and enjoy the outdoors.

Your poorly-timed laughter or ill-considered jokes can harm your reputation between the 2nd and the 8th of this month. Don't be tempted to laugh at jokes which belittle or denigrate others. Consider the consequences before slinging any barbed quips. Carefully examine your motives before teasing people. To be on the safe side, keep your humor self-deprecating and gentle. Only indulge in risqué jokes in the company of your closest old friends. If you behave in an unbecoming manner now, you risk alienating people who formerly admired you.

You and your partner seem to have opposing schedules lately. He or she seeks affection at precisely those times you strive to meet important deadlines. You look for love when your partner has already made commitments to be elsewhere. You feel frustrated and start to twinkle inside about what other options exist for satisfying your needs. If you can wait until the week of the 17th, the two of you will find your timing aligns again. In fact, there's a perfect opportunity for an evening of heightened passion around this time.

Household plumbing is likely to create a problem for you around the 25th. If you live in an apartment building or condo, your bathroom may cause a leak into your downstairs neighbor's flat. If you have a house, there may be flooding in your basement. It's possible you'll have to keep a plunger next to the toilet for a week or so until you can get a plumber to get to the bottom of the problem. Renters may find that landlords become testy about this glitch and try to blame them for the issue. If you own your home, prepare to bite the bullet in terms of expense. Plumbers don't come cheap. Landlords either.

## CAPRICORN September 2014

Someone younger than you challenges your authority around the 5th. This may occur either at home with one of your offspring, or at the office with someone junior to you. Don't blow up like a puffer fish and demand they obey you. Instead, take a kid gloves approach. Talk the person down and through their behavior. Although it may be difficult to prise out the reasons behind the youngster's combative behavior, ask a few key (discreet) questions. Are they doing well in school? Have they had any turmoil in their family lately? Do they like the way they look? Is there anything they need that you can provide? Don't cut off communication. Be kind. Befriend.

It benefits you to look toward the future this month. Either you or your partner feels the temptation to overspend around the 12th. This may feel safe because of promised year-end bonuses at work. But there's a strong possibility those funds will have to cover an emergency expense later in the season. Curb any desire to purchase luxuries right now. Instead, put money into a savings account. Make up a monthly budget and stick to it. Schedule a thorough physical check-up now. If you haven't already, carve time out of your week for regular exercise. The year 2015 holds some potential health dangers for you. Take precautions now to ensure you remain in tip-top shape.

A discussion around the 20th with that unusual new friend of yours makes you re-think some of your beliefs. You're surprised at how liberating it can be to let go of rigid opinions. Flexibility has never been Capricorn's style. But by dropping your guard around too tightly held fixed ideas, you will realize that some of the tension you've been experiencing was coming from within, not from other people. It may take all month, but if you allow for vulnerability, you will have the courage to espouse change, let go of prejudices and replace them with sound ideas.

Life may give you an integrity pop quiz around the end of September or early October. You find a wallet full of cash. Or a server in a restaurant undercharges you. How you handle this surprise test will set the pace for future ethics puzzles you will come across before the end of the Horse Year.

**CAPRICORN October 2014**

If you decide to host a Halloween party, try to get your invitations out early. The three-week period (October 4th thru 25th) preceding Halloween brings another glitch-prone Mercury retrograde phase. As usual, try not to sign any contracts, make major purchases or schedule any surgery during this time frame.

You're likely to feel creatively fertile this month. Use this energy to plan a unique Halloween party. Or come up with an amazing solution to a problem you've been facing at work. Or decide to go back to writing that half-finished novel in your desk drawer. Whatever you get around to doing in October, you will be fearless and energized.

Some of this spiffy feeling spills over into your time with your partner. You proffer small gifts in surprising ways. Perhaps you tuck a book of poetry or a small box of chocolates into your partner's suitcase when he/she goes off on a business trip. You suggest activities which breathe new life into your romance. If he or she felt a bit taken for granted before, now your sweetie is touched by the tenderness and playfulness you're bringing to your love life. Single Capricorns will find themselves very popular now. If a crush formerly saw you as invisible, he or she will ogle you with fresh eyes. Grab at this chance to get to know this person better.

You're a bit dismayed to discover your work colleagues don't share your sense of renewed enthusiasm. They are still stuck in old patterns. Don't express anger or sigh with impatience. Use savvy diplomacy to help others see the value of your new ideas. Chronic miscommunication between you and one individual in particular can hinder your progress. Rather than burning a bridge here, see if you can repair this potential crack in the foundation. Admit your part in past disagreements. Demonstrate your newfound flexibility.

There's a strong possibility that someone in your family anticipates a blessed addition around this time. This event will shake up old patterns. Perhaps a new child is on the way for someone who was formerly childless. Or a dyed-in-the-wool bachelor or bachelorette may up and decide to tie the knot. Maybe that old maid aunt or uncle has decided to move in with a lover. This approaching event derails the family status quo and can draw harsh criticism. Choose not to be counted among the naysayers who throw cold water on impending joy.

## CAPRICORN November 2014

Strategy is your middle name early this month. You will have to think several steps in advance. That schemer (maybe an ambitious Libra or an unscrupulous Scorpio) at your office is trying to cast aspersions on you. Previously, you managed to neutralize the threat this person poses by keeping them at arm's length. Now a personnel change at work means you will have to labor more closely with this weasel-like individual. Change the password to your office e-mail account - pronto. This tricky person isn't above snooping and real sabotage. Why not suggest to the powers-that-be that he or she transfer the nuisance to Peru? Or award them a special assignment which promises to keep them traveling full time? If you play your cards right, the weasel's new assignment can be made to look like a promotion. He or she will no doubt find the prospect of advancement irresistible.

If you have any animal companions in your home, take extra precautions with them this month. There's a possibility your furry, scaled or feathered companion could go missing. Make sure your dog or cat has an identification chip embedded in case the poor thing gets out all alone without any tags. If you have a small pet that lives in a cage, check and double-check to make sure he/she doesn't escape. Certain small pets may find their way into the walls or wriggle out a crack between window and sill.

A seemingly chance meeting with an ex-lover around the 16th may not be so accidental. Don't be too quick to confide in this person on the basis of past closeness. Turns out he or she may have been stalking you online for weeks. Do some online sleuthing of your own to make sure you know the whole truth about this person's reputation. Does their Facebook relationship status match up with what they initially told you? Tread carefully now.

You run the risk of feeling like jittery around the end of November. Your thoughts will grow jumbled and your acts somewhat haphazard. You might snap at innocent people. To temper this irritability, try yoga. And learn how to meditate. Make spirituality a priority in your otherwise tension-filled life.

## CAPRICORN December 2014

You may take on the burden of someone else's financial crisis this month. A parent or a grown child may have a medical emergency. Or someone you love could face homelessness. You won't want to see them suffer any unfair consequences. But do remember that offering help may mean using your end-of-the-year bonus or dipping into savings. Part of the challenge of helping this person will be to bravely ignore others' advice. Your friends may counsel you not to do the victim any favors. They want to persuade you that the person in need created his/her own problems. Let compassion rather than criticism from outsiders guide your choices.

A work colleague or neighbor unexpectedly confides a personal matter to you around the 10th. He or she is feeling shaky and insecure about something less than legal they have done. Could be nothing more than running a red light. Overcome your usual emotional reserve to offer this individual some support and advice. You have grown in wisdom over the Horse year, moving past old prejudices. Now that you have overcome your earlier fear of change, you can feel safer offering warmth to those who really need it.

You make headway with your creative project in December. Perhaps you reach a milestone, such as completing a novel, deciding to enter your epic poem in a contest or offering your painting to be exhibited in a gallery. Perhaps you will only show the finished product to someone special who offers insightful praise as well as practical advice. The message? Don't be afraid to expose your work and obtain some notion of where you should go next.

The holiday rush will do everything in its power to interrupt the recently renewed connection with your partner. Turn down some invitations. Leave heady celebrations early in order to take time for a few extra intimate evenings in front of the fireplace at this jolly time of year.

Capricorns rarely expect life to be easy. But this year has certainly handed down many challenges. Do not be discouraged. Start to plan now for the financial abundance of 2015. Research possible investment opportunities. Buy a new house or refurbish the old one. Also, research places you might visit for a spectacular vacation with your sweetheart. The coming New Year will bring plenty of rewards for your hard work and generosity.

## CAPRICORN January 2015

Take some time to renew yourself in this gap between the beginning of the Western New Year and the commencement of the Year of the Goat on February 19th. Grab a mental health day or two off from work. For your day off, make a lists of activities. Call it: "Enjoyable things I used to do but don't have time for anymore." Select some items at random from the list and force yourself to devote your time off to these pleasant activities.

Get together with your new friend from last year around the 12th. It is important to perpetuate this camaraderie. He or she challenges you and prevents you from growing stale. The middle of January is also a good time to update your appearance. If you're feeling daring, get a new tattoo or a discreet piercing. Or change your hairstyle or hair color. At the very least, buy some new clothes. Select your new outfit from a store you normally deem a bit too far out for your style. Capricorn is a sign known seeming to age in reverse, becoming more youthful with each passing year. Do not let preconceptions about "acting or looking your age" limit you.

Single Capricorns have a marvelous opportunity for meeting Mr. or Ms. Right this month. If no social invitations do come your way, try hunting up someone online. Internet dating no longer carries a stigma. A 2013 study actually found that marriages between people who met online were likely to be more stable. Remember that your mission is to find the right person. Not to gain dating site popularity. The quality of responses you receive counts more than the quantity. Choose someone who shares or at least appreciates and respects your interests. Define your boundaries way ahead of meeting in person. Talk extensively with potential dates before meeting them face-to-face. Arrange all initial in-person meetings in a safe public place such as a coffeehouse. Remember. The Year of The Goat starts late (Feb 19) this year. If you keep at it, you have a good chance of finding romance before the Chinese New Year comes barging in.

# AQUARIUS 2014

## OVERVIEW FOR THE WOOD HORSE YEAR

*Altruistic Aquarius,*

*The Year of the Horse may stun you, in the beginning, by appearing to be nothing but a bumpy ride. But do not despair. Don't give up. Stick with it. Things do get better. By the time this Horse year concludes, you are likely to be both wiser and wealthier than you were in the preceding year. One of your challenges will be to develop a deeper understanding of reciprocity, balance and intimacy. Some of you may have had a tendency to place blame on others or to expect more from them than you are willing to give. A few of you may have used screens (computer, smart phone, TV) to filter out one-on-one human emotions. This year will give you a chance to grow into a cozier way of relating. You may have to shift your perspective to see yourself as the standoffish one, rather than pointing the finger at others.*

*In short, this Horse year will help you to deepen your ability to perceive others' needs. You may discover that face-to-face conversation can be far more exhilarating than social networking or e-mail or texts. If finances have been an area of tension for you, the situation will change this year. You may find a new job or develop a lucrative sideline. There's also a strong hint of a windfall, possibly an inheritance. One way or the other, you will increase your fortune this year. Then you can finally develop a cause you have always believed in. One which may just be able to make a dent in the woes of the world. sw*

———— ᖾᖱᖾᖱ ————

## THE CHINESE YEAR AHEAD

## AQUARIUS 2014

**AQUARIUS February 2014**

The start of the Year of the Horse may find you irritable. You might decide to do a purge of Facebook friends, eliminating those who don't share your political opinions. Not on Facebook? Then think about giving a piece of your mind to the nosy neighbor and telling off your sister-in-law who is always razzing you about your choice of wardrobe. You suddenly feel alienated from the culture and politics of your home country. You may even research moving to another country. If you do decide on exile, be sure the country has national health coverage for all.

Around the 10th of the month, you and your live-in partner may quarrel about money. Perhaps he or she has been contributing the lion's share of the household income and feels resentful. Or else your incessant hints about changing passports may actually frighten them. One or both of you may have been underemployed and underpaid for too long. You, however, have an unyielding urge to acquire a luxury item - a technology toy or a lavish flat screen with surround sound and hundreds of buttons to play with. Your better half wants to rein in the spending until one of you gets a better job or wins that lawsuit or lands that big contract. Remember, you won't expire if you continue to use the old version of the iPhone or Xbox or whatever gadget you feel you need. Don't push. Compromise. If you absolutely crave the rush you get from buying things, pick up a fabulous bargain at a charity sale or score at Goodwill.

Delay and frustration are likely to characterize your financial situation this month. The Mercury retrograde period (Feb 6 to 28) may result in miscommunication about payments. A check mailed to you could get lost. Or someone may offer you a job, then call back to say they need to wait for their business partner to get back from Brazil before hiring you. Try not to become discouraged about this slow cash influx. Choose a learning project to keep your mind occupied. Study up on something that will both challenge and advance you. If you're still thinking of becoming an ex-pat, concentrate on learning the language of your projected new country. Memorize those verb conjugations. You'll be needing them.

## AQUARIUS March 2014

Single Aquarians, or those whose romantic partnerships are relatively new, may hear some discomfiting news from an old flame the first week of March. This ex-lover tells you to get tested for a sexually transmitted disease. Try to handle this situation in a mature manner. If you both chose to practice unprotected sex, there should be no pointing of fingers - no guilty or innocent party. Get tested. If you have a disease, share the news discreetly with your current partner. Honest communication is crucial in this situation. Accompany your current main squeeze to be tested as well. Only fair. Chances are slim you have the illness. The planets are aligned now to favor Aquarian good health.

You could achieve 15 minutes or more of fame around March 16. Possibly a comment you make on Facebook or Twitter goes viral. Or perhaps your podcast or blog receives notice from somebody well-known. Suddenly, you attract public attention. Your comments and opinions wield influence, at least within a particular subculture or corner of the internet. Enjoy your celebrity. If possible, leverage it to improve your financial situation. Do try however to avoid taking a scornful tone about anyone. As rapidly as you became a hot shot, you can un-become one. I know you Aquarians disdain those you deem unintelligent. Do remember that people who grow famous and set about mocking others quickly become the targets of mockery themselves.

Toward the end of the month, you hanker to shock people. You may decide to express this through a change in your appearance. You might shave your head. Or dye your hair purple. Get a new tattoo that expresses your viewpoints or tastes in a humorous way. Wear some accessory or item of clothing more associated with the opposite gender than your own. If your community or workplace is too conservative to make any of your chosen outlandish getups an option, then draw the curtains at home and dance naked while wearing an outrageous mask or wig. It is healthy for Aquarians to feed their wild side every once in a while. Just make sure you do it a way that doesn't appall anyone but yourself.

## AQUARIUS April 2014

Someone may question your integrity around the 4th-7th of this month. Deny the allegations, and then let it go. Holding a grudge against this mistaken person will only deplete your energy. Focus your attention on your own life now and develop all plans according to schedule. This particular individual is a known gossip. Spending a minute of your precious time trying to expose their calumny will only keep you connected to him or her. Troublemakers want you to pick up the bait and enter a dialogue. Don't go there. Watch this seedy character grow smaller in your rearview mirror as you continue on your own path.

Add some extra spark and imagination to your sex life around the 12th of April. Your sweetie may feel that he or she is not getting enough attention. Focus less on your desires and more on what he or she wants. Talk with her/him. Try to discover any secret fantasies he or she hasn't shared with you yet.

You run a risk of straining yourself through overexertion around the $15^{th}$-$19^{th}$. If you lift weights, be careful not to attempt too great a challenge. A ligament is quickly pulled from over exertion. A tendon can be damaged in a wink. It's also possible you might put your back out lifting furniture or heavy boxes around the house. Don't try to prove anything. Pushing your body too ferociously can too easily result in a period of forced inactivity. Then, while you are confined to your room and only getting around with a crutch, depressing thoughts rise up and punch you in the nose.

If you've ever dreamed of being a superhero, you will get your wish in a small way around the end of this month. The universe will call upon you to come to the rescue of an animal. Perhaps you will remove a thorn from the paw of your own pet. Or you may find a starving or injured stray animal and take it to a vet for care. Or you may simply be moved to adopt a homeless animal from a shelter. Whatever happens, post your heroism to your Facebook wall as a proud accomplishment. Listen for the cyber applause.

**AQUARIUS May 2014**

Your partner and friends may remark on how moody you seem from the $1^{st}$ to the $4^{th}$ of May. You are accustomed to thinking of yourself as calm and rational. But you tend to grow disgusted with the world when things do not evolve as you see fit. Often you do not realize how harshly critical your sarcastic comments seem to others. Do not blame them for having hurt feelings. It is important to pay closer attention to the effect of your words on others.

Part of the mood swing problem may stem from lack of sleep. Sleep deprivation affects one's state of mind. Your irritation with the fact that the world is going to Hell in a hand basket can affect your sleep habits. Even if you get eight hours of snooze-time regularly, the effects of stress can leave you exhausted. Try going to bed earlier at night. Give up those wee hours' marathon sessions of downloading music or re-watching your favorite old TV shows. Instead, drink some tart cherry juice to encourage slumber. Put some fresh sheets and pillowcases on the bed. Turn off the TV, the computer and even your smart phone. Schedule nothing for the morning. Permit yourself to sleep until noon if necessary. Mid May for Aquarians is kick back time.

Face it. You have been feeling unappreciated this month. For a while now, you have been hoping more friends would offer greater support for your job-hunt or your creative project. But have you been asking for help without giving it? Take some time around the $22^{nd}$ of this month to find out how you can assist your friends in achieving *their* goals. Maybe you can offer a lead on an apartment for that friend who is looking for a new place to live? Perhaps some of your friends simply need encouragement. Be generous with your praise. Do not act as if you were the tough professor who never gives out an "A" grade. Acknowledging others' talents and assisting them in realizing their dreams does not, in any respect, detract from your own achievements. On the contrary - giving others a leg up is enriching.

**AQUARIUS June 2014**

If you have any concerns related to your health, try to attend to them before the $7^{th}$ this month. That is when the Mercury retrograde period begins. For you Aquarians, it may affect communication matters related to health, as well as routine chores and romance. There could be confusion and crossed wires on these topics for you. This three-week period of relative confusion starts July 7 and ends on July 1. Patience, remember, is a virtue.

Toward the middle of June, the planets align to make you look foolish. Check the mirror carefully each time you leave the house. Make sure you are not prone to any wardrobe malfunctions. Avoid speaking either too brusquely or impulsively. You could end up eating your words with a heaping side serving of crow. If you followed last month's advice about being helpful and generous with your praise and assistance, this phase will proceed more easily for you.

Near the 25th, someone may ask you to offer aid in an area outside your usual bailiwick. Maybe a sick friend asks you to weed her garden. Or possibly your partner asks if you can build shelves to organize the bedroom closet. You may not know a dandelion from a dahlia or how to find the hitting end of a hammer. Rather than refuse this person's, request, recruit some help. If you cannot afford to hire someone to aid you, find a knowledgeable friend or read up on the skill in question online. During this spring and summer, it is especially important for you to develop your ability to help others in practical ways. You can be accused of drifting off into your own Lalaland, ignoring family and friends whenever it suits you. Turn that around now by showing that you, too, can play the game.

Your partner may reveal a surprising secret about his/her past sometime around the 29th: They were married twice before. There's a child of theirs dangling out there somewhere with an ex-partner. They have a criminal record. One of their parents killed the other. Don't show shock and blurt out a hostile, crazy reaction. Avoid taking a judgmental tone. Take some time to absorb this new information. You may want to make some adjustments to your relationship after this bombshell hits.

## AQUARIUS July 2014

You should be infused with enthusiasm for improving your health around the 6th of this month. Avoid letting your personal zeal develop into criticism of others for their weight or dietary choices. Instead, remain focused on yourself. Wear imaginary blinders to help you avoid judging others. Your success is not diminished by their failure. Stick to your own regime and scotch tape your mouth shut about them. You are going through a phase where your condemnation of others can harm your own reputation.

Your financial situation is likely to improve around the 11th of July. If you have been job-hunting, you may be offered employment. Or a hobby or side-project may become more lucrative. Use part of the fresh income to treat your partner. Or, if you have no partner, do a favor for a great old pal or a parent by taking them on a short vacation. He or she has helped you through difficult times. Let your companion take the lead in deciding where to go for this pleasure trip. The planetary alignments will smile brightly on a journey you take from the 19th to the 28th of this month. You and yours will have an absolutely scrumptious time.

Don't go overboard spending the whole windfall on your trip. Better not to try a trip to the Caribbean or the Seychelles. Settle instead for a short jaunt to a local resort or a chummy road trip. Do save some of those funds for later this year. You have a few months coming up where your income will just cover household expenses. You will be happy to have that extra lucre to spend when the lean months come along.

Toward the end of this month, someone whom you previously banished from your life may try to wriggle their way back in. It may be an ex-friend or lover who betrayed you in some way. It could be a family member who was the source of a wicked trauma you experienced. This person will try to play on your sympathies. Maintain rigid boundaries. You should of course resist the temptation to hurl insults at this individual. Doing so will only open up old wounds and end up upsetting you all over again. Let sleeping Dogs lie - especially this one. Once burnt, twice shy is the best approach here.

## AQUARIUS August 2014

You may feel excluded as August begins. You could discover that a friend deliberately timed a gathering while you were out of town. Or you may learn that someone whom you trusted has been gossiping about you. Do not confront this person. People who behave like this tend to be accomplished liars who secretly enjoy harming others. If you are frank about your unhappiness, they will smile and pretend to care, but will not change their behavior. Instead, display utter insouciance. Smile and let others perceive you as carefree. Be a bit more mysterious about the details of your life. Avoid sharing personal information with just anybody. Without actually prevaricating, permit the naysayers, gossips and other lowlifes to wonder. Make people think you have tapped into some hidden source of happiness. Then, without making a big announcement or production, gradually disconnect from the negative character in question.

Toward the middle of the month, you may find yourself feeling someone else's pain very deeply. Maybe a story in the news will attract your sympathies. You might find yourself actually crying when reading about people losing their homes in a natural disaster or losing a loved one as a result of an act of violence. Or someone whom you know, a co-worker or friend of neighbor, may experience a dramatic loss which moves you deeply. Whatever it is, you find your usual sense of detachment evaporates. Thoughts of those who suffer may even keep you awake at night. Avoid wine and spirits as the ingestion of alcohol when you are hypersensitive can make things worse. Try drinking sleepy herbal potions one hour before bedtime.

You and your significant other may enjoy an especially passionate time around the 21$^{st}$. Your increased sense of open heartedness and vulnerability may unexpectedly increase your partner's desire for you. And they may surprise you by being bolder and taking the lead more than usual. Relax. Enjoy the change of pace. Instead of being the head honcho instigator, slip away to paradise as a swooning passenger. The best way to unwind from hyper sensitivity is to spend a lot of those excess feelings in bed with your main squeeze of the moment.

## AQUARIUS September 2014

You'll have to keep your nose close to the grindstone this month, Aquarius. Whether it's for school or the workplace, you are destined to grasp the meaning of real hard work. However you go about this labor, it won't feel terrific. You may find yourself growing resentful as you toil for hours on tasks which provide no immediate reward. Rather than throwing in the towel, think ahead to your long term goal. Pace yourself. After a certain number of hours of application of elbow grease, reward your inner worker bee. Breaking up the workload gives you the strength to go on. Remain disciplined. Don't let your taste for rebellion overthrow your need to complete this project. You can email your friends or post a public notice on Facebook about how disgusted you are with current drudgeries. Venting to family, friends and Facebook cronies will let some of the anger out. Then you must get back to work.

Relationship snags may be added to your work woes around the 18$^{th}$ of the month. Your partner or lover complains about your behavior. He or she thinks you are selfish and unreasonable. Do not fall into the trap of treating this like a debate. You cannot "win" an argument with your partner on points. The goal is not "winning" but rather mutual understanding. Take the time to listen to what your sweetie has to say. Chances are, at least some of their gripes make sense. In order to understand their point of view, you may put your brain in front your ego. Acknowledge any mistakes you have made without offering excuses. Be respectful of your partner's feelings. Avoid saying anything condescending. Share your own concerns without accusation. Seeking to cast blame will only throw oil on the flames. Make reconciliation and compromise your goals in this discussion.

After the two of you once again find common ground, the make-up sex is likely to set off fireworks. Be sure to also take the time in the next few days to express your appreciation for your sweetie. Surprise him or her with a special dinner or a gift. Or offer your honey a foot massage after she/he returns from a hard day at work.

**AQUARIUS October 2014**

Don't be surprised if confusion arises in messages related to the workplace or school this month. Mercury is going retrograde again. This particular Mercury retrograde lasts from October 4 through 25. It ushers in a period where it is unwise for you to travel far from home, sign major documents or purchase electronic equipment. Don't let the minor snafus of this period ruffle your feathers. These apparent backward movements of the planet named for the messenger of the gods is always temporary. We just have to wait it out.

Looking for a way to cure some of the world's ills? Why not volunteer your time at a soup kitchen or spend some hours every week manning a suicide line? Your special Aquarian brand of altruism works wonders every time.

Fortunately, this uncertainty will end on the 25th. That's good news for you because the end of the month should be a fabulous social time for you. Your calendar will be overflowing with opportunities for fun. Aquarians on the lookout for romance will find an abundance of interested candidates eager to scoop up their affections. This will be one of those periods when your pheromones become an irresistible elixir, drawing people to you as if by magic. It won't even matter if you forget to comb your hair or spiff up your wardrobe. People will find you irresistibly attractive no matter how you look.

However there is one caveat. One of your new admirers during this time may try to persuade you to step outside your usual boundaries in some way. Do not bend your usual rules for this individual. This person is likely to be extremely charming as well as physically attractive. This charmer may try to sweet-talk you into setting aside your personal rules "just once." Do not give in to this temptation. Avoid this character's blandishments. The more time you spend with them, the more hypnotized you will become by their appeal. If you drop your guard and follow this person's lead, the consequences are could be ruinous to your equilibrium. You are already a tad loony by nature. Aquarians are the kookiest of people. If you let kooky become wacko, the route back to normal may steal some of your very precious time.

**AQUARIUS November 2014**

The universe will gift you with an enchanted day and reminder of the joys of childhood sometime on or about the 5th of November. If you are a parent, you may have a wonderful time visiting a park, zoo or museum with your offspring. Or a neighbor or friend may unexpectedly ask you to baby-sit, creating an opportunity for you to share in a child's delight in finger-painting or fairy tales. Possibly you'll decide for a change of pace to watch a children's film on your own some night. Give yourself permission to let go of the sardonic side of your personality and fully enter into this opening for playfulness. You will find that you are mentally and emotionally re-charged by indulging in childlike pastimes.

A neighbor needs your assistance again. You have been most generous to this person over a period of months. They have gotten used to calling on you for aid and may indeed be abusing your good nature. It will be delicate to wriggle out of this person's grasp. But I advise you do so. Contact one of their family members to shoulder some of the burden.

Your sense of ethics will be tested sometime after the 14th of the month. You may find someone's smartphone or a wallet full of cash. Or your bank statement may arrive with a sizeable mistake in your favor. If you are still experiencing a sense of financial strain, you may feel very tempted to take what you can and hope no one discovers your actions. I won't tell you what to do. But I will warn you that this year is one of heightened karma for you. Seeds you plant this year are very likely to spring into full flower very quickly, for good or for ill.

Toward the end of this month, everyone around you may seem insecure. Since your own confidence will be high at this point, you may find yourself impatient with others' neediness. Hold your tongue. Remember that the truth of an observation does not always justify spilling its beans out loud. You are a caring person and rarely intend to hurt people. But sometimes you forget that words can cause grave injury - especially those close to you.

**AQUARIUS December 2014**

A lack of tact on your part could make things difficult for your partner this month. If you speak out carelessly, he or she may have to face consequences - possibly with a boss or parent. Try to stick to just one glass of wine at awkward social events you attend now. Or even better, choose to drink just soda or juice. Sobriety - especially at holiday time - helps eliminate the risk of verbal *faux pas.*

A film you see around the holiday period may make an especially deep impression on you. This movie may open your eyes to some previously unsuspected human injustice. You may even feel inspired by this cinematic experience to get involved in a volunteer project. Begin researching worthwhile organizations online so you can offer your services next month. You have always longed to be of some use to the poor or under privileged of the world. Make time to help out at a soup kitchen or enroll in a program which offers aid to people in areas struck by disaster.

That project that sucked up so much of your time back in September may earn you some recognition now. Amazingly, you don't even have to lift a finger or ask for this special attention. Whether it's a good grade in class or a holiday bonus or even a promotion from your boss, your earlier efforts will be rewarded this month.

Amidst all the holiday celebrations, you could have to attend a funeral. An older relative - not someone you are very close to - may die this month. There's a strong possibility that you have an inheritance coming your way. In addition to some valuable property, you may also be given some papers pertaining to your family's history. Do not dispose of these documents. If you do not want to examine them now, keep them in a secure place. When you do feel ready to review them, these papers will shed light on the behavior of some of your relatives. Learning this information will help you make peace with some parts of your own past. Old emotional scars will finally be on the road to healing. You will finally feel strong enough to end a generational cycle of recurring trauma.

## AQUARIUS January 2015

As a result of that successful project back in September, someone has set you an even more daunting task for this month. If you passed Calculus I, you may have been placed in Calculus II. Or your boss may have decided you could handle an even more formidable project. Interestingly, you may not feel up to the challenge. You feel heavy. It's as if you have been asked to translate the complete works of Shakespeare into ancient Greek. The project may cost you tears of frustration. You may fling your textbook or assignment against the wall. Ask for assistance. Or delegate parts of your project to a co-worker. If you still feel stymied, sometimes the correct path is to simply let go of what you cannot handle. It makes no sense to bang your head against a wall. Tell your boss or professors that your areas of expertise lie elsewhere. If nothing else, the experience will have taught you something about yourself. By process of elimination, you are gradually finding out where you are an absolute genius and where you are a dolt.

Romance has been eluding you. Make some effort to find a companion with whom you click on a lot of different levels. Creating satisfying sex is always one important hurdle in a love affair. But try to hook up with someone who is intellectually and astrologically compatible with you as well.

You may decide to sell that valuable property you inherited. Consult more than one person for advice on this topic. Be wary of the suggestions of people who stand to earn a percentage from your sale. Instead, seek advice from people you know who have long real estate experience. Some of your friends may have been buying and selling houses for years. Ask them to share their insider knowledge of how the market works.

Follow up on your resolve from December to get involved in volunteer work. Most Aquarians have very strong social principles. Taking positive action in regard to your ideals will help you feel more useful and energized. Also, your benevolent efforts will introduce you to a large group of people who share similar beliefs to yours.

# PISCES 2014

## OVERVIEW FOR THE WOOD HORSE YEAR

*Starry-eyed Pisces,*

*If it does all it promises, this wood Horse year will morph every Pisces from a minnow into a whale. In this workaholic year, you will learn scads about your own power and strength. By observing and then participating in the general hubbub, your sense of confidence will grow. What you have always known as your potential, will slowly become reality. As this process moves toward its goal, you will face the challenge of acknowledging that you have cut a set of large, sharp teeth. Now you have to relinquish the tendency to view yourself as the innocent victim in every conflict. This growth process may require a reassessment of your relationships, both past and present.*

*Your previous idols may topple from the pedestals where you placed them. Former enemies could become allies. Romance and creativity play prominent roles in your life this year. You may enter into some new field of creativity you have not tried in the past. You and your sweetheart (Yes! I said Sweetheart) may unite your imaginations for some kind of innovative project. Of course, daily life and its vicissitudes will bounce in from time to time and demand your attention. There will be money troubles and family quarrels. But you will be surprised more than once at how much muscle you have developed this year - merely by existing, pitching in and taking charge of your own life. sw*

———————e ·e ·e———————

## THE CHINESE YEAR AHEAD

## <u>PISCES 2014</u>

### PISCES February 2014

Mercury will be in retrograde motion most of this month. Between the 6th and the 28th, the communications technology you use may be temperamental with connections fading away at inopportune moments. Getting from home to work or vice versa may involve unexpected difficulties. Don't let this wonky period perturb your general equilibrium.

Aside from minor disruptions, you will swim in the waters you love best this month. Artistic visions and dreamy romance come your way. A stalled creative project of yours revives. Ideas for new creations are as abundant as tadpoles in a pond. Someone offers you assistance, providing the support and structure you need for your imaginative notions to reach fruition.

You may meet a fellow creative spirit early in February. If you are currently unattached, you and this individual may start a romance. Even if circumstances do not allow for that, you will help kindle each other's creativity. You feel a deep soul connection to this person. You may find that the two of you can communicate through dreams. Or you may even find that telepathic messages flow easily between you and this highly sensitive person.

Whether with this new chum, or an established partner, romance sizzles for you around the 10th through the 21st. You can use this energy to concoct yourself a sweet Valentine's Day. Probably best to celebrate privately rather than at a restaurant. The auguries show you are likely to make the kind of fireworks which glow brightest in *tête-à-tête* situations. You are on the precipice of a new sexual universe. You and your partner will want to try something new, perhaps tantric sex. Whatever it is, I see you attaining new heights of ecstasy and intimacy.

An older relative or a mentor who has aided you feels unappreciated. It is important that you carve some time out of your schedule to show this person how much you value and respect him/her. If you do not take pains to show how thankful you are, the consequences may extend well beyond bad karma. Any perceived selfishness on your part during the last week of February can have grave repercussions down the line. You could be cut out of a will. Or well before they die, you could lose the respect and affection of a special someone who has been both a buttress and personal guide for you for many years.

## PISCES March 2014

From the 4th to the 10th of March, you face a new challenge in your personal growth. A few years ago, you fell under a pernicious influence. It may have been a teacher whom you looked up to, or a group you idealized, maybe it was a past lover, probably someone older than you. Whoever or whatever it was, you later discovered your faith had been misplaced. But you do recall, you let this person separate you from a true and trusted friend. Your misplaced loyalty caused you to hurt a kind and gentle soul. Let go of your resentment. Find the person you hurt right away and make amends. Don't be afraid to show your vulnerability. You humility is proof of your strength.

Exercise caution around people who lavish praise on you. I know, Pisces, that you seek a world full of peace, love and understanding. The people who tell you that you possess amazing talents and insight may appear to embody the harmony you desire. But your yearning for a perfect world can mislead you. Consider this: pouring sugar into a fishbowl causes the fish to gasp for breath and then die. Same goes for excessive flattery of someone as susceptible as yourself to compliments. Too much fawning can cause you to swerve off course. Seek out a few real friends who will tell you the truth, even when the truth is not entirely pleasant. I offer this advice because I see you in particular danger from flattery around the 16th-22nd this month.

Time now to weed the phonies out of your personal life. Some of them may secretly harbor ill will toward you. If you are offered new investment or employment opportunities from people who shower you with praise, step around them. What seems too good to be true probably is.

The romantic fires from last month continue to burn brightly this month. You and your partner have another of those doorways into a new dimension of pleasure on the 27th. Explore some mutual fantasies. But remember the importance of communicating your wishes clearly. Don't assume your honey can read your mind all of the time. Whispered secret desires and breathless encouragements can help to enhance the lovemaking experience. Use everything you already know about sex. And, while you're at it, why not learn a few new tricks for the future?

## PISCES April 2014

Your home life becomes complicated around the beginning of the month. You could acquire an unexpected roommate. A friend may lose his/her home. Or a relative may come to you for refuge from a tense domestic situation. Go ahead and follow your generous impulse to let them move in with you. But do remember that helping people out of scrapes also requires attention to practical considerations. Discuss the ground rules carefully. Make sure they know your hospitality is only temporary. Advise this person that he or she has to take care of their own dishes and laundry.

Make sure they contribute to living expenses. Or, if they have no job or income currently, offer a barter arrangement. Permit them to help out with household chores or childcare. Be patient with your friend. You are used to being the most emotional person in the house. You may have to relinquish that title for now. Your guest has already endured much and may need to emote and vent even more than sensitive old you.

Around the 16th, a family member may experience a health crisis. This person has helped you a great deal in the past. Even though you already have much on your plate, you must aid this ailing relative. Make arrangements to shift your work schedule. Have your temporary roommate or another friend watch your children. You must make sure this person does not think you have abandoned them.

Your partner's work situation changes. Things are tense at his/her workplace. It appears the bosses there are intent on eliminating anyone who appears to slack off. He or she must work longer hours than previously. You are both so busy that you communicate mainly through texts, e-mails or notes jotted on a scratch pad on the dining room table. Most of these exchanges will naturally be about practical matters. Be sure also to intersperse the reminders about changing the cat litter with a few romantic messages. Or leave a small, thoughtful gift in your partner's briefcase or lunch-sack. Don't let the romance wither under the pressure you feel right now.

**PISCES May 2014**

On or around the 1st, life rewards you for past good deeds. You may receive an unexpected cash gift. Or you may collect some kind of prize. Celebrate with a party. Invite a cross-section of people, including a few old friends you rarely see. Ask folks to come who may provide an opening for your unexpected houseguest to find new quarters. You might even want to make it a costume party. Let everyone get outside their usual role by dressing as some imaginary creature. Make sure there is music and dancing. The first two weeks of May are a great time for you to help everyone welcome the new season.

Later this month, use some of the money to handle those changes you have been contemplating at home. You will want to shed old negative energy. This should start with practical modifications. Clean out the gutters. Clear out your closets. Throw away moldering papers and books. But being a Pisces, you will also want your home to reflect your artistic side. Paint the walls a luscious color that inspires you and lifts your spirits. Construct a mobile from beautiful found objects you have picked up on your nature walks. Hang the mobile from the dining room ceiling. If you have a small child living in your house (or visiting frequently), paint one wall with chalkboard paint so he/she can draw on the walls with impunity. Transform your home into a fun place to live.

After months of feeling stuck and frustrated with your work situation, around the 23rd things suddenly improve. Your employer notices your contributions in a new and favorable light. Bonuses, plum assignments, even a raise all seem like distinct possibilities now. But do keep your feet firmly planted on the ground and your eyes open. Someone at your workplace resents your being favored by the boss - and the green-eyed jelly fish is not who you think. In fact, it's someone you thought was an ally. When you realize who envies you, you'll be disappointed. Gradually see less of this non-friend. You do not need detractors.

**PISCES June 2014**

Mercury takes another of its thrice-yearly backwards dances in the sky this month. Between June 7th and July 1st, you will feel the usual disruptive effects. This time there may also be some hint of threat to your finances. Take a few extra precautions during the first five days of June. Count your change carefully after purchases. Don't walk after dark in questionable neighborhoods. Steer clear of any dubious business ventures. During this time, you are more likely to brush shoulders with dishonest and possibly dangerous people. An alert attitude should get you through this period unscathed. But do take precautions. Don't carry large sums of money. Take one debit card with you at a time. If you have a purse, keep it slung around you and not just on your shoulder. Wallets should not protrude from back pockets. An ounce of prevention...

The week of the 8th is a good time to take stock of your health. If you have been ignoring any symptoms, now is the time to look into them. Visit your physician for a thorough check-up. Use vitamins or herbal supplements to nip any problems in the bud. There's a possibility of health problems for you around December as well. Preventive action now can ensure you remain healthy throughout the year. Pay special attention to your feet as well as your respiratory and circulatory systems. These are vulnerable areas for most Pisceans.

Mid-June provides excellent opportunity for you and your partner to deepen your romantic connection again. Schedule a weekend getaway for just the two of you. You both need a break from routines and worry. I feel there may also be an issue your partner needs desperately to discuss. This may be related to some area of his/her personal insecurity. Provide an opening for her or him to confide in you. Demonstrate through your words and actions that it is safe for your lover to reveal areas of personal doubt and vulnerability.

Your psychic senses will be especially acute from the 26th through the 30th. Pay attention to your dreams. They are likely to contain messages worth heeding. Keep a pen and small notebook by your bed. Write down your dreams as soon as you awaken. Mugwort tea before bed helps make dreams more vivid and memorable.

## PISCES July 2014

A youngster may come to you feeling insecure and threatened. Does it have to do with bullying? An embarrassing physical problem? A feeling of shame? Or fear of an adult in the child's entourage? Take the time to bolster the little one's confidence. Help them regain a feeling of being safe and protected. Be careful not to appear critical. You may also have to take further steps in regard to this matter. A therapist or school counselor may come in handy.

You have a new work assignment around the 11th. It requires you to hit the ground running. You have tight deadlines to meet. Your boss wants it done yesterday. Everything else goes on the back burner. Unfortunately, you don't get much help. Those co-workers assigned to assist you can't be counted upon. The tools and/or information given to you to do the job also prove unreliable. You may have to make do with brief naps rather than eight solid hours of sleep for a while. Organization plus hard work and lack of sleep will ensure that you succeed. And as a Pisces, you see a tiny bit of martyrdom as absolute proof that you deserve success.

You have a sneaking suspicion a neighbor has been spying on you. Truth be told, it's quite innocent voyeurism. But it's plenty annoying - and even disconcerting. Rather than deal directly with the nosy interloper (avoid direct strangulation and /or slashing of tires) treat your windows to a new, more substantial drapery effect which you can close tightly at dusk. If there is nothing more to peep at, the voyeur will desist and settle for peeking out the other side of his house.

Your partner has a puzzling health problem. The doctors try to treat it multiple ways but the symptoms persist. Perhaps alternative medicine will work. Ask friends for recommendations.

Find a doctor of Traditional Chinese Medicine. Going to this new healer not only improves your partner's health, it brings a valuable new contact into your lives. Someone who will help both of you. The person in questions could be this acupuncturist, or someone who works in their office or maybe even someone you meet in the waiting room. Somehow the connections you make via this alternative practitioner will become an important addition to both your current and future existence.

## PISCES August 2014

As August begins, you wrap up last month's big project successfully. Everyone at work is impressed. Of course, a few of your friends get tired of you boasting how you sacrificed yourself to meet the deadline. But you feel proud of your accomplishment. Unfortunately, the financial reward for this success may be delayed.

Sometime from the 7th-12th, you receive a puzzling text or e-mail. The person knows your name and writes as if you know them, but you can't tell who it is. You respond, only to discover when they reply that it's an old friend from your past. This character may have behaved in a dishonest way to you. Or they may have ended the friendship abruptly for no apparent reason. At any rate, you don't quite trust them. Clear the air immediately. Ask outright why they are contacting you. Chances are this kind of forthright behavior will scare them off of their hidden agenda (if they have one that is). On the other hand, if you shy away from being forthright, this person may start gradually winding up to charm you and eventually ask you for a favor or even for a loan. Don't waste time on this matter.

Around mid-August, you could face some expensive repairs to your home or vehicle. It's something you can't afford to put off for long. Safety becomes an issue. You may have to bite the bullet and dip into savings. Or cross your fingers and charge the expense to your credit card. Get multiple estimates and references from friends as to both the honesty and quality of service offered by their favorite carpenter, mason, plumber or mechanic.

Sometime after the 20th, a long-simmering family matter may finally erupt. Resentments will be aired. Family skeletons emerge from the closet. Don't try to stuff them back in—the closet lock won't hold anymore. If you try to paint yourself as the sweet innocent who never realized the problems existed, you'll only make matters worse. Accepting your share of the blame doesn't mean you will accept the role of scapegoat.

## PISCES September 2014

You and your partner may quarrel about money sometime around the 3rd-8th. This probably relates to some income stream which has unexpectedly dried up. Try to develop clear policies about how to handle things. Nobody enjoys keeping records - least of all dreamy Pisces. But boundaries and rules can make monetary matters less stressful. Be realistic and tough-minded about where you can cut expenses. Budget for a month ahead. Know where your money is going and why.

From the 17th through the end of the month, you become a social butterfly. Suddenly, your calendar fills up with engagements. As you are sticking to a budget now, you may have to recycle some items creatively to concoct suitable outfits for all these occasions. Some recent changes in your body's shape or size mean you can't wear the same clothes you did last year. Have recourse to your sewing skills or find someone who can do alterations for you. If you don't sew or can't afford a seamstress, why not haunt the aisles of your local thrift shops or vintage clothing stores?

Or, ask older relatives if they have clothes from decades ago sitting in a trunk somewhere. Spiff these up with a few modern accessories and you will shine brightly on all occasions.

A lucky relative or close friend has a new romance. Much as you want to, you can't make yourself care for this new person. Don't disregard this feeling as prejudice. Your Pisces intuition is giving you a warning. Be polite but maintain your boundaries. Avoid entangling yourself with this individual and remain silent about your perception for now. Warning your friend of the new lover's shady past or disreputable background will only create a Romeo and Juliet situation between the couple. Remember some of your own past romantic mistakes. Recall how angry you became if anyone tried to pull off your precious rose-colored glasses. Love is blind. Give your friend time and he or she will soon perceive the facts about their dream boy or girl. At some point later on, you may have to be ready to help your good friend get over their broken heart. Such are the wages of devoted friendship.

## PISCES October 2014

Your live-in companion or significant other undertakes a new health regime. Early October may find the two of you going on a juice fast, giving up gluten or getting up early to go to boot-camp fitness classes. You actually enjoy the challenge of this new routine. You feel invigorated. Your partner on the other hand, is a bit grumpy about it. Don't let him/her slack off, though. With exercise, nothing is more motivating than a pal or a trainer or a lover who is keeping you honest about how much and how often you work out.

This month's astrology forecast includes another of those times when Mercury seems to go into reverse. Mercury will be retrograde from the 4th to the 25th of October. Behave as you would if you observed a truck backing up close by. Exercise a bit of extra care in all daily activities. Don't buy new electronic devices or expect the ones you own to function properly during this retrograde.

An exciting idea for a creative project comes to you in a dream or while on a long solitary drive in the second week of October. You feel a great deal of enthusiasm about this idea. You even wax a bit resentful when work obligations interfere. There is a class, workshop or seminar you want to take related to this artistic endeavor. But you worry that doing so will make the financial tension between you and your partner worse. You think your idea has the potential to earn money at some point, but your partner feels it is too much of a gamble and balks at seeing you spend savings on what they see as trite or even worthless.

Although funds remain tight, an opportunity for travel arises in the latter half of the month. A close relative may gift you and your partner with plane tickets, or your boss may offer you the use of her vacation home. By all means, take advantage of this opportunity. Getting away will enable you and your partner a chance to see past tiffs more objectively and perhaps even laugh some of them off. While on the tropical beach or comfortably ensconced in the boss's vacation home, the two of you may cook up an idea to improve your financial picture for 2015. You return from the trip feeling united again. You sense that you now face your problems together rather than letting those issues split you apart.

## PISCES November 2014

A close friend whose counsel you rely upon announces plans to move away next year. She/he will be hundreds or even thousands of miles distant. The reason for this move is a happy one. You know the two of you will keep in touch. But you also know it won't be the same as getting together regularly in person. You feel sad and a bit apprehensive. You probably ought to say little about your feelings. No use making your pal guilty about leaving you when they are so joyful about it themselves.

Begin thinking about how you will fill the empty space left by your friend's imminent disappearance. Take up some serious study. Learn a language or attend a class in creative writing or dance. If you don't do something to distract yourself from the impending loss of your crony, you may sink into a mini depression by the end of the year.

Some individual could make your home life difficult around the 12th. If you rent your abode, it could well be a landlord. Or it may be a neighbor. Whoever it is, they interfere with your life in an irritating fashion. Lashing out at this person will only backfire on you. For now, the best you can do is screen your calls and limit your contact with them.

Children occupy more of your time this month. They may be your own offspring, or they could belong to friends or relatives. Possibly they are your students. Toward the end of November, you have a wonderful time helping them with a project. You also help sort out a disagreement between the children. As a result of the enthusiasm you show for their activities and your sensitivity to their feelings, these children admire and look up to you.

You and your partner continue to feel the renewed sense of closeness from last month's trip. The two of you find creative new ways to maintain this feeling. You may watch a DVD about couples' massage and start to give each other regular massages. You might make a trip to an adult toy store to select some fun items you can play with at home. The tension between the two of you melts away.

**PISCES December 2014**

A sense of grayness enters your sensitive soul as December begins. A loss you experienced sometime in the past two years comes back to haunt you. Don't suppress these feelings. Give yourself at least one whole day to grieve. There is no shame in crying. Tears are not weakness. The body cleanses itself of pain by weeping. Use art and nature to help you heal. Listen to music. Write a poem about your feelings. If the weather permits, go for a walk in a garden or on a forest trail. Or spend some time communing with an animal companion. If you love horses, this is a marvelous time to go riding. The connection between you and the horse provides a natural form of healing.

Occasional sadness is normal and even healthy. You don't have to paint a false smile on your face. But if these feelings threaten to overwhelm you, seek help. See a mental health professional who can help diagnose your condition and offer appropriate help. You may have to go through a period of experimenting with different medications or treatments to see what works.

There's a good chance your mood will lift around the 20th. You reconnect with your past in a consoling and positive way. You may have dinner with a relative you haven't seen in a long time. Or you could unexpectedly hear from an old school friend on Facebook. Warm reminiscences help you dispel any remaining feelings of gloom. Also, a child will help ease your heart with an unanticipated gesture of sharing.

The holidays will finally see you rid of your melancholy. You are inspired to make a special festive effort this year. Invite your dear friend who is leaving town after the new year to come to a special surprise dinner in his or her honor. Get everyone to bring small easy-to-pack presents. Drink a toast to the good friend's future in their faraway new home.

Someone makes an odd and perhaps comical mistake about you toward the end of the month. Maybe a waiter at a restaurant mistakes you for a celebrity and asks for an autograph. Or perhaps you receive a misaddressed e-mail requesting your services as a clown at a children's party.

## PISCES January 2015

In January, you will through some kind of spiritual reawakening. You may find yourself re-connecting with the religious tradition in which you were raised. Or you may start to study another form of spirituality. Perhaps you begin meditating. If you already meditate, you may find that you attain a new level in your practice. At any rate, 2015 starts with a major shift for you. It is, however, a change few people perceive right away. With time, others will be surprised and pleased at how you seem to have come out of your shell. You will be invited more interesting places by the kind of enthusiastic people you have always sought to surround yourself with.

This invisible inner change gives you a deeper sense of confidence. You feel more resistant to tension. When your co-workers display their most malignant behavior, you remain unperturbed. When your partner feels anxious or testy, you are able to remain loving and calm. You feel as if you have a new secret identity: Buffy the Stress Slayer.

You finally receive a long-overdue reward for that pressure cooker project of last summer. A promotion seems to be in the wings. You and your partner might make plans to participate in a volunteer vacation later in 2015. You like the idea of visiting a new place and helping the people who live there. You may also decide to adopt a pet from a local shelter. Your heart may be stolen by a sweet, affectionate three-legged dog or a beautiful cat who likes to sleep at your feet all night.

Think about taking up a musical instrument this year. What instrumental sounds move or inspire you? Consider what types of musicians you would like to play with—do you picture yourself improvising with jazz musicians? Jamming with hopeful rock stars? Joining in a drum circle? Also find out what kind of musical instruction is available in your area. Perhaps that interesting looking man you see sometimes at the corner store is a great guitar teacher. A deep involvement in music will support the other changes in your life and bring you more and more self-confidence.

# YOUR MONTHLY FORECASTS
for
# THE CHINESE SIGNS
for 2014

# RAT 2014

## OVERVIEW FOR THE WOOD HORSE YEAR

*Ravenous Rat,*

*Rat and Horse typically quarrel – over everything from how money is spent to how to raise geraniums. Despite the Horse's odd attraction for you, as soon as you two strike up a relationship, the fight is on! Arguments can be productive. But in the case of Horse and Rat, perpetual spats take up much of your precious time and get neither of you anywhere positive. So rather than live this year in permanent tumult, try staying out of the limelight. Do not try to gain more power. Not now. Leave political office off your list. Forget asking for a raise or bidding on that promotion. Leave the major decisions making to your live-in lover or spouse. Do not try to get your little claws around the reins this year.*

*If you are too visible and/or grabby in a Horse year, you might face both financial and emotional bankruptcy. The Horse hates to be dictated to. And you like to be boss. As you can see, this year bodes disruptive chaos – unless of course you wisely choose to stay out of the spotlight. As you will not be parading or appearing in public all that much, why not plan to have the cosmetic surgery you have been postponing in this pragmatic Horse year? Next year promises to bring you back into the public eye. So you might as well do everything you can now to improve your appearance, spruce up your wardrobe and scissor that old-fashioned hairdo into some kind of contemporary coiffure. sw*

---

## THE CHINESE YEAR AHEAD

### RAT 2014

## RAT February 2014

The planet of communication and transportation will stage one of its backwards-moving periods most of this month (the 6th until the 28th). Prepare to deal with electronic glitches and delays getting from point A to point B. Postpone any non emergency surgery or contract signings. This month, however, Mercury's retrograde period may bear some unusual fruit for Rats. Rats are planners .Mercury Rx is the perfect time to plot and plan and scheme and ruminate.

You may bump into an ex-friend around February 2nd. The encounter will necessarily be awkward. People you knew back then had always disliked this character. You allowed yourself to be drawn into some intrigue about this ex of yours which besmirched his or her reputation. Later he or she confronted you about your behavior. The discomfort quotient of this chance reunion could be heightened by the fact that you will be wearing a gift this ex gave you. Something you cherish and found too elegant to put aside after the relationship ended - a brooch, tie, shirt or handbag. You have two options here. You can offer your old lover a polite nod and walk quickly away. Or, in an attempt to bury the hatchet, you can stop long enough to apologize for your unkind deeds of the past.. Either way, this spontaneous meet up will be upsetting.

The alignment of the stars may create an opening for your creative project to gain you some recognition. Maybe your article for a professional journal will be mentioned on a high-profile blog. Or you may be invited to speak as an expert on a local television talk show. Or, by some fluke, your sage remarks on Facebook will go viral. This achievement could lead to a long series of successes for you. It will probably occur between the 16th and the 20th. Make sure you are prepared. Mind your manners. And be certain you have your finest attire ready and waiting in the closet.

Your partner will prove his or her worth, rising above and beyond the call of duty to help you in a minor crisis. Perhaps you leave an important document at home on the day of a crucial meeting. Your partner will drive home to fetch it and bring you what you need. Or you lose your car keys and call your partner from a parking lot miles from home. Whatever mini-crises arise, this month your partner will frequently come to your rescue.

## RAT March 2014

An older relative offers you a generous gift in early March. But there will be strings attached. Could be he or she will buy you that new car you need to replace your old beater. Of course, in return, Aunt Matilda or Uncle George wants your first-born child—or at the very least to have that child named after them. Maybe this person offers to give you and your partner a down-payment on a new home. The catch is that you will be obliged to visit this elderly relative for most of your holidays. Go ahead and say yes. Nothing is free in this life. Besides, as a canny Rat person, you can always find some wiggle room in any agreement. Name your son or daughter after this bountiful relative. You can always nickname the child Butch or Sissy.

You may suffer a bereavement this month. If you have an aging animal companion, be prepared to say goodbye around March 11. Only a handful of your closest friends will truly understand how deeply you feel this loss. If you have children, this loss will be especially hard on them. To help your kids (and yourself) move through this grief, do something creative in honor of your departed four-footed friend. Besides burying the pet in the backyard or in some place sacred to your family. Hold a ceremony honoring the departed critter. You might also make a photo collage showing pictures of the animal from youth through old age.

An ex from a long time ago may get in touch with you sometime after the 20th. You thought matters between the two of you had long been concluded fairly. It turns out this person thinks there remain some thorny loose ends to tie up, possibly of a financial nature. Even though where you're concerned it's by now, all water under the bridge. Don't quibble about the details. Clearly this character wants back into your life at all costs (yours). Be generous. But don't spoil this critter. That's how the trouble started in the first place. You were too nice. Write a check. Then remind them gently never to darken your door again for money or any other purpose.

## RAT April 2014

At a party in the beginning of this month, while you are mingling with the other guests, you notice something disturbing out of the corner of your eye. A person whom you know slightly may be flirting with your significant other. Even worse, your partner will not appear to be dissuading this interloper's advances. You feel your blood pressure rising. But in addition to anger, you will also feel mystified. You know full well that this potential romantic rival is not as attractive as you. He or she may be older, stockier and less well-dressed.

Yet your sweetie is laughing and chatting apace with this person. When this trespassing character places a tender hand lightly on your partner's arm or shoulder, it remains there. He or she does not pull back. What to do? If you're a man, you will be tempted to pummel the geezer. A lady? You'll want to weep or scream. It may be best to insist on leaving the party early before they start exchanging phone numbers and email addresses. Your partner may have had too much to drink. Or he or she could really be pushing the envelope on this flirtation. Refrain from exploding while you are still seething inside. Direct confrontation is not the best way to handle this matter. Deal with it in the morning when your defenses are up and your temper has cooled.

One of your Facebook or other social network friends may ask you to get involved in a charitable group project toward the end of this month. It may be planning a fundraising gala event or participating in a bike ride or walk related to some illness. Go ahead and accept this invitation. You will make several valuable new connections.

Over the next couple of weeks, when the air has cleared around the unfortunate touchy-feely party incident. You may find yourself using your own best connections to smooth over any difficulties your honey may be facing at work. Listen attentively to his or her anecdotes about what happens during the day. Take the time to arrange special intimate dinners at home, followed by a passionate evenings in bed. The planetary energies of the 16th are particularly helpful in opening new dimensions of your relationship and diminishing your main squeeze's temptation to flirt.

## RAT May 2014

The elements at play during the second week of May might combine in a few different ways. The basic ingredients could include you and your partner being in separate cities - you attending a concert or sporting event - and a celebrity noticing you at this event. You may be invited to a private party afterwards. At this party, a very attractive famous person will pay a lot of attention to you. Ultimately, you will receive an invitation to her or his hotel room. I'm not sure how you will respond to this celebrity's flattery. Will you still hold some resentment toward your partner for last month's flirtation? Will you decide to repay tit for tat? That seems to me like a game that could backfire on you.

Give a dinner party after the 23rd of this month. Of course you won't invite that person who flirted with your significant other. But do send out invitations to an interesting mix of people from different spheres of your life. Make the event large enough to feel convivial yet small enough that you can serve gourmet fare without breaking the bank. The planetary energies of the final week of May provide Rats with an excellent opportunity to network and impress influential people.

There may be some sad news related to your partner's family around the end of May. It could be related to mental health. Perhaps a sibling, aunt or uncle will have some kind of breakdown. Or it could emerge that this person has been cutting her or himself for several months now. Be supportive of your sweetheart now. He or she will naturally feel shaken by this new development.

## RAT June 2014

Have you backed up all your files? Laid in a hefty stock of patience for dealing with misapprehensions ? If so, then you are probably well-equipped to deal with another of Mercury's annoying retrograde phases. This one takes place between the 7th of this month and the 1st of July.

Don't sign anything binding. Make plans. Negotiate. But delay concretizing deals till after 1st of July.

The travel bug will bite you hard around June 6th. Go ahead and plan a getaway of some kind. If you and your partner are not financially flush right now, opt for a brief luxury trip rather than a protracted vacation. The luxurious surroundings will leave a more lasting impression. Besides, at a deluxe hotel you are more likely to rub elbows with people high enough up the social and professional ladder to aid your own progress in some way. Pack your most elegant attire. Don't go down to breakfast in the morning until you have completed your *toilette*.

That celebrity you flirted with last month may surprise you by getting in touch sometime around the 24th. He or she wants to see you again. Is this beginning to sound complicated? It's heading that way for sure. Think strategically about how to handle this situation. You don't want to make an enemy of this VIP. Turning them down could wound a hypersensitive ego. On the other hand, would a *groupie fling* with this character be worth ditching the security of your current relationship?

Use your refined sense of ethics to decide what to do around the increasing attention you are receiving lately. Your longtime companion could be drifting away simply because you are so much more social these days. Moreover, the publicity you got back in April starts to set off a chain reaction. More people get in touch with you, wanting your comments and input. You may receive invitations to serve on some important committees.

Unfortunately, you may have to turn some of these invitations down or at least postpone them. At the end of May you could suffer some kind of mishap which affects your personal appearance. Perhaps your hair makes some kind of drastic mistake. Or that new tattoo or piercing becomes infected. Or you break out in a rash. You have become so popular that you can no longer expect be an anonymous Rat person with a bad dye job. You might have to lie low for a few days.

**RAT July 2014**

As you head toward home after work around July 10, you may glimpse that bimbo/him-bo who flirted with your partner. The thought flashes through your mind that he or she may have just left your house after a tryst with your significant other. You can't find definite confirmation either to prove or disprove this possibility. Your sweetie seems distracted, but that could be because she or he is anxious about family matters. Are there two coffee cups on the counter because your partner misplaced her/his first cup? Or was your partner just sharing a cup of coffee with someone? Take a few deep breaths. It doesn't really make sense to become anxious or angry about what only could have or might have happened. Again, don't bring up this incident until you are certain it's based on fact. No use arguing over a paranoid fantasy you might have concocted out of a glimpse.

You may notice some unusual symptoms around the 12th of the month. You won't feel sure if you are sick or if it is only stress. Make an appointment with an acupuncturist. Healers trained in Traditional Chinese Medicine learn how to take the pulse not only of the heart but also of the liver, gallbladder, small intestine, kidney and bladder. Doctors of Chinese Medicine can also tell much about a person's health by looking at the tongue. These diagnostic tools enable them to detect incipient health problems before they are discernible to western MD's.

A distant relative whom you haven't seen in years may get in touch with you. He or she is in town and wants to get together with you. Could be a cousin or even a second or third cousin.

Maybe the two of you played together when you were younger. If you happen to have an opening in your busy schedule, by all means arrange to meet this person over coffee or lunch. The reminiscing you do will bring up precise memories that you didn't know you still had. This type of meeting allows for a re-reconnection with a part of your personality that you tend to neglect. It's fine of course to live in the moment. But harking back to your childhood can also be extremely enriching.

## RAT August 2014

You may experience another of the drawbacks of becoming more well-known as August begins. It will probably involve social media in some way. You could receive a spate of negative messages on your Facebook page. Or someone may call you to task for a hasty tweet. It's even possible that an unflattering photo of you could become a meme. Hold your head high. But remember also to show a willingness to laugh at yourself. Be your most charming self as well as sporting your most resplendent attire. This half hour of fame won't last forever. Soon someone else will become the *scandale du jour* and you will be able to relax again.

Mid-August you continue to wonder about your partner and that flirt. You could feel strongly tempted to snoop into their personal belongings and private business. The prospect of checking into your partner's e-mail records or mobile phone will magnetize you. You already scan your significant other's Facebook page on a daily basis to see if that horrible rival person is commenting on your sweetie's posts. Would you like it if your partner were to spy on you? Endeavor to respect his or her boundaries as well. Do not let yourself become suspicious about what might or might not be happening behind your back. Remember: the best way to keep a bird who lives in a cage is to leave the cage door open.

Your newfound popularity will start to pay off in cold hard cash around the 23rd. Until you feel certain this will become a regular stream of income rather than an occasional windfall, be conservative with these funds. Put more than half of the fresh money into a savings account.

It may be time for you to bring a new animal companion into your life after your loss earlier this year. He or she may actually come to you. There is a strong possibility you will find an abandoned animal in your neighborhood. Or someone you know may have to give up an animal because of family issues. This friendly critter will need to be seen by a vet right away. Bring inoculations up-to-date and be sure he or she is in fine fettle.

## RAT September 2014

You only confided in a handful of friends about that flirtation with the famous individual a while ago. But during the first week of September you discover that one of them has blabbed. Now the tale is becoming overblown and distorted. When you think about people maliciously gossiping about you, it incenses you. Instead of plotting ways to get even with the gossips, stop and think. Early this year you encountered someone you gossiped about in the past. That individual asked you why you behaved that way. But he or she never retaliated. Distance yourself from the rumor mongers. But don't declare war on them. Keeping the peace will help even the karmic score.

Your partner's troubled relative seems to be having a hard year. He or she may have just emerged from a treatment center. This person has no idea how to re-gain employment and/or independence. After living with other family members for a brief period, this individual may ask your partner if they can stay at your home. You can readily observe that your partner feels his relative's pain very deeply. Although you may well have a few qualms, come the 11th of

September you feel duty bound to agree to let the mixed-up family member stay in your guest room for a couple of months.

In addition to the strains of having a new pet and a houseguest with mental health issues, you discover in the latter half of the month that your home needs major repairs of some kind. So now you must hire a contractor and then face a few weeks of household chaos while a team of workers troops through every day but Sunday. By mid-October the cloud of dust will be lifted and the dog will have stopped peeing on your houseguest's slippers. On the other hand, it looks doubtful the resident relative will be gone.

## RAT October 2014

Here comes another Mercury retrograde. It will last from the 4th of October till the 25th. I'm sure you're already familiar with the usual warnings—anticipate hassles and delays in matters related to communicating and traveling. Don't firm up any important agreements. Wait until later for major medical procedures, etc. But Mercury retro does have its positive side. You can negotiate, initiate and make plans for the future with reckless abandon. But whatever you do, don't commit to marriage or sign up for anything else you can't wriggle out of easily.

That extra money is continuing to flow in as October arrives. You can use it to cover the renovation expenses on your home. You may also decide that both you and your partner require a wardrobe re-do. Try not to go overboard. Select just a few elegant pieces you will wear frequently. Look on E-bay or hit swanky resale shops to see if you can find used designer duds at a bargain price. Sign up to receive notices of special private sales at upscale department stores in your area.

There's a strong chance you will overreact to some perceived slight at your workplace during the third week of October. You might interpret something someone says as a snub. If you lash out with harsh, angry words, you will only look foolish afterwards. Instead let everyone see your charming, delightful side. Train yourself to react with a winning smile whenever you feel uncertain of someone's motives. You can always show your teeth eventually if and when the situation proves to be worth riling yourself over.

You and your partner leave your houseguest and new pet at home while you dress up in costumes and attend a big bash one of your friends is having at the end of the month. Probably Halloween party with elaborate decorations. You both have a fabulous time. In fact you two might have too much of a good time. Your companion may end up passed out among the coats on the host's bed. You could experience a quarter hour of worry and confusion before finding them. As you search, you won't know whether you are more worried that something happened to your partner, or that your S.O. is in a back room kissing the dreaded flirt. Of course, in retrospect, the entire event will assume a humorous aspect as it is occurring whilst you are dressed up as a Fairy, a Clown or a Duck.

Several weeks have gone by without mishap regarding the vague flirtation you were so anxious about. This might be a good moment to bring up the subject to your lover. Time to clear the air and get some closure around what will probably turn out to be but a mirage.

## RAT November 2014

Your houseguest has been worrying you for a while. He/she is easy enough to get on with, but aimless and lost. You don't really approve of anyone spending all day playing video games and watching daytime telly. But you hold your tongue and keep your counsel. Your significant other is, of course, more patient with their relative than you are. But when you discuss it, both of you agree that you have begun to feel frustrated with the lack of privacy in your home. The guest never seems to leave home except for occasional trips to the convenience store for soda and candy. You have hinted they go out for a walk or use a guest pass to visit your gym. But he or she seems oblivious to these suggestions. Could be depression revisited. Make certain they are taking their medication.

Your matchmaker side emerges around the 12th-16th. You will find yourself assessing romantic possibilities for every person you know who is not already part of a happy couple. You may decide that your colleague who insists she/he loves being single needs to meet your neighbor. Beware however. They may not play for the same team. You might even decide that the perfect way to get that houseguest out from underfoot is to fix him/her up with a semi-depressed wallflower you used to work with. After all, you might find yourself thinking, *they can talk about mental health issues together.* Try to restrain your Rat-like instinct to pair everyone up. You may think you are only being helpful, but others may perceive you as interfering. Rats often busy themselves with the affairs of their entourage. Resist the temptation to be so relentlessly meddling.

I hope your thriftiest self triumphed over your love of luxury when you shopped for clothes last month. If not, you may have to dig into savings to cover some unanticipated expenses around the 19th. It may well turn out that the final bill for your home renovations is much higher than the original estimate. There's also a possibility that either your vehicle or your partner's will require some costly repair work. Rein in the spending.

**RAT December 2014**

You and your partner confer more seriously about your houseguest in early December. The two of you will come to the realization that the person needs structure as well as compassion. Your partner begins researching online for job-training programs and group homes for people coping with mental health issues. Now that you have stopped being so suspicious of your partner, the two of you will have begun to re-establish a sense of intimacy. Deciding together about how to help the despondent relative by shifting him or her to a new residence will help you feel like a team again.

Arrange for your houseguest to move out after the holidays. You can't very well exclude them from the festivities. Do the research now to find an opening at a group home. Or perhaps one of your partner's other relatives can host the patient for a few months. Be sure to discuss the plan with all family members. You may be pleasantly surprised at how many folks reach out to host your current burden.

Make certain the person doesn't feel rejected. Just explain that you and your companion need to spend more time alone together. You want to re-build and re-structure your partnership. I know you like to be ultra-social during the holiday season. If you do hold a holiday gathering at your place, do so in the late afternoon. You will want to be available early enough to have time to re-kindle your romance at home. There are a few days on either side of December 18th which are particularly beneficial for healing your relationship.

You could receive a mysterious package around the end of the year. Someone will send you a very generous gift for your home. Without a card. You will have no way of tracing the giver. Did your celebrity friend remember you nearly half a year after you met? Did that wealthy but controlling older relative decide to give something without any strings for a change? Whoever sent the gift, it will be a lovely and useful addition to your home.

## RAT January 2015

Your star is on the rise again. That brief flurry of local media attention you experienced last year starts again around the 7th of January. Some of the accolades you earn now are a result of the new connections you made through that charity project last year. After the learning experiences of last year's ups and downs, you feel more ready to step into the public eye. There are definite signs your income will be rising throughout 2015. You feel more secure in your relationship with your partner as well. The two of you may contemplate buying a new property together. Looks as though you will move. Could it be you will purchase a second home as a weekend getaway? You will enjoy the search for this property at weekends during the months to come.

Around the 15th, you get some iffy news about your partner's health. He or she may be diagnosed with a chronic condition. The doctors may discuss the a few different approaches and medications. They will explain the pros and cons of different ways of coping with this health challenge. Suddenly, the two of you will be awash in medical literature as you learn the terminology and treatment options of this previously unfamiliar condition. Your partner may find the new information about his/her health disorienting and even a little daunting. This will be a difficult time. You will have to supply emotional support. Be patient and forbearing. It may take a few months for him or her to recover a sense of emotional equilibrium. But your relationship will benefit because you will triumph over this medical accident.

Some kind of incident involving your car may occur at the same time as you are dealing with your partner's health concerns. No one will be hurt. But the car may sustain serious damage. Possibly some careless driver hits your car while in a parking lot. Or a thief may break a window to steal your belongings. Make sure your insurance policies are up-to-date. And don't leave anything temptingly visible inside your car when you leave it sitting somewhere locked up.

# OX 2014
## OVERVIEW FOR THE WOOD HORSE YEAR

*Obdurate Ox,*

*Because of the general tone of diligent labor which characterizes all Horse years, this Wood Horse year will be fortuitous for Oxen. It's no secret. Oxen love to work and work hard. You enjoy an exceptional capacity for exertion – both physical and mental. Work energizes you. Why? Because you live for results and are not much fussy about how you get those results – even if you have to struggle uphill with a thousand pound boulder on your weary shoulders – reaching the destination is always worth the effort.*

*So when Horse years come around, you are favored and applauded and praised for your unparalleled work ethic. When the Japanese took Koreans as slaves in a darker period of their history, it was commonly said: "We worked them like Horses and Oxen." Nobody works harder than you two - in tandem! So in this Horse year you may be working your buns off, but the results will be precisely what you were after. the Horse's influence protects and preserves The Ox. 2014 may not prove to be the most jovial year in your life . . . but then when you have such rich and tangible rewards from your work, who needs fun? sw*

---

## THE CHINESE YEAR AHEAD
## OX 2014

### OX February 2014

The Year of the Year of the Horse may commence with financial disappointment. Your boss could announce a freeze on salary increases. In fact, it is even possible your employer issues an edict for across-the-board pay cuts. Accustomed though you are to discipline and thrift, this will nonetheless be alarming. You may have to make some hard choices about what small luxuries to eliminate from your day-to-day.

Do not let the tension from this financial challenge affect your health. Sweat out those negative feelings with vigorous exercise. See if your health plan includes a discount on a gym membership. Or check to see if any local dojos are offering special discounts on martial arts classes. If these options are out-of-reach, check some exercise DVD's out from the local library and leap around your living room every day for half an hour. Perhaps you could try commuting to your job on foot or bicycle instead of driving.

Mercury makes one of its backwards treks through the sky this month. This occurs from the 6th until the 28th of the month. These periods are the worst possible times for making major purchases so put off any plans you have to acquire a new vehicle, home, computer, refrigerator, washer or dryer, etc. Moreover, expect computer glitches and travel delays. Do not sign any documents which could have inextricable clauses during this time.

A younger person - a teenager or a fledgling adult, comes to you for advice around the 21st. This youngster could be your own child or the offspring of a close friend or sibling. Turns out he or she has acted out in a rather disturbing manner. Bottom line, this youngster faces some potential legal trouble. Resist the temptation to point out or gasp at the folly. Delivering a lecture will only make you appear pompous in the kid's eyes. If you offer practical advice untainted by judgment, the youngster will take your wisdom more seriously. Be a chum. Not a judgmental "adult".

Toward the end of the month, someone you least expect to, announces they see you as a potential spouse. You may have indulged in a mild flirtation with this person in the past. Or he/she could be someone you regarded solely as a friend-with-benefits. To your utter surprise, you will discover this person has always had strong romantic feelings for you. She or he will express these feelings as a result of a move related to his/her career. They were thinking you might actually accept their proposal and move with. It doesn't look like it's in the cards. You have bigger fish to fry. Be gentle and diplomatic in your refusal.

## OX March 2014

You will win some kind of small prize from the 4th to the 9th of March. It may be a pair of tickets to a concert or sporting event, or perhaps dinner for two at a local restaurant. Share your good fortune with that friend of yours who has been depressed lately. Sharing time with you will help lift his or her spirits. Try to be patient if this pal wants to rail against the unfairness of life and tell you (once again!) their sob stories. Not everyone possesses your Ox-like stoicism. Often simply by listening to someone's woes, you help them unscramble their thoughts. If your friend repeats the one about how his father took his dog away too often, tactfully change the subject. If that doesn't work, begin spouting a few of your own childhood miseries.

You are likely to have some serious plumbing or water infiltration problems at home around mid-month. Be sure to get more than one estimate on repairs. You will find a wide variation in what different contractors charge. Do not make your choice solely on the basis of the lowest price. Get references from other people who have used these peoples' services. Try to suss out which expert is the most honest.

Toward the last week of March, you may hear some grim news about an ex of yours. He or she has fallen on hard times. The catalogue of this person's dissolution will be quite long. They may actually be living in a car or at a homeless shelter. He or she could be facing legal woes, perhaps a bitter divorce or a messy bankruptcy. It is possible she/he also has serious health problems. Given how badly things ended between the two of you, you probably won't feel inclined to offer your help. But try not to indulge in any vindictive satisfaction either. Instead, use your knowledge of your former lover's problems to let go of any lingering anger you still harbor. Having done so, at month's end you should feel lighter and freer. You will also know for sure that the breakup was not at all your doing.

## OX April 2014

It's highly probable during that the first week of this month the universe will play a bit of an April Fool's joke on you. Unfortunately, you will have to endure the laughter of others but it won't seem funny to you. You will take a bit of a spill. Might be down a few stairs or merely tripping over a rug or a chair But the way it will occur could make those present chuckle. You may even observe a few stifled titters when you relay the tale to your friends. Don't be offended by a few random giggles. The humor here is due to the contrast between your usual dignified reserve and your slapstick pratfall. No fault of your own of course.

Choose your words with extra care at the office around the 12<sup>th</sup> of April. A co-worker may try to engage you in a conversation which will veer off course into some controversial topics. Even if you think they are not present, a superior may be listening. If you seem to agree with some of your co-worker's extreme opinions, it could affect your supervisor's assessment of you. The best course may be to appear too busy to engage in idle chitchat. For this week, keep workplace conversations focused on work topics.

A visit to your home by an acquaintance may clue you in to some good news around the 17<sup>th</sup>. This person will remark on something you own, letting you know it carries more value than you thought. It may turn out that a book, a painting or an inherited piece of glassware or ceramic that you've owned for years can be sold for a nice chunk of change. Have it appraised by a reputable firm. And before selling it, get a reliable second opinion

If you decide to go ahead and sell this precious item, spend a portion of the money on something frivolous. You are usually exemplary in the way you handle money, always putting some aside to save. You generally purchase only what you need, often used or at least marked down. Indulge yourself in something fun for a change.

## OX May 2014

Someone in your social circle may suffer a loss around the 8<sup>th</sup> of May. It could be the death of the spouse, parent or child of a close friend. Offer practical help, such as preparing food or driving members of the grieving family to the funeral home or ferrying them from the airport. Proffer your shoulder for your friend to lean on as he/she absorbs the shock of this loss. It is possible that some negative characters will try to spread gossip about the deceased. Nip this in the bud. Tell these nasty people in no uncertain terms that their behavior is unacceptable, rude and inappropriate.

A new romance may blossom for you the third week of May. You will probably meet this person through your job. You will naturally hesitate at first as you usually keep your love life separate from your work. But you will doubtless experience a powerful sense of chemistry when you are near this individual. Events may move very quickly. This new lover will differ from your usual type. You may find yourself both thrilled and surprised. In some way this guy or girl represents a type you previously thought you couldn't tolerate. It could be that his/her political or religious views are the diametric opposite of your own. Or she/he may have some physical trait you formerly found distasteful. Yet for some mysterious reason, you will find him or her irresistible.

Toward the end of May, a visiting friend with a vivid imagination may ask you if your home is haunted or has a poltergeist. You will probably laugh off the very question. Then you will start to notice some unusual occurrences. Lights might flicker in your bedroom. You could hear something that sounds like footsteps in an empty room. Objects you leave in one place may mysteriously migrate to another location. Even you, with your strong preference for rationality, may have a hard time finding a logical explanation for all of these curious events. My mother used to call those weird flying objects "resentments". Are you still resentful about something you thought you had long since gotten over? Check your dreams for signs.

## OX June 2014

I hope you are not waiting with bated breath by the mailbox for some desperately needed check, dear Ox. I'm afraid payments, as well as other missives, are liable to be late this month as

Mercury retrogrades. From the 7th of June until the 1st of July, delays and glitches are likely to be the norm rather than the exception.

Your muscles ache. Your brain cells seem to move sluggishly. Almost anyone else would read these as signs of fatigue. They'd schedule a break pronto. Oxen, on the other hand, tend to take for granted that they must always toil on no matter how weary they feel. Change this pattern of self-abuse through overwork. Take some time off now. Treat your need for R&R as an emergency. Don't wait for illness or injury to enforce rest upon you. Think of this mini vacation as a form of preventive healing.

The second week of June offers a marvelous window for you to re-discover some form of fun you have forgotten. Is there a hobby you used to enjoy but abandoned because it took too much time away from work? If so, this is an excellent opportunity to revive this pastime. Perhaps it's time for you to participate in some of the pleasures of your childhood. Climb trees. Draw pictures on the driveway with colored chalks. Catch fireflies in a jar. Have a tea party with your dogs. Schedule a field trip to some place that gives you back a sense of childlike wonder: the zoo or perhaps an aquarium or planetarium. Restore a sense of playfulness and joy to your life.

Between June 22nd & 25th you may hear from that person who revealed her/his giant crush on you back in February. It will likely be a tentative e-mail or perhaps a jaunty Facebook message. He or she is coming back to town and would like, once again, to get together with you. This admirer feels uncertain about whether you return their feelings. If you are truly not interested, beg off with a reasonable excuse. Be honest—but not brutally so. Or, if you are still curious and maybe even a bit keen, go ahead and schedule a coffee date. Right now your life is full of surprises in the romance department. No harm in taking advantage of the extra attention. Good for the sometimes faltering Ox ego.

## OX July 2014

You could very well decide to make some kind of commitment between the 6th and the 11th. Not obvious if it's that infatuated admirer who recently came back to town, or that unusual individual you met at work back in May. It may be someone else entirely - a third entity. It's odd. You felt unsure of this person at first. You weren't sure if it was a practical match. But you may also have wearied of putting in the extra time and effort involved in looking for a partner. For you, having someone readily available both to share the chores and share your bed makes sense. You are a person who prefers reason to swooning emotion. It is similar in an interpersonal way, to growing and cooking your own vegetables rather than wasting money at restaurants. Whoever you're committing to has demonstrated that he/she appreciates your strength, tenacity and honesty. Another of the attractions these person offers is that she/he is wise enough to let you choose the terms of the relationship. Besides, the sex is damn good.

Your new sweetie would love for the two of you to spend time together cocooned together in romantic bliss. But you have increased demands at work starting around the 17th. Your boss has delegated an important project to you. As always, you step up to the new responsibility, never shirking any work. You hope that this may lead to a promotion. You know you can handle the responsibility of authority and supervising others. You know you deserve more of a leadership role. Go ahead and   prove your worth by applying your nose to the grindstone, working longer hours and not asking for any remuneration for same. Model employee time.

One of your neighbors is being inconsiderate. He or she may play loud music late at night. Or possibly this character fails to pick up the poop her/his dog drops on your yard. Maybe visitors to this individual's home regularly block your driveway with their vehicles. You may have to demonstrate to this person that you will not accept this trespass onto your boundaries. Insist firmly that he or she cease this thoughtless behavior immediately. No need to raise your voice. Simply display your brute strength of character. If an Ox puts his or her foot down firmly enough, nobody messes with them.

## OX August 2014

Your new partner nudges you to join her/him in an activity that you have always avoided. You are proud of the fact that you are a strong-minded person with vehement opinions. But sometimes this means you slam your mind shut about certain less comfortable topics. There's nothing actually wrong with this pastime your sweetie wants you to try. It's not immoral or illegal or bad for your health. You simply decided some years ago that sky diving or tango or kite surfing was a bit frivolous. Perhaps the idea of it secretly scares you a bit. Why not permit yourself the luxury of outgrowing this prejudice? Go ahead. Give it a whirl. Do not pretend to being trying this adventure just to please your companion. Do it for the sake of your own personal growth.

You may feel both horrified and helpless around the 20th of the month. That depressed acquaintance of yours may start dropping hints about suicide. Insist they see a therapist ASAP. Inform this person's closest family members about this downward emotional spiral. But do be discreet. Don't openly break the patient's trust. They need to believe you are on their side - and you are.

Your ability to shoulder a heavy load is receiving favorable attention from your supervisors. That promotion you hoped for may be within reach. However, I sense there's a rival lurking in your workplace. This competitor could be a Tiger, a Rat or a Horse. He or she is vying with you for the same position of authority. This person does not have your talent for hard work. But they have oodles of charm and hope to capitalize on both their charisma and their undeniable good looks. Unfortunately, this person's charisma lacks integrity. Of course, you will not be able to expose their duplicity. Like a weasel, this individual frequently wriggles out of the consequences of his/her actions. This time, they may resort to underhanded tactics to achieve their goal. He or she may attempt some form of sabotage around the 25th. Make sure you do not leave any documents or files in places where this tricky character has access.

## OX September 2014

Turn your attention to your health as September begins. Some chronic wellness issue that you thought you had under control may flare up in some way. Or perhaps an old injury starts to give you pain again after a period of respite. Go see your most trusted physician. Be leery, however, of any doctor who wants to solve your health problems through long-term prescription drug use. If the doctor starts writing endless prescriptions you should take them, say thanks and leave. Check for a complementary health clinic in your area which combines allopathic medicine with alternative healing modalities such as homeopathy or plant compounds. With chronic illness, acupuncture and Chinese herbal remedies often completely alleviate the problem.

Your sweetie will surprise you with an unusually thoughtful gesture around the 12th. You will feel deeply touched. You may also feel slightly embarrassed. This romantic expression of affection is one you have never considered performing for anyone. Accept this sign of her/his feelings graciously. Think about how you can expand your own skill set of emotional warmth. Perhaps next month you can delight them in turn with a creative token of your increasing endearment: a special book of love poems or a garment they have been coveting. Jewelry or fancy sports equipment would be appropriate as well. Write a sweet message on the card. I know. It's uncharacteristic of you Oxxy. But it's an exercise well worth the effort.

You may quarrel with an old friend in the third week of this month. Perhaps you express your controversial political or religious views too strongly at a gathering. You fail to consider that your friend has very different notions on this subject. They respond with unexpected ire. Their fury only makes you angrier. Slow down. The rift can be repaired. But do not expect your friend to be the only one who bends. You also must demonstrate some flexibility. You will have to compromise. If you display your usual obstinacy in this situation, you could lose a valuable friendship.

One of your animal companions has a health problem that has not yet been detected. That malady could become serious if you do not take him or her to the vet before the end of September.

## OX October 2014

Mercury will be retrograde from the 4th through the 25th of October. What happens during Mercury's apparent backward movement can flummox you and upset your applecart. As you know by now, during Mercury retrograde electronics go on the blink, travel delays occur apace and we must never sign binding documents or plight our troths during these periods. One more caveat - give Mercury time to relent. Don't rush into anything life changing till November 1st. Meanwhile plot and plan. Scheme and ponder.

Your unstable friend - the one who has been experiencing emotional turmoil - may stage a scene of some sort around the 5th of this month. She or he may engage in a loud public monologue on an inappropriate subject. Or this sad person may act out in some way, perhaps undressing at a party or threatening someone. Although you have always offered sympathy and support, your patience with this pal is dwindling. You feel that you have survived as much or more pain than this person has experienced. Yet, you never indulge in personal theatrics. You are not the type to take on a role of co-dependent *vis à vis* someone else's problems. If it's alcohol or drugs that are behind the public acting out, suggest a 12-step program. Say it once. If the person laughs in your face and resists vehemently, it may be time to distance yourself.

Your workplace rival may have won the first round of your competition. She or he lands a plum assignment that you were convinced had your name on it. Funny thing is, your adversary makes the mistake of underestimating you. Their gloating about this victory only deepens your determination to gain a larger prize. Unfortunately, your tendency to cut people off without a word can hurt you now. You dislike pretense. However, for now, you must affect a mask of bland friendliness toward this competitor. If you go silent and sulky, you risk appearing surly and unprofessional.

The last five days of this month offer an opportunity to show your sweetie that romantic gestures are not beyond you or your notoriously stodgy repertoire. Demonstrate to your partner that you have noticed his or her personal tastes. Design an evening tailored precisely to your honey's preferences. Take your partner to a restaurant which offers her/his favorite dishes. Afterwards, go to a concert or attend a play by their favorite musical artist or playwright. Or spend a weekend afternoon doing whatever your sweetie most enjoys - whether it's the scaling the climbing wall at a gym or getting a couples' massage at a spa - force yourself to not only do it. But enjoy doing it.

## OX November 2014

Those mysterious occurrences in your home may start up again around the 1st. You are still dubious about your fanciful friend's notion that this is a haunting of some sort. However, your animals and perhaps even your sweetie seem spooked by the strange events. Missing knickknacks. Disappearing plates. Papers circulating where they were not last time you looked. To allay fears, you could have someone come in and check the pipes and wiring in your house. If that doesn't stop the odd activity, it can't hurt to follow the advice of spiritualists for banishing unwanted invisible guests. Sprinkle some salt in the corners of your home. Let your mystically-minded friend say some prayers or incantations. It can't hurt. And it may indeed even help lay those perceived ghosts.

Check into good deals on last-minute trips. The second week of this month offers a wonderful chance for you and your sweetie to enjoy some time together away from everyday responsibilities. Even if you just take a weekend at a rented cottage in the country, it will do you both some good. You often fail to notice how big a toll you pay in stress from your hard work. And that tension has a deleterious effect on your relationship. Your partner will enjoy spending time with you when she/he can be your top priority. Be especially attentive to your sweetie. Why not ask about his or her work or studies rather than dominating the conversation.

A few years ago you suffered a traumatic personal event. One of the friends who helped you during that time may come to you for aid toward the end of November. The two of you may have quite naturally drifted apart since that challenging time in your life. Each went his or her own way. Now it's your turn to offer assistance in whatever degree you are able to this former pal. He or she may need to lean on you temporarily - sleep on your couch for a few nights, move into your guest room for a week or so or even borrow some cash to get by till they get back on their feet. You know this person's heart is in the right place. Feel free to let go of any minor reservations you may have had and dole out help altruistically.

## OX December 2014

Even if you usually skip office parties, be sure to make an appearance this year. Your workplace rival will try to use office holiday festivities to showcase her/his charm and get an advantage over you. Appearing aloof from your co-workers now could be counted as a point against you. I know you have little interest in clothes and appearance, but take some time now to look your best. Get a haircut. Ask your most stylish friend to help you choose an outfit that makes you stand out as both elegant and tasteful.

In the past you may have spent the holidays working, perhaps even giving up paid vacation days. This year take time off to spend the festivities with your partner. The planetary alignments for the second half of December create a sparkling opportunity for Oxen to enjoy intimate pleasures. You will have to switch off your workaholic side. Staying home from work should not simply mean more time for household chores. Curl up on the couch with your sweetie and watch a few DVDs. Cook together. Then eat fun snacks and drink wine in bed after a marathon session of lovemaking.

Try to steer clear of any holiday parties where your theatrical (cuckoo) friend may make an appearance. Those eternal scenes will only grate on your nerves. You always want to be able to DO something about them. But you know you can't. Send a holiday card. Or call and have a brief conversation to show that you still care. Maintain some connection but keep it loose - and distant. You cannot become this pal's personal savior. Anyone who wants to heal from trauma has to make a decision to survive, just as you may have in the past.

That young person you helped earlier this year may get in touch with you around the 19th. He or she may want to thank you for your advice and support. It is also possible this youthful character will seek your counsel on another, more romantic matter. Seems they have taken up with someone much older and are even thinking of marrying. Your job? Make them wait 18 months before committing. A year and a half of closeness ensures that all the warts have been viewed and all the red flags disabled.

## OX January 2015

You could face a health setback around the 6th of this month. This is not set in stone. You are not inevitably fated to be ill in early January. But you will be more vulnerable during this time. Taking precautions with your health throughout 2015, and especially during December, can ensure that you experience nothing more severe than a head cold or a paper cut. If you do succumb to some health issue, don't play hero and pretend it's nothing. There is nothing heroic about continuing to drive yourself to death when your body needs rest.

Your partner may seem restless and anxious around the 10th of January. Most likely the root of this behavior lies in her/his workplace. She or he may hesitate at first to confide in you. Probe gently about what is bothering your partner. Do not offer any bits of advice unless they are requested. Demonstrate that you can be a good listener. Sometimes your honey simply needs to vent and to know that you actually care about their innermost woes.

Your partner may also be experiencing some girth issues. Around the 14th, he or she decides to go on a strict diet. Why not show your support by undertaking this new health regime with your sweetie? Life will be a lot easier if meals together do not require two separate menus. It will be simpler too for your partner to stay motivated if she/he does not have to watch you eating foods which are restricted on this diet program. No stringent diet is ever a *bad* diet. But some are more slimming than others.

The last two or three days of the Year of the Horse may bring some mixed news about your workplace rival. Your boss may decide to have the two of you share responsibilities on an important new project. It's even possible the two of you will have to share an office for a while. Take this in stride. Or appear to. The more closely you work with this adversary, the more opportunities will crop up to display the rival's sloppy work habits and show up their surly manners.

# TIGER 2014
## OVERVIEW FOR THE WOOD HORSE YEAR

*Intrepid Tiger,*

*In Horse years, Tigers are not always lucky. The Horse truly loves you and approves of your zany energy. But sometimes – only sometimes – misfortune befalls Tigers in Horse years. Don't panic. This bad luck is not life-threatening. But it does mean you will have to labor harder under somewhat adverse conditions in order to reach the kinds of summits of success for which you are so famous. I don't mean to imply that you won't have enough money or that you or some beloved family member will fall ill and die. But small events will arise as obstacles and may cause you grievances.*

*More specifically, this Horse year can impinge on your natural good health. Here, because luck is not always on tap in Horse years, you will have to work harder to keep fit, avoid sugars and starches to stay thin and double up on the workouts at the gym. Walk everywhere. Take the stairs. Leave the car in the garage. Ride your bike to work. If you happen to be married or in a long term relationship now, take your loved one on an exciting journey somewhere new and instructive. In Horse years, you will enjoy entering a whole new culture together, bringing back souvenirs, taking photos and maybe even making new friends. The mood will be jolly this year. But the work may prove problematic. sw*

---

## THE CHINESE YEAR AHEAD
### TIGER 2014

### TIGER February 2014

One of your sources of financial security may disappear around the beginning of February. If an older relative has been permitting you to live rent-free in a family-owned property, he or she may suddenly decide to seek paying tenants instead. Perhaps an income property of your own goes empty. Or if your partner's income has given you the freedom to pursue your artistic dreams, he or she could become unemployed. Could even be an investment which previously paid good dividends will go sour. One way or another, this month you will be thrown back on your own skills and resourcefulness. Not to worry of course. You're a Tiger.

Don't waste time bemoaning this change. Consider it a challenge and hit the ground running. Work your connections. You have many talents. You also have a slew of allies who will be delighted to give you a leg up. You may have to be less choosy than you have been in the past. I know you prefer to work on projects which fulfill you. For now, you might have to take a plain job which is a bit boring. Or perhaps you can cobble together some self-employment projects and one or two part-time jobs. You can gradually eliminate the less appealing or lower-paying assignments as you find newer ones which offer more money and interest. You will be out of this thicket fairly quickly if you resolve to work through it instead of trying to head it off at the pass.

Mercury goes retrograde on the 6th of February and remains on its apparent backward course throughout this entire month. Keep communications simple. When Mercury is retrograde tangles occur. Avoid signing any compromising contracts or making long term commitments. There are glitches aplenty now. Any new employment you take on may prove to be of a temporary nature. Allow extra time when driving to appointments. Traffic delays become more likely during these phases. If you plan to fly anywhere, be sure to bring plenty of reading material in case changes in flight schedules leave you hanging out in the airport for several hours. Unless necessitated by emergency, do not undergo any surgery until after the retrograde period ends on February 28.

### TIGER March 2014

A few years ago, your generous side was overruled by your less noble desire to be free of worry and care. A friend or family member in need came to you for help. You responded with kindness at first. You permitted this person to think he or she could rely upon you. But your vanity interfered. Perhaps you felt that being around such a needy person dimmed your dash and luster. Or your sweetheart of the moment didn't like the needy character. For some reason, you began to criticize them. Perhaps your partner disparaged this needy friend as well. Eventually you actually dumped the poor thing. Now, sometime around March 4th, a similar opportunity will come your way. I don't think the same person will be returning. But it does look like the universe is offering you a second chance to display your finer qualities. This time don't let your generosity be thwarted either by your own selfish impulses or those of any member of your entourage.

An ex may get in touch around the 19th. Although you have a solid union as well as a tangy sex life with your partner, you may harbor secret regrets about this former lover. This person is a bit older than you. He or she may be someone way more important in the world than your significant other - a politician, a diplomat or a savvy leader in the business world. Your relationship with her/him probably lasted several years. You view that period with some nostalgia - as a kind of peak time in your life. The two of you attended important functions together. You learned many things from him/her - not only in a sexual sense but about the world. Go ahead. Make plans for coffee or lunch. It's fairly clear that you will gain clarity during at this innocent appointment and find that you see this older ex in a completely different light now. You will no doubt discover that the feelings you have at this meeting are more wistfulness than attraction. Although you can still see how a younger version of you found her/him irresistible, now you see why your current significant other turned out to be a better choice.

### TIGER April 2014

For a long time, you have enjoyed a balance of independence and intimacy in your partnership. You knew you could rely on your significant other to remain loyal. But back then, the two of you didn't live in each other's pockets. Perhaps your partner traveled frequently for work. Or you spent three weeks out of four in your country home while she/he lived in your condo in the city during the work week. Now all that has changed. Maybe you or your sweetie recently decided to retire or became unemployed. Or one of you may have switched to freelancing or telecommuting and work from home.

The excessive togetherness is driving you crazy. Tigers do not like to be confined or interrupted. You certainly like him/her cuddling you in the bedroom. But you are not keen to have them hovering by your side while you're making phone calls or working on your laptop. Do not expect your sweetie to understand your frustration via telepathy. He or she may see no problem with the two of you both sharing the same dwelling full-time. Although it may irritate your lover, speak out now of your need for separate space. Perhaps the two of you can work out a schedule which allows each of you some private home time. One of you can work on the first floor of your home while the other works on the second floor.

An important family birthday celebration will require some effort on your part. Either you will be asked to open your house for this party. Or you will have to order all the food or even bake the cake. Take this in stride. Offer to do more than you are asked. The person whose birthday it will be has always been more than kind to you. This is a golden chance to make a real difference for them.

Someone whom you admire greatly will proffer you an honor around the 22nd of this month. Could be that a teacher whose classes you have taken asks you to co-teach a special workshop or seminar with him/her. Or maybe the person whose charity work inspired you to join a volunteer group requests that you serve on the board of directors of that organization. Accept graciously.

## TIGER May 2014

You may be involved in some kind of dispute related to children the first week of May. Perhaps you will have to take the co-parent of one of your own offspring to court about child support. Or there may be some family disagreement about where the young children of a sibling, aunt or uncle of yours will stay while the parent goes to a rehab center or into hospital for a prolonged stay. It is even possible that you will observe one of your neighbors abusing a child and contact the authorities. Even though you may feel a certain rage around this issue, try not to show animosity toward the other adults involved.

Racism or another form of prejudice might mar an otherwise pleasant social occasion around the 16th of this month. The ugly comments may be directed at you or at someone close to you. This is not the time to remain silent for the sake of peace and diplomacy. You want to make it clear to the bigots that their ugly words will not be tolerated. Let the offenders know their behavior is entirely unacceptable. However, try to resist the temptation to triumph over them by insulting their appearance or intelligence. Stooping to personal insults about the bigots themselves will only bring you down to their level. Eviscerate their prejudices at first, by seeming to agree. Nod your head until they trip themselves up or utter some gross stupidity... then pounce with your knife sharp reason and intelligence and annihilate their inanity.

A recurring pain which has plagued you on and off for years may flare up again around the 20th. Your usual means of dealing with this may not prove effective this time. Think outside the box. If the painkillers your doctor prescribed are not helping your aching back, perhaps you need to make your spine more limber. Try yoga. If possible, opt for private sessions with an instructor skilled in yoga therapy. She or he will know which stretches and yoga positions benefit which parts of your body. If you hate the idea of yoga, join a stretching class. Tigers are cats... remember?

## TIGER June 2014

Here comes another Mercury retrograde period. It will start on the 7th of June and end on July 1st. Exercise the usual precautions related to this period when the planet of communication and travel seemingly goes backwards in the sky. Do not permit your awareness of astrological influences to turn you into one of those people who fear Mercury retrograde times. These periods do offer some opportunities. These are opportunities for re-organization, revising and recycling. Do research during Mercury retrograde. Use this time to practice playing a musical instrument. Or learn how to play bridge or even poker! Distract yourself from decision-making and you may even enjoy Mercury's usually irritating backward journey.

You may be forced out of your home during the first week of June. Don't worry. It's not permanent. I don't foresee eviction or the bank re-possessing your house. The planetary alignment however may bring about a need for some kind of extensive work on your house or apartment which will necessitate your temporary re-lodging elsewhere.

Uninvited guests of the six-legged variety may have to be removed by fumigation. Or some kind of mishap like a tree branch crashing onto your roof may result in serious renovation work. Ask around to find out which of your friends or relatives can put you up while your home is in the hands of the exterminators or the repair and construction crew. The task of finding a temporary shelter may be trickier than you anticipate. Could be all your friends who have a decent guest room are already booked with out-of-town visitors. You may find the only viable option is to bunk in on the sofa of a generous friend with a studio apartment. Or you may be offered a musty basement room in the home of a relative whom you rarely see. If you can afford to, you might consider staying in a hotel. Cohabitation can be dicey. There's always a chance you and your host/ess may have vastly different living habits resulting in a bit of friction. You will be able to return home before the 13th of the month.

## TIGER July 2014

Your partner might have to make a trip to the emergency room around the 7th of June. It's something accidental. He or she suffers an injury from a fall while bringing boxes down from the attic or working on the roof. Or it could be severe abdominal pains from an intestinal complaint. . It's nothing so serious as a heart attack. The physicians at the hospital will bring things under control. You may, however, experience several hours of anxiety before that happens. Your love mate will need to take things easy for a while. Don't chide him or her for clumsiness or for bearing up so heroically when the pain was so bad. Just be happy they are on the road to recovery.

One of the fringe benefits which enhanced your existence may disappear this month. A change in somebody else's life means some kind of minor sacrifice in yours. Perhaps you were able to schedule annual vacations to your favorite world capital because a friend hosted you at his/her townhouse. Now your friend is divorcing and losing that home. Or maybe your sister worked at the most luxurious spa in town and got you discounts on luxury treatments. But she is switching jobs. Try not to feel disappointed about these alterations. With your charm and savvy, more price cuts and perks are already lining up in the wings, waiting to be chosen to enhance your lifestyle.

A creative project you put together yourself earns you some kind of acclaim toward the end of July. How this will manifest depends on where you have been focusing your energy. Your contribution to a local bake sale sells out ahead of everyone else's. Or a gallery showing of your artwork earns rave reviews in the local paper. Or else you participate in some kind of group performance and everyone claims that your solo performance was the highlight of the evening. You could even enter an essay competition and win first prize. In any case, something you do well will earn you applause by the end of July.

## TIGER August 2014

In the first week of August you may pull out your checkbook planning to make a generous contribution to a political cause that you strongly support. Uh Oh! You discover that your bank balance is much lower than you thought. Somehow your expenses have caught up with and threaten to overtake your income. Apply all your creativity to this problem. Attack it from both ends. Scour your brain for new possible streams of income. Also consider what expenditures you can reduce. I'd guess that haunting thrift shops is a better choice for now than ordering online from expensive retailers. Do not consider buying used clothing as coming down in the world. Instead, think of this type of shopping expedition as a sort of treasure hunt. It takes a bit of digging through racks of ordinary looking apparel before you come upon an amazing find - a designer shirt or a luscious cashmere sweater for a song. But the thrill of paying ten dollars for something worth a hundred pounds is well worth the time spent stalking your prey.

Flirtation is in the air around the 15th of August. An attractive person connected to one of your part-time jobs or creative projects has been paying you compliments. You often notice this person gazing at you with admiration. He or she seems to appreciate your wit and intelligence as well as your physical attributes. You do not intend for this to turn into an affair. But you feel invigorated by the positive attention you are receiving.

This attention is especially welcome as your sex life with your partner has grown dull to non-existent lately. Since that surprise trip to the hospital last month, he or he seems uninterested in romance. Although you are sympathetic to your significant other's health challenges, you also feel a bit forsaken. You think your honey could at least muster a spare compliment about your latest haircut or new thrift shop frock. If your lover hasn't regained any vigor for an energetic session of lovemaking, it is time now to discuss it openly and see what is really bothering them.

**TIGER September 2014**

One of your parents or perhaps another older relative has been mentally deteriorating for quite some time. Around the 6th, the matter may become urgent. This person, who has developed an advanced case of forgetfulness, may do something which endangers his or her life. Of course their spouse feels frightened and inadequate. No one person is up to the job of sole caregiver now. Something will have to be done. Perhaps the older people can move in with another family member. Or maybe the family can hire trained aides to come in and help out. You are likely to have to face facts and search for an assisted living facility. All the family members affected by this decision will have to hold a meeting to deliberate. There will be disagreements. People tend to be highly emotional about this kind of transition. Use your skills of diplomacy to try to bring everyone to a consensus. Careful research of the different options will be necessary. This is not a matter which can be decided overnight.

Your older relative's declining mental abilities might well remind you of the importance of exercising your own brain. Why not sign up for a membership on one of those websites offering brain-boosting games and exercises? This month is also an excellent time to resume some kind of study. Purchase a foreign language audio course and use it every day. Or look into extension classes at the local university. Have you always been interested in the natural sciences? Take a class in botany. Most people these days can only identify a handful of tree and plant species. Expand your knowledge base. Maybe you can buy a telescope and some books about astronomy. If you can't afford a course, at least take up crossword puzzles. Focus on enhancing your cognitive skills in some useful way.

If you plan it right, you might be able to slip away with your lover for a romantic weekend in September. You might still not share as much passion as you would like. But the time away from the chaos of your current home situation will give you both the space you need to talk things through. If you can't manage to get your spouse or partner to open up, you may have to insist on embarking on some couples therapy.

**TIGER October 2014**

From October 4th through the 25th, the planet Mercury will be retrograde again. Heed the same old rules: No signing of binding documents, no purchases of major appliances, hard or software. Expect delays and snafus at every juncture. Keep your head when obstacles loom. Spend tons of time plotting your next attempt at changing the world.

Bonding with an animal will soothe the tension you may experience the first week in October. If you have a dog, take them for a nice long walk to a large park where you can let them off the leash. When you get home, spend time petting your canine companion. If you're more of a cat person, buy some new toys for your feline friends. Afterward, hone your skills in scratching furry little heads until your kitties purr in ecstasy. No animals dwelling in your house? Head for the local shelter and sign up for an afternoon of volunteering. You may even decide to adopt a new roommate while you're there. Research studies have shown that living with a pet can lower blood pressure and stress levels.

An opportunity for travel comes up around the middle of the month. Someone else is picking up the tab. Perhaps your partner's boss treats a group of employees to a spa getaway. Or possibly your rich aunt has noticed how difficult things have been for you so she offers to underwrite a trip to Portugal or Belize. Maybe you cannily found a free publicity trip offered by the owners of a resort for travel writers and got the local paper to sponsor you. Whatever you do, you will certainly enjoy be enjoying yourself mid October.

I hope that most of your indiscretions are at least a few years in the past. That will minimize the embarrassment you feel when something secret becomes public toward the end of October. If you ever made a silly sex tape, it could end up on the internet. Or could be an old friend from your wilder days will post photos on her Facebook page of the two of you partaking of some illicit substance. So long as you're not planning on running for public office, this information probably can't harm you. Keep an insouciant smile on your face. This will let people know you're enjoying life too much to worry about tempests in every little teapot.

**TIGER November 2014**

Your love life suddenly waxes hot and steamy during the first two weeks of November. Your sheets will play host to some wild creatures emitting passionate roars and whoops of joy. It's not clear if your significant other emerged from her/his phase of disinterest; or you changed your mind about that flirtatious individual from last August. Maybe you will stumble on someone new. Are you rotating through a selection of lovers? Multiple lovers would certainly explain the degree of heat that will be generated in your bedroom. Something unexpected may emerge from all this sensual activity. It might well be a pregnancy (Take precautions if babies are not a desired result). Or, if you are juggling more than one lover, you may be discovered by the one who really matters. In any case, this two week *sexcapade* looks like it could be a game changer.

Take a look at your wardrobe this month. The holidays a nigh. You will no doubt be invited to a few parties, and you want to look your best. Money is still rather tight so it's time, once again, to hie yourself to those thrift shops and haunt bargain sales in department stores. You'll see. You will wow everyone with your $20.00 Harris Tweed sports jacket or a handsome glittery sweater you paid peanuts for at the Goodwill or charity store.

Later in the month, you befriend someone visiting your country from a foreign land. You will find this person most intriguing. He or she will become something of a teacher to you, revealing entire new continents of knowledge. You may feel inspired to draw on the information this new guru imparts in your own classes or creative projects. This bubbly, vivacious person may claim to own an ability to predict the future. He or she will foretell fabulous success for you. They could also come to your home and cook you a fabulous meal, recreating the cuisine from their homeland. You may invite this person to a party to meet your friends. At that event, this character could take a surprising step. He or she will ask one of your unattached friends to enter into a pretend marriage to enable them to remain in your country. This move on their part could cause you some embarrassment. Wait and see.

## TIGER December 2014

A good friend may be the victim of a violent crime during the latter half of this month. She/he may suffer both physical and emotional trauma from this incident. Naturally you will want to offer him or her all the help you can. They may feel unwilling to return home after this incident. Offer your guest bedroom. Be patient and sympathetic. Your pal will be very emotional over this disaster. Off your home and hospitality as a refuge where your friend can heal from this traumatic event. You may want to suggest that they see a counselor to learn how to deal with their frightening experience.

At holiday gatherings this month, cut way back on your alcohol intake. The roads will be packed with police stalking their prey in the wee hours after such festivities as you might attend. If you want to drink, do so at home or at a place you can saunter home from safely.

Your enjoyment of the holiday season could be diminished by a severe cold. You will be coughing too much to be the *beau* or *belle* of any balls this month. Rather than hack your way unhappily through too many parties, it may be better to stay home. Rent some favorite old movies and watch them curled up on the couch drinking gallons of juice. Only attend events where you absolutely must put in an appearance. If the cold lingers for more than a couple of weeks, see a doctor. A course of antibiotics may be indicated.

Jealousy rears its ugly head around this time. You will discover, via the grapevine, that one of your friends is dating a discarded ex of yours. Although you don't care for this former lover anymore, your pride is somewhat bruised. Don't lie to yourself or to others about these feelings. Nobody will be fooled, by your long, elaborate explanations as to why these two people are all wrong for each other. If you cannot admit the truth to yourself, at least stop gabbing to friends about what, to them, is obviously a visit from the green-eyed monster himself.

## TIGER January 2015

The approaching Year of the Goat (starts February 19) may require that you are ready to switch directions in a jiffy. Streamline your life in preparation for the beginning of a new Chinese year next month. Is your home littered with magazines you subscribe to and never read which have gathered dust ? Cancel those subscriptions immediately. Donate the un-read magazines to your local library. Also jettison any programs on your DVR that you recorded months ago and never got around to watching. If you have been wasting too much precious time on Facebook, limit yourself to five minutes a day to catch up with your friends. But lose the habit of spending hours there. Moreover, give yourself a strict time budget for any websites which have become time wasters.

Feng shui experts purport that getting rid of clutter makes room for new energies to enter your life. You are likely to find that after cleaning and organizing your home environment, you find new creative inspiration. You have a brilliant idea for re-painting a room in your house, possibly involving a mural. You start writing a children's book. You wake up in the middle of the night with a fabulous notion for a new painting that came to you in a dream. You start sketching this immediately. You pick up an instrument you used to play years ago and start composing a song.

The last two weeks of the Year of the Horse offer a marvelous opportunity for mending broken fences and building new bridges. If your relationship with any of your neighbors has fallen into disrepair, correct that now. Invite them for lunch or brunch. Be sure to inquire about their dietary restrictions. It won't do to serve ham to vegetarians or a pork chop to someone who keeps kosher. Make light, pleasant conversation. Steer clear of controversial topics. See how the atmosphere brightens on its own. Life has a way of giving back what we offer it. Your neighbor will suddenly soften and begin to co-operate with you about that garden project they so vehemently vetoed last year.

# CAT/RABBIT 2014
## OVERVIEW FOR THE WOOD HORSE YEAR

*Distinguished Cat/Rabbit,*

*Horse years are notorious for their thunderous rhythm and amazing speed. Some might term these years 'dynamic'. I tend to think of them as wild and wooly. There is a LOT going on and it's usually about work. Unlike the sedate, rather languorous Snake, the Horse is a large, nervous, muscular beast whose capacity for labor is legendary. Horses can raise their own food and build their own houses and bake their own bread and raise kids and pets – all the while juggling three plates on sticks in the air over their heads. They are stunningly talented and beaver-busy all the time.*

*This, of course, is quite the opposite of you Cat/Rabbit people who enjoy quietude and seek (as long as there is someone to do the gardening and muck out the stables) the tranquility of the countryside. So you will no doubt find the pace of the Horse year irksome. You may be surprised – even shocked and frightened – by the degree of headlong interference which occurs in your backyard during this Horse year. You might be reading a book under a tree in the park and suddenly be turned upside down by someone "working" there. Or you could be sunning on the beach and out of nowhere be instructed to "move along" by the life guard. Horse years are famous for invading peoples' peace and quiet. Don't be alarmed. Be careful. And if you don't want your life meddled with in some aggressive manner, don't make any waves. sw*

---

## THE CHINESE YEAR AHEAD
## CAT/RABBIT 2014

### CAT/RABBIT February 2014

Business affairs may assume prominence in your life early this month. You will have several decisions to make about property, bank accounts, investments or loans. This might be in relation to opening a new business of some sort. It could be that you have decided to augment your regular income by launching a small sideline. At any rate, financial matters will consume much of your time. You may have to organize this project on your own more than you anticipated. Someone who usually serves as your guide or mentor in these type of matters may be unavailable to come to your aid. Not to worry. You can do it by yourself. It will just take more time.

Read the fine print on any documents related to the above-mentioned business matters with excruciating precision. Delay signing anything of importance between the 6th and the 28th of this month when Mercury backpedals again. These retrograde periods of the planet ruling communication and travel are the worst possible times for making long term commitments. Use this time to concoct plans and do research about future projects.

You may quarrel with a friend around the 17th of February. Turns out you assumed that you and this pal were on the same page about something crucial. Your casual reference to this supposed shared opinion causes your friend to announce that she or he sees the matter very differently. Stop and consider your chum's viewpoint. They may simply be stating some boundaries they feel you should respect. No need to end the friendship over this. Don't withdraw into your safe Rabbit hole. Acknowledge the misunderstanding. Then change the subject.

Looks like you will have a wardrobe mishap on your way to a business meeting or social gathering toward the end of the month. A bird poops from overhead. An essential button might pop or your zipper could break, leaving you more exposed than is acceptable. High heels could snag and crack off in the crevice of a sidewalk. Your shoelace might break in two. Pack a quick change of clothes in your briefcase or pocketbook.

Nothing is more annoying to you than conflict. You seek the quietude of a peaceful environment at any cost. The end of February will not be your favorite period of 2014. There are signs of a hurly burly around money and relations of the family variety. Someone thinks they ought to have inherited something they did not. Another person, cousin or nephew, brings it up at a convivial meal - and the fight is on! You will want to retreat. But your job here is to be the diplomat and soothe the savage beasts.

## CAT/RABBIT March 2014

You have a secret admirer. This person finds you very attractive but hesitates to approach you. You do tend to appear a bit aloof. You may think of it as shyness. But it seems more like standoffishness. If you want something to happen between you and this newcomer, you will have to make the first move. You have noticed her/him before. You see this individual on a regular basis. He or she may be in your weekly spinning class. Or perhaps it's that attractive neighbor who takes the same bus as you. Go ahead and strike up a conversation. Make an observation about how late the bus runs or offer a compliment on this person's T-shirt, tie or watch. Your admirer will feel flattered that you broke the ice. Once the two of you start talking, you will discover you have much in common. There's a definite potential for romance here. But I suggest you take things slowly. Develop a strong friendship first. Let flirtation remain an undercurrent rather than the driving force of your relationship at first.

A friend you haven't seen in years may contact you around the 14th of March. He or she is considering a move to your neck of the woods. Maybe you can help with this move in some way. Use your contacts to help them find a job and/or a place to live. At the very least, you can be a tour guide, showing your old crony around town. There are no coincidences. People come in and out of our lives for a reason. Be generous. He or she will prove useful to you in many ways in the future.

I hope you do not have claustrophobia. There is a chance you will briefly be stuck in a small space during the last five days of March. To avoid this, you might want to take the stairs rather than the elevator. If you go to a small storage room or basement, make sure to leave the door ajar behind you. If you work in a restaurant, check that the walk-in cooler door doesn't shut behind you.

## CAT/RABBIT April 2014

During the first part of April, someone you feel ambivalent about will invite you to a cultural venue - art gallery, museum exhibit or a play. Because you consider the individual rather lackluster, you may be tempted to refuse. I'd urge you to re-consider. This invitation will yield unexpected benefits. Perhaps you will derive creative inspiration from what you see. Or you may meet someone very influential who can assist you in significant ways. Being in the company of this tedious individual for a small spell will be but a piddling price to pay. He or she may even assume a role in making this event beneficial to you. Perhaps they will introduce you to that VIP you needed to meet right now. Or an observation this person makes about the play or art exhibit will kickstart your imagination in some very fruitful way.

A precept or idea which has shaped much of your personal philosophy will be shaken by some unexpected events occurring on or about the 21st of this month. Try to look at this as an opportunity the universe is offering you for a mental spring cleaning. The way you were looking at an issue proves to have been narrow and old-fashioned. As science fiction writer Isaac Asimov once said, "Your assumptions are your windows on the world. Scrub them off every once in a awhile, or the light won't come in." Do away with prejudices. Welcome new ideas.

The health of a sibling or close friend may become a concern around the 29th. He or she will receive a wake-up call in regard to some bad health habits (smoking, drugs, burning the candle at both ends etc). Avoid any "I told you so" statements. Offer sympathy instead. Show compassion for the pain and difficulty your pal experiences. Be supportive of any healthy lifestyle changes she or he decides to make. But do steer clear of preaching or proselytizing. Use the carrot, not the stick to help your sibling or buddy chart a course toward general well being.

## CAT/RABBIT May 2014

You may have some kind of discomfiting dealings with an authority figure around the 8th of May. Perhaps you will receive a speeding ticket. Or else the tax authorities send you a stern letter. Could be something to do with your property as well. The representative of law and/or order that you encounter may exercise his/her power in ways unduly harsh ways. Exercise your native tact and prudence in this situation. Devious behavior, stuttered excuses or a high-handed response could cause you serious trouble later on. This matter has to be handled delicately and with aplomb - both of which you are generously endowed with from birth.

You could experience tension around the middle of the month. An offer to aid a friend in need will interfere with your personal space. Have you taken on more than you anticipated? Perhaps you invite your pal to live temporarily at your place after she/he is ejected from home by an angry spouse or lover. Then, of course, it takes your friend an eternity to find a suitable new abode. Plus you discover he or she is forgetful or disrespectful of your preferences. Maybe they leave dirty dishes in the sink overnight. Or your friend wakes up hours before your rising time, starting the day with a medley of enthusiastic toilet flushing, booming shower singing and clanging pots and pans. I know you dislike confrontation. But it may be necessary to have a tactful chat with your friend. Otherwise you could continue to feel distressed and out of sorts till the cows come home.

Around the 25th, you may be pondering how to re-invent your life in some way. Perhaps you'll fantasize quitting your job to return to school. Or you might decide you can live less expensively in another country. Do some research before giving your notice, accepting to go for that MBA or buying a plane ticket to Uruguay. You do have a knack for landing on your feet. Just make sure you know the possible consequences of the leap into the void before takeoff.

## CAT/RABBIT June 2014

Mercury goes into reverse from the 7th of June until the 1st of July. The usual retrograde warnings apply. Sign no documents. Make no life-changing promises. Expect travel snarls and electronic breakdowns.

You may find yourself spending time with an ex this month. Could be a person you see somewhat regularly. Perhaps you have children together, work together or have common financial interests. This month will put you in closer proximity with this former lover than you have been since you were a couple. Maybe both of you will attend your child's graduation. Or due to a shortage of rooms the two of you have to bunk together on a "family" holiday. You may both go to inspect a property you own jointly preliminary to selling it. I have a strong hunch that your ex will try to use this situation to re-kindle the romance. Giving in to her/his romantic overtures would definitely make your life more complicated. Resist those blandishments diplomatically but firmly. In other words, just say no... in the nicest way possible.

Planetary energies indicate you might be hit with a wave of sadness around the 26th of June. Something you see or hear will trigger memories of old pain. You may find yourself brooding about the times when life treated you unfairly. Allow yourself a day to indulge these feelings. Stay in bed and cry or go somewhere and brood. And why not write down what is making you so sad? Journaling can be a marvelous pick-me-up. Give yourself some time to move past this pain. If your despondency persists, make an appointment with a with a mental health professional. Depression should be treated, not ignored or repressed. By the time August rolls around, you should be feeling like your jolly old self again.

You no doubt observed that all of the above remarks revolve around the past re-entering your life. Forcing us to deal with our own history is one of the ways that Mercury retrograde may manifest. Not to worry. This Mercury retrograde only lasts 3 weeks. Use this time for negotiation and planning. Make no major decisions.

**CAT/RABBIT July 2014**

The situation between you and that secret admirer you befriended earlier this year may heat up in the beginning of this month. Your first evening of romance, however, may fall short of your romantic dream when you discover that the two of you are not sexually compatible. Perhaps one of you has a particular kink or fetish that the other doesn't share or sympathize with. Or your romantic pace is like classical music whilst she or he prefers a rock or hip-hop vibe. The two of you would have to do some fine-tuning and adjusting of your relationship before you could hope to become a couple. Compromise and accommodation are often necessary when we pave the road to romance. Could be you will both decide you are better suited to be sweet friends than mismatched lovers.

Your heart and your head could be in conflict around the middle of this month. You will have a decision of some import to make. Something about a relationship with a family member or an in-law. Your intellect will guide you in one direction. However your feelings may suggest a different course. To gain clarity on this issue, I advise you either to mediate long and hard before acting. Or better still, seek counsel from someone objective, older and more experienced in these dealings than you.

At a party around the 28th, someone you barely know will confide something very painful and personal to you. The moment will be awkward and uncomfortable. You feel torn. On the one hand, you feel empathy for this person's woes. On the other hand, part of you feels it's unfair for this person to dump these intimate revelations on you. You will be squeamish about some of the details he or she shares with you. This individual probably needs your kindness and a listening ear. He or she probably chose to confide in you because of your calm, sensitive demeanor. Lend an ear, nodding your head when necessary or offering brief expressions of sympathy. If they hang around and start repeating their tale of woe, make sure you have a ready, credible excuse to escape.

**CAT/RABBIT August 2014**

Your powers of concentration will likely reach their zenith around August 7th. Utilize this period to take care of any tedious chores you usually postpone. Read a book you put aside before because it seemed too difficult. Put that foreign language disc in your computer and memorize a few new verbs. Your attention span is at its best. This makes it an excellent time for negotiating with any slippery individuals too. You can zero right in. No one can get the better of you in a transaction now. Do not waste the gift of this extra mental energy on games. Your brain is hungry for challenges. At this time you are capable of handling matters which might normally discourage you.

You may feel hungry for more beauty in your home around the 19th. All the carefully chosen objects you placed around your house bore you now. You feel the need for the new. Visit a local art gallery. If you cannot afford a painting, look for a reasonably priced photograph or small art print. Or haunt the charity shops in your neighborhood, keeping your eye peeled for something lovely. The trick to great finds in thrift and resale stores is to be open to what presents itself. You may start shopping for old photographs, but stumble across a striking pair of carved candle holders. Learn how to creatively recycle objects for new uses. Perhaps a colorful children's board game with great vintage graphics can be framed and hung on a wall. Spark up your environment. It's good for the soul.

You may feel concerned about your health toward the end of the month. You could experience some diverse and unusual symptoms. Do try to avoid looking up your symptoms online. Many medical websites have a scare-mongering attitude toward health. They mention so many dire side effects that they can make you believe you are going deaf and blind and have only two months left to live. Make an appointment with a reliable physician. Ideally, try to choose a doctor who incorporates holistic health methods as well as allopathic healing. This kind of MD is less likely to treat every ache or pain with a prescription or surgery. He or she can try to find the source of your ills and will help you focus on overall wellness and prevention.

## CAT/RABBIT September 2014

You find yourself developing a fascination with a new field of interest as September begins. This topic never previously intrigued you, but now you are moved to learn all you can about it. Perhaps you devour books on architecture. Or you purchase an app to help you identify different species of butterflies. You attend lectures or field trips in your area to learn more about this riveting new subject. You may even begin planning a trip for next year to further your knowledge of this area. Perhaps you're researching butterfly sanctuaries in Costa Rica. Maybe you'll look for tours of the most innovative buildings in Asia. Enjoy your new interest. Even if it's cooking or needlepoint or fly fishing, it will lead you in surprising directions and make you some dazzling new friends.

A close acquaintance may try your patience around the 14th. You notice that this person only calls you when he/she needs help or wants to complain about their circumstances. Do not let this person take advantage of your good nature. Unfortunately, divulging your true feelings may not be the best idea. She or he may wax angry and defensive. If you'd rather not listen to another whine-fest, it may be better to make yourself scarce now. Wait a couple of weeks. Then call and make plans to meet for coffee. Plan ahead so the conversation remains geared to happy subjects. Compliment the person. Praise them for the progress of their favorite hobby or the accomplishments of their child. When your pal is beaming and talking animatedly, mention casually how glad it makes you to see him/her in good spirits. Continue to emphasize positive topics in all your conversations with them. If the tone turns to whimpering, pay the bill and hurry away to that important meeting you just invented. Your rapid departure should make them understand that you will not tolerate their victim speeches - ever!

Toward the end of this month you may misplace some small important item. It may be your cell phone or the case for your car keys or a computer memory stick containing important documents. You will have a brief period of panic about this loss. Do not worry. Whatever it is will turn up in less than 48 hours.

## CAT/RABBIT October 2014

Keep your eyes open wider than usual on any visits to yard sales or thrift shops around the 4th. You are liable to stumble upon a fabulous bargain. It may be an item which normally wouldn't particularly interest you. But you are canny about antiques and valuables and recognize this as a worthwhile purchase and a departure from the usual junk you find there. Go ahead and snap up this find. Think of it as an investment. You can gain a profit by re-selling it. Perhaps not right away. But with time, it will increase in value.

You may see or hear about a former co-worker or neighbor under sad and surprising circumstances around October 16th. This won't be someone you knew well. Perhaps you even found this individual slightly irritating. But now you cannot help but feel compassion. You may see this person at a subway stop panhandling for change. Or you may discover while reading the news that this person was the victim of a violent crime. Better not to get involved. There are more reasons than you know which have led this person to their current circumstances.

One of your bosses or teachers notices your excellent work. This character may take you under his/her wing in some way. You have often felt that the prizes go to those flashier than you. This new mentor's attention to your progress will help assure that you receive your due.

How long has it been since you played host/ess? You excel at creating ideal settings for entertaining. The planets are lined up to shower blessings on any gathering you host toward the end of this month. Maybe you can make it a Halloween party, complete with costumes and playfully *macabre* decorations. Invite one or two of your best friends to help you plan the affair. You and your chums will have great fun preparing the party food and décor. This shindig is bound to be a huge success. There's also a strong possibility that one of your friends brings along someone new. This new person will find you amazing and want to get closer to you. They don't look like an interloper. More like a keeper.

## CAT/RABBIT November 2014

Yet another of those annoying Mercury retrograde periods occurs starting on the 4th and lasting until the 25th of October. By now, most of you probably know the drill about what to avoid as well as how to reap the possible benefits of these periods. Mainly, don't sign any life-changing documents or make major purchases until Mercury goes direct on the 25th.

Someone whom you consider a friend may snub you around the 2nd of November. This may be a Rat or Tiger buddy of yours. Perhaps you see this person at a restaurant. He or she is dining with some local bigwigs. You stop to say hello. Your friend responds curtly and does not offer to introduce you to the VIPs. I'd let this go if I were you. You know that friend is a bit of a social climber. Also, he or she tends to compartmentalize his/her life. If you say you felt slighted, you know you won't get any sympathy or understanding. Your erstwhile friend will only accuse you of being thin-skinned. For your own good, see less and less of them. When they ring up, be busy or otherwise engaged.

Around the 25th, you may accidentally learn something about a relative that shocks you. Perhaps while you are visiting your aunt, she asks you to fetch her sweater. You can't find it in the living room but think she may have left it in her bedroom. When you open the door, you cannot help but notice a sex toy sitting on the bedside table. Perhaps you catch a glimpse of a dildo or a pair of handcuffs. Maybe while looking for television remote at your parents' home, you find a bong. Or it's possible you'll overhear a conversation at the grocery store which reveals that your grandparents have a polyamorous relationship. Try to take this information in stride. Say nothing. After all, it is none of your business.

A power outage in your home or a blackout in your area may leave you temporarily without electricity the last week of this month. Make sure you have sufficient candles and matches or lighters in your home. Put them somewhere accessible - not on a top shelf where you might fall trying to retrieve them in the dark. You might also want to invest in a mobile phone charger that runs off your car battery.

## CAT/RABBIT December 2014

Usually your diplomatic skills go unheralded. You quietly make suggestions which help balance the conflicting desires of those signs more prone to swollen egos. Around the 14th of this month however, your cleverness and tact earn you some kind of recognition. Someone perceives your talent in making sure that Tigers, Dragons and Roosters don't come to blows in their battles for power. This appreciative person will at the very least give you some perceptive compliments. It's even possible he or she might see to it that you receive some kind of reward for your efforts - a gift or a trip to somewhere you have longed to visit.

You and that admirer from your October party have been spending time together. Around the 18th, the relationship may blossom into romance. This individual may be another Cat or possibly a Goat. You feel safe and comfortable when you are with this individual. The two of you may prove to be compatible on many levels, physically, mentally and even spiritually. You enjoy the sex. But equally enthralling to you are the long conversations in bed about everything from how to cook the perfect omelet to the meaning of life. Unfortunately, when your new sweetie introduces you to her/his family, you do not experience that same sense of harmony. These relatives of your lover offend your cat-like sense of decorum. They may be loud and boastful. So long as your new honey does not morph into his family when in their company, don't worry. People cannot choose their relatives.

You are likely to have at least one or two big parties to attend as 2014 draws to a close. This is a great time to impress everyone with your sense of style. Put together an elegant outfit by combining some of your charity shop finds. Banish any signs of the stress you have experienced by getting a massage and a facial. Get a fabulous new hair style. Perhaps it's also time for a new hair color. Push the boat out and splurge. There is no better morale booster than knowing you look your best.

## CAT/RABBIT January 2015

You are likely to feel fatigued in the week following the western New Year. Your indulgences over the holidays, even if they were minor, could have thrown your system out of whack. Try doing a brief juice fast, just over a weekend, to cleanse your body. All you need is a juicer and some fresh, organic fruits and vegetables. Do this over a weekend where you don't have any other plans. You may feel even wearier at first. But after a couple of days, you will find that you have regained vitality. When the juice fast is through and you start a new week with renewed vigor, you will find you are more productive as well.

Back in 2013 or 2012, you completed some kind of creative project. You released it into the world, only to be disappointed in how it was received. Now suddenly that project gains positive attention. You will naturally feel pleased that this child of your imagination receives its moment in the sun. This turn of events may also result in another stream of income for you. Buy yourself some kind of gift to celebrate. If you have enough funds, perhaps you can plan a trip to an exotic venue. Why not take your new sweetheart along? Nothing like a steamy foreign place to raise the level of passion between two lovers.

You may receive an intriguing proposal around the 16th of this month. A close family member, perhaps one of your grown children or a sibling, may suggest that the two of you start some kind of project together. It may be a creative endeavor, perhaps one of you taking photographs or doing the illustrations for a book and the other supplying the words. Or it might be a small business of some sort. Do not make your decision based solely on your affection for this relative. Think carefully about whether the two of you balance each other in terms of practical abilities.

The Goat year starts on February 19th. Get ready to indulge your creativity and grow your personal fortune through artistic endeavors.

# DRAGON 2014
## OVERVIEW FOR THE WOOD HORSE YEAR

*Dauntless Dragon,*

*You Dragons often find yourselves flummoxed by Horse years. First of all, these years are notoriously fraught with tension. The Horse is a strong, yet troubled soul whose sense of self can be easily disrupted by the slightest setback. You, Dragon, might just be part of one of those setbacks as you are not daunted by the prospect of conflict with anyone – least of all a Horse. You sense the Horse's force. But sometimes you don't intuit the Horse's skittish fragility. Horses are powerhouses of talent. But they don't always seek to shine. They are not so interested in hogging the stage as you are. But they do want and need and actively seek recognition for the deeds.*

*This year I suggest you chill. Hang back a bit. Look around in your own life and wonder to yourself just how much progress you have been making over the past couple of years. Then, on tiptoe, return to the fray without making waves or awakening the Horse's aggression. You will be able to make enormous progress in Horse years and enjoy gobs more time with your family . . . if only you can keep the lid on that your flamboyance. Horses need understanding. Sentimental people like you are capable of largesse and compassion. Use those talents this year and you will float right through unbridled. sw*

―――――― ℯ ⸲℮⸲℮ ――――――

## THE CHINESE YEAR AHEAD
## DRAGON 2014

**DRAGON February 2014**

As Mercury transitions into reverse gear this month, we all must prepare to lose a trickle or two of time going over old ground. These retrograde periods of the smallest and fastest moving planet of our solar system can tie communication and travel matters in knots. This particular retrograde period commences on the 6th of this month and lasts until the 28th. Don't sign or promise anything you can't get out of.

Around the first week of this month, an acquaintance whom you had been considering as a potential friend may fail to qualify as a member of your inner circle. He or she will boldly disrespect your boundaries. Continual prying questions from this individual will test your patience. They are far too curious about your private life. Being a Dragon, it might be difficult to rein in your temper. Respond to these inappropriate queries with obfuscation and misdirection. Afterwards, you can go home and un-friend this person on Facebook, or delete his/her number from your phone directory. Reply politely but a bit distantly if she or he tries to contact you again. They will (eventually) get the hint.

Around the 12th, family matters will demand your attention. There may be a problem related to the health or living conditions of one of your close relatives. You may be called upon to offer your input in some concrete way. Providing assistance with medical or household bills or taking the patient into your home for an extended convalescence are noble acts. But be careful not to let your sentimentality get in the way of your best interests. You might make sure your relative's household expenses don't pile up while she/he is unable to work. You may even roll up your sleeves and pitch in, taking care of a few chores to help the children and spouse of the sick person. But be careful not to promise more than you can reasonably deliver without totally disrupting your own life.

Your partner's eyes may gleam with green-eyed jealousy around the 26th. I don't know whether or not you've done anything to excite his/her suspicions. But I strongly advise you, if you want to maintain this relationship, to soothe your sweetie with gestures of pure, syrupy, cloying hearts and flowers romance. Take some time away from your projects. Woo your honey anew. Plan a candlelit dinner. Take him/her dancing or to a concert (choose your partner's favorite music, not yours) or a play. Listen attentively to your lover as if every word emerging from his/her mouth were diamonds and rubies. Give gifts that you know will delight your partner. Send sweetly loving messages via text throughout the day to reassure your honey of his/her paramount place in your thoughts even when the two of you are apart.

**DRAGON March 2014**

Your boss or one of your clients may reward your stellar work efforts with some kind of bonus. It could just be money. Or it could be an offer of a pair of tickets to some highly sought after event. It might also be a plane ticket to Paris or London. Whatever blessing befalls you from this circumstance, share it generously with your partner. Your magnanimous gesture will melt the very fiber of the green-eyed monster.

You may decide around the middle of the month that at least a portion of your Dragon cave needs sprucing up. Nothing ordinary or boring will do. Perhaps you decide to re-do the bedroom in vivid violet. Or maybe you will determine that you need to add an infinity pool to your yard. Sketch some plans which convey the drama of the effect you want to create. Then seek out a reliable contractor to handle the nuts and bolts of making your redecorating or renovating vision a reality.

An eccentric colleague or co-worker may clue you in to an investment opportunity around the 20th. Don't ignore this chance simply because this person is a bit of an oddball. He or she is likely to be offering you an excellent chance. Naturally you will want to do your research first. But this quirky new placement of your money promises to be an excellent way to earn a great return on your money.

An awkward situation may arise at a gathering of your partner's family around the 29th. One of your significant other's relations may flirt with you or even make a pass. This individual may be a different generation from yours. Perhaps a niece or nephew, aunt or uncle. Extricate yourself gracefully. You would be a fool to involve yourself in the complications of this type of affair. The big question remains whether or not to divulge the situation to your partner. If the overtures directed at you stopped with subtle flirtation, I'd suggest silence. However, if this person became aggressive, it is important that your spouse know what happens. For example, if she or he hears about the incident from someone else, it could imply that it was you looking for trouble with the Aunt Martha or Cousin Jake - not the other way around.

**DRAGON April 2014**

Your partner may come to you wanting to discuss their desire to help a friend who is struggling through hard times. Perhaps the poor soul has become homeless and needs a place to stay. Or she or he is broke following a bitter breakup and needs to borrow a significant sum. Offer your blessing for this charitable endeavor. But put a cap on both time and money allotted to get this unfortunate person over their hurdle.

If you are a parent, be particularly attentive to your offspring's emotional needs around the 14th of this month. Don't assume that a sad face or a cranky tone of voice are signs of immaturity or moodiness. Your teenager or young child may be experiencing a difficult emotional trial involving kids at school. Be available to listen. If she or he does not open up about these problems, then work on strengthening your child's self-esteem. Many times parents will offer criticism but don't compliment their children unless they achieve something stellar. Parental love and unequivocal approval provide fuel for children to overcome difficulties. Remember, not everyone is born with your redoubtable Dragon confidence.

Be cautious in high places toward the end of the month. There is an increased chance of injury from a fall of some sort right now. Such a fall could mean anything from a twisted ankle to a broken rib or a punctured lung. Take the stairs at a reasonable pace rather than careening downward two or three steps at a time. Also be very attentive if you have to use a ladder for any reason. Hire someone else to do that roof work for you or at least postpone it until next month. Decline any invitations to go hiking along steep paths. Not the optimum time to go rock or mountain climbing.

Putting off going to the dentist about an on and off painful tooth or gum problem is not going to make the problem disappear. Taking care of dental matters and curing mouth irritations is crucial to your well being. If you have an infection in your mouth, it can spread to your whole body. Get thee to a dentist.

**DRAGON May 2014**

You may put your thorny green Dragon foot in your mouth early this month. You will be in a jovial mood. So you go ahead and make what you think is a jovial comment. "Isn't that a ridiculous T-shirt you're wearing?" or "My mother died just after she wore a dress (shirt) the color of yours." Your interlocutor will recoil in horror and let you know in no uncertain terms how they receive the remark. Stop and think, Dragon. That other person is not too thin-skinned and overly sensitive. You occasionally open your maw a bit too wide. Mull over your words. How would you react if someone blurted the same comment to you? Remember. Apologizing can actually be an act of bravery. It takes courage to admit you were clumsy and gauche. Humility is not your strongest suit. Confess anyway. It's good for the soul.

If you find yourself feeling grumpy around the third week of the month, the fault may not lie with the people around you or their actions. Instead of breathing fire at everybody, why not get out and exercise? Find a track you can use at a gym or local high school and try jogging. Or if you're more of a Water Dragon, locate a pool you can use and swim for at least a kilometer. Or call a friend and schedule a game of tennis or handball. At the very least, put on some energetic music and dance up a storm in your living room. You need to move, to get that upbeat mood of yours firing on all cylinders again.

An alluring new person may appear on the scene at your job. This individual displays his/her keen appreciation for both your myriad talents and your considerable physical charms. She or he also knows how to stand up to your haughtiness without inciting your anger. You may find yourself seduced by the possibility of an affair. If you do fall in love with this irresistible creature, do so discreetly. The entire work staff is watching. You can create jealousies among people you never even dreamed envied you. Some will always seek revenge.

## DRAGON June 2014

Retrograding Mercury brings its usual bag of hassles this month starting on the 7th. Avoid committing to lifelong entanglements. Sign no documents. Take no prisoners. Try to postpone major purchases as well as elective surgery until after this bumpy period ends on July 1st.

You may be disenchanted with your job around the first week of June. Activities which you formerly found intriguing and challenging now seem boring. Office politics may have something to do with this. Someone has been casting aspersions. Someone quite a bit weaker than you. You know you could easily defeat this character. But you aren't sure it is worth the effort. You may begin to look around for a job change of some sort. Maybe even in the same company - away from the aspersion caster.

Plan a getaway around the 17th of this month. Even if it's just a short break, take a real vacation. Leave all electronic devices at home. You need to restore your spirit and be free of the distractions of constant messages, emails and calls. Find inexpensive airfares online. Take your partner with you or go solo. Don't ask that flirtatious colleague to accompany you. You want to be entirely free to vacate. Your new sweetheart might be tempted to talk to you about work.

Around the 22nd, your partner may quarrel with that friend he or she has been helping out. You had a hunch. And you were right. Their patience for that person's problems grew thin. You may have to step in and play peacemaker. Or, better still, sit them down for a three-way meeting wherein you get to express an opinion or two. You might actually be able to talk the sad sack guest into leaving for Peoria or doing some couch-surfing for a few months whilst you gain back some privacy.

The last few days of June may find you venturing into unknown territory in some way. An odd turn of events will find you in a place you never anticipated. If you are a sleek, sophisticated city Dragon, you may find yourself attending a rodeo or a mud wrestling show. Or, if you're more of a rustic Dragon, circumstances may somehow propel you to an opera or theatre performance in Manhattan, Paris or some other cosmopolitan city. Perhaps you're an atheist Dragon who somehow finds him or herself manning the barbecue at a fundamentalist church picnic. Whatever befalls you, it will make you feel like a fish out of water. If, however, you relax and let go of some of your preconceptions about the folks you are cavorting with, you may actually have a good time.

## DRAGON July 2014

During the first ten days of July, you may hear of the passing of a social or work acquaintance. Although you were not particularly close to this person, this death will have an effect on you. It may be that someone very close to you had a strong attachment to the deceased person. Your friend will go through a deep personal transformation of some sort as a result of this loss. This in turn will affect your relationship with them. Try to be sensitive to your friend's feelings. Offer sympathy and support. If your pal needs to talk about his/her deceased friend, lend a willing ear. It is, after all, quite normal to wax emotional over such a stunning loss.

Another friend may experience a much happier sort of change toward mid-July. He or she will announce plans to get engaged or married soon. You will likely be invited to be one of the wedding party, perhaps serving as best man or bridesmaid. If you sing, you may be asked to contribute a song to the ceremony. Be sure to let your crony know that you are touched and honored to be included in this happy event.

In the middle of July you will receive a surprise visit or call or email from an old acquaintance you had plumb forgotten about. You two shared part of your respective childhoods in the same school or neighborhood. Perhaps you were in a scout troop or a equestrian club at the same time. You will spend some delightful days in the company of this enchanting character. He or she is probably a Snake or a Pig. In any case, they are someone you will never again forget.

There's a strong possibility you'll be involved in a minor fender-bender in the latter half of the month. No one will be seriously injured. However, it may turn out that either the other driver or one of the passengers in the other car turns out to be someone well-known. It could be a mega-famous person or a long-lost celebrity who turns up on those "whatever happened to" websites. Could be one of the local talking heads. This person's involvement will lend an additional note of interest when you recount the accident to your friends and family.

## DRAGON August 2014

A professional rival of yours may surprise you by asking you out to dinner early this month. If you spend too much mental energy racking your brain to figure out the person's angle, you'll miss some very obvious signals. She or he doesn't want to poach your clients or steal your job. This supposed enemy is actually trying to get you into bed. Relax and enjoy the meal while you decide how to respond to this surprising overture. You may feel intrigued—and even aroused— by the element of risk involved in a dalliance with this person. Consider the fallout before entering into a liaison with this critter.

You may enjoy a brief interlude of minor fame around the 13th of this month. Maybe your auto accident with that celebrity last month garners some delayed media attention. Or you may be interviewed for one of those "person in the street" reactions to some newsworthy event. It's also possible the fame will relate to you in a more direct way. Could be your business receives a favorable write-up in some popular publication or website. Spiff up your wardrobe before you make any TV appearances.

It may be your turn to experience avid jealousy around the 18th. You catch a glimpse of your partner laughing and joking with an attractive person. You know this individual is notorious for his/her sexual exploits. Your significant other seems to be under the influence of this character's inimitable charm. It riles you no end. But your pride stands in the way of an instant reaction. Watch for signs of betrayal. But don't go all paranoid. Your lover may just be networking for professional reasons.

Some member of your family may have a mishap involving water around the 27th of June. If you have very small children, do not turn your back even for a second while they are in the bath. If you own a swimming pool, make sure that people do not run or otherwise behave carelessly there. Remind any of your relatives who enjoy boats and water-sports to wear a lifejacket.

## DRAGON September 2014

A ratty-looking stray dog or cat may turn up on your doorstep around the 2nd of September. Do what you can to comfort this bedraggled creature. Give it food and water. Provide it with some kind of shelter. If you cannot take it into your home, at least fashion a crate bed and add an old blanket of some kind to shelter it from the elements. Take it to a vet's office or shelter to have it scanned for a microchip which might lead to an owner. If the animal does not have a microchip, try to find it a home. Have the vet take care of any ailments the animal has developed while living outdoors. Take it to a groomer so it appears more attractive, and then take its photo. Post the animal's photo on a website like Petfinder or even on your own Facebook page. Social media increases the opportunities to rescue abandoned animals.

You may argue with your partner around the 15$^{th}$ of this month. I fear jealousy may be the root cause of your disagreement although one or both of you may invent some decoy reasons. She or he is having none of your high-handedness. Your significant other demands that you treat her or him with more respect. There may be other demands involved as well, perhaps even couched as ultimatums. You will feel your independence is at stake and may even be ready to walk out. I suggest you avoid making things final right now. Take some time so that both parties can cool off. Reconsider. Try imagining things from your partner's point of view.

You may find yourself beset with requests for financial assistance around the 21$^{st}$. A grown child or a sibling who has been unemployed for some time may need your help to avoid eviction or foreclosure. A close friend's business fails, leaving her or him unable to the bills for a spouse's mounting health expenses. If you cannot afford to assist everyone with money, see if you can offer some other kind of help. Perhaps you can use your contacts to help one of them find a job.

**DRAGON October 2014**

Remember, Mercury is retrograde right now. This is the worst possible time to purchase anything of major significance. Although the Mercury retrograde period lasts only from the 4$^{th}$ to the 25$^{th}$ of this month, I always advise my clients to wait an interval after the end of a retro phase before proceeding full steam ahead.

There may be concerns related to a child you know early this month. This could be one of your own offspring, a niece or nephew or maybe the son or daughter of a close friend. You will hear complaints from teachers about the schoolwork and behavior of this child. He or she is not a bad kid nor lazy or unintelligent as some of those involved might try to claim. This child may actually have a learning disability which has not yet been diagnosed. If this relates to one of your own children, do not discipline the child for poor grades or unusual interactions with schoolmates. Instead, seek an expert to evaluate possible learning disabilities. If the child in question belongs to a relative or friend, gently suggest this tactic. The youngster will do much better once she or he receives assistance tailored to his or her needs.

Both your libido and your sexual charisma will likely rise off the charts around the 18$^{th}$ of October. Erotic thoughts take over even when you are at work or sitting in a traffic jam. Other people respond to you as if you were the last popsicle left in a heat wave. You may find yourself postponing meeting and/or social engagements in order to romp with someone in a secret murky venue. The planetary portents do not reveal whether that someone is your partner or another individual. You might even entertain the idea of multiple partners, either separately or in bed with you at the same time. If you really want to engage in kinky sex, do so with extreme precaution. No amount of memorable sex play is worth contracting a serious illness over.

Your judgment center is likely to be compromised at the end of the month. If your car breaks down, think about whether to pay for extensive repairs or wait till the climate improves and get a new one. Meanwhile, take public transportation or cabs. Or why not just walk more often? Forego springing for any fancy restaurant tabs or giving in to real estate temptations. Postpone any major spending until at least the second week of November.

## DRAGON November 2014

You may be involved in a hiring project around the 10th of this month. You will spend time looking at resumes and either making, or at least contributing to, a decision about a new employee. Make sure you make your choice based purely on professional qualifications. If you pass over the best candidate because of race, gender, age, sexual orientation, religious affiliation or even weight/appearance, there could be negative consequences down the line. You or your firm could face a lawsuit or negative publicity regarding discrimination if your decision is made without absolute integrity.

The general tone for Dragons this month is quite uneven. Either due to your quick temper or your fixed opinions, a casual discussion about something relatively lightweight and inconsequential - a cartoon or TV show - could turn into a heated political disagreement around the 22nd. This conversation may be with your family or among your in-laws. Try to see at least three steps ahead in every dialogue at this time. Be prepared to head off arguments at the pass. Even your lighthearted banter about a frivolous subject can rapidly devolve into a debate about something highly controversial. One party may end up stomping out of the room and refusing to talk to the others for months. Watch for prickly subjects. And keep an eye out for folks who try to get your goat with snarky remarks and/or cutting comments about your appearance.

You are not a religious nut. And you are normally quite accepting of people having unusual beliefs. However at a gathering around the 28th, you may find yourself in a debate with someone who strains the limits of your "live and let live" attitude. This person will tell you something which mingles base, selfish personal motives with both traditional religion and woo-woo. She or he may confide that the Virgin Mary revealed in a dream how to cheat the tax authorities without getting caught. Or this character might announce that she/he learned the password to access an ex's voice mail by communicating through a Ouija board with a revered teacher from the Zoroastrian tradition. This person may indeed have severe mental or emotional problems. Terminate the dialogue as quickly as you diplomatically can to avoid becoming yet another character in his or her fantasy world.

## DRAGON December 2014

In a post-coital conversation with one of your lovers the first week of this month, you may learn about an unusual "six degrees of separation" sexual situation. Perhaps the ex-spouse of your bed partner was once the secret lover of a famous politician or athlete. Or maybe in college your lover dated someone who had a high school romance with a person who later married a famous rock star. For Dragons whose western sign is in water, there may be a slightly gruesome angle to this connection. For example, your lover may once have had a fling with a person who later died in some infamous violent incident. Or the ex-spouse of your sexual conquest might have mysteriously disappeared over a cliff one dark and stormy night. Choose your flings with good taste and discernment this month.

For a long time, you thought someone you work should have his or her name next to the dictionary definition of part of the human excretory system. Around the 15th of the month, you may accidentally learn something which inspires a lot of sympathy for this person. You may discover that the boss who screams at employees suffered years of sexual abuse as a child. Or you may learn that the co-worker you suspect of pilfering goodies from the office fridge is dying of a particularly painful form of cancer. In any case, the jackass in question might have some valid reasons for their misbehavior. There is not much you can do about their deportment. But knowing they come by it honestly, can serve to reduce your irritation.

Some extra money, perhaps a dividend from one of your investments or a year-end bonus at work, will brighten your financial picture toward the end of this month. Given the planetary portents for you for 2015, I advise saving or re-investing most of this money. Use just a little to buy some treats for yourself and those you love. But keep mum about the exact amount you garnered. Otherwise you might be besieged with people wanting financial aid. These funds should be used wisely and responsibly to secure your future and that of your family.

## DRAGON January 2015

The commencement of a New Year on the western calendar may inspire you to perform a blizzard of cleaning. You might tackle some area of your home or work life which has become a bit disorganized. Maybe you finally realized you will never again fit into those clothes from high school which have occupied the bulging closet in your spare room for more than a decade. No use punishing yourself for not being the same size as you were at 18. Give those clothes either to a charity shop or to a young friend or relative who may actually see them as vintage gear. In the same cleansing mode, you may finally decide to go through those files which have been collecting dust in the attic. Best to decide to throw out old paperwork. Organize those piles of photos which are all sticking together in those old cartons. And finally, make sure to protect yourself from possible identity theft by either burning or shredding any documents which detail your private information.

Around the 12th of this month, you may be hit with an unsettling realization. Some mental block shifts slightly. You now perceive that a long-standing grudge you have nursed stems not from the other person behaving badly but from your own stubbornness. You could not see that you were the offender - not the offendee. Several years may have passed since you were in touch with this individual. But it's never too late to make amends. Look them up online. Send a brief message of reconciliation. Acknowledge your mistake simply and humbly, without excuses or accusations. Even if she or he does not reply, you will feel better for having proffered the olive branch.

Unless your checking account is looking particularly plump these days, you may want to hide your credit cards toward the end of the Year of the Horse. Freeze them on the bottom of the remotest ice cube tray in the back of your freezer. If not, you could make some very dumb impulsive purchases of items you do not really need. Anything you buy at this time could seem quite silly to you within just a few weeks. Steer clear of any stores or websites which tend to be temptation zones for you. By all means, avoid breaking into your savings or investment accounts to satisfy your bizarre January spending urges.

# SNAKE 2014

## OVERVIEW FOR THE WOOD HORSE YEAR

*Sentient Snake,*

*Many people assume that Horses and Snakes don't harmonize. Many people are right. This year will be choppy at best for Snakes as the Horse is not even-tempered and doesn't much care one way or the other about his subjects' well-being. Horses are rankly pragmatic. They just want to DO things their way. They are talented and savvy. And they are artistic. But not necessarily altruistic. You Snakes are motivated by compassion and philanthropy. You sincerely believe in your ability to contribute to the betterment of mankind. So Snake dissatisfaction is common in the ego-centered Horse year environment. You will feel as though you just can't get going on any project and keep at it without obstacle after obstacle being thrown up and roadblocks appearing at every turn.*

*You might moreover be entangled in a legal battle over a contract or real property. As the climate in Horse years is unfavorable to positive outcome for Snakes, you will not stand much of a chance of winning. Better try some tricky tactic to get the lawsuit delayed until next year when the gentle Goat will rule – a more clement climate for Snakes involved in legal tussles. Obviously, this year will not be your favorite. Take your frustration on a long holiday somewhere warm and tropical with your main squeeze in tow. Should your significant other be (for some weird reason) a Horse, I advise that you leave him or her at home. Maybe you should think about seducing someone more philosophically inclined. sw*

───────── ❧❧❧ ─────────

## THE CHINESE YEAR AHEAD

### SNAKE 2014

**SNAKE February 2014**

Mercury goes retrograde on the 6th of this month. You, wise Snake, are usually calm and centered enough not to become agitated by change, including the apparent backward movements of the planets. But this time around, the shift of the planet of communications may have an effect that only Luddites can escape. Mercury's reverse motion will take place mostly in Aquarius, the zodiac sign most strongly related to technology. Do what you can to minimize the impact on you. Back up your computer documents daily. Don't neglect to re-charge your phone. Mercury goes direct on the final day of this month. However, sometimes the tail end of the retrograde period can have a sort of whiplash effect, like a car braking and then changing direction. Maintain precautions until at least a few days after the retrograde ends.

Too many people have begun to copy your look. Those style choices which seemed so *avant garde* last year have started to appear a bit banal. You are not the type who enjoys seeing yourself cloned. For you, imitation is not so much the sincerest form of flattery as an encroachment on your turf. So around the 12th of February, you are likely to begin to make changes. Perhaps a completely new *coiffure* along with a subtle change in hair color? Or invest in a few new wardrobe essentials to give you a truly chic look that no one else has. Hone your trademark look until it is so inimitably you that no one can even try to steal it.

Your partner may seem a bit sulky and distant toward the end of the month. They could be feeling neglected. Have you been taking your significant other for granted? Perhaps your enthusiasm for your work and creative projects has made you forget to attend to your lover's needs. Arrange some kind of special romantic treat - a weekend getaway for just the two of you. A road trip to a place which holds fond memories for both of you. Make arrangements to leave the kids at home. Turn off your phones. Give yourselves time to remember what you found so fascinating in each other.

**SNAKE March 2014**

The first week of this month is a sublime time for you to become involved in volunteer projects. Look around and see if there is an organization seeking adults to mentor or tutor young people. Perhaps you can join a Big Brother/Big Sister program. Also check to see if a community center or local library needs tutors for an after-school program. Maybe a professional organization in your field has a mentorship program which will afford you the opportunity to share your expertise. This kind of volunteering will be a marvelous way for you to offer others the benefit of your accumulated wisdom. You can inspire and offer practical advice to someone younger. You will enjoy this relationship and the child or teenager will benefit greatly from your help. Assisting someone within the framework of a volunteer program offers you the opportunity to apply your innate helping instincts without worrying the recipient of your aid might encroach on your boundaries.

Your talents will receive the positive attention they deserve around the 3rd week of March. Your employer may offer you a prestigious project, along with a raise and promotion. Or, if you are an artist or performer of some sort, your work will become more prominent as well as more profitable. Perhaps a director will ask to use one of your band's songs in an upcoming film. Negotiate to get yourself the best possible deal. Be sure to draw on your immense store of tact when making demands. Don't sell yourself short. But make nice to get what you want out of the deal. "You catch more flies with honey than with vinegar" may sound a tad corny. But that old soft-soaping you Snakes are so famous for really does work like a charm.

A good friend of yours may come up with some exciting news around the 25th of this month. His/her announcement may relate to something personal like becoming engaged or expecting a new child. Or she/he may have achieved some sort of honor like a fellowship or an award. Applause and celebration are in order. Offer champagne.

**SNAKE April 2014**

The alignment of the planets around the 7th of this month forebodes possible bone breaks or fractures for Snakes. You might want to avoid engaging in any activities with a high potential for injury. Steer clear of extreme sports activities such as rock climbing, downhill skiing, skydiving or zip-lining. Wait until later to take that class in martial arts or flying trapeze gymnastics you've been considering. If you regularly ride a bike or go roller blading, do not forget to wear your helmet or other protective gear. Exercise additional caution even in everyday activities. Look both ways before crossing busy streets. Take stairs at a more sedate pace.

Around the middle of the month, you may meet an intriguing new person. Although this individual may have a flirtatious manner and offer you many compliments, don't mistake him or her for a new conquest. Instead, you will find that she/he feeds your creativity in some way. This person may turn out to be a new collaborator with whom you can develop exciting projects. Maybe he or she is a poet whose words mesh perfectly with your music. Or the two of you may develop some other type of symbiotic relationship. Perhaps you'll introduce him/her to a gallery owner friend of yours. In return this person provides you with a new rehearsal space in a building she/he owns. It may be best to keep this relationship non-sexual to avoid inflicting drama or jealousy on what promises to become a very mutually beneficial interaction.

Have you been avoiding an old friend lately? Someone in your circle becoming too needy? This person may try to confront you around the 22$^{nd}$ of April about those e-mails, texts and voice mails you have been ignoring. You may find that it is no longer possible to so cunningly slither behind the shrubbery. You may well have to make it plain to this pal that you simply cannot become his/her full-time personal social worker.

## SNAKE May 2014

Someone might misinterpret a friendly or casually flirtatious gesture of yours for something much more serious around the 2$^{nd}$ of this month. A smile you offer to a server at a restaurant may result in him or her giving you a phone number or e-mail address. A compliment you pay a co-worker on his/her new haircut could precipitate an invitation to share a romantic dinner. Declining this person's overtures diplomatically won't do. He or she might stick at least a toe, if not an entire foot, over the line into stalker territory. That waiter could use your credit card information to look up your Facebook profile and send you a friend request. Maybe your co-worker starts leaving little gifts on your desk. You may have to defend your boundaries with an iron fist.

A relative of yours may come to you seeking monetary assistance around the 17$^{th}$. He or she is truly in dire straits, perhaps facing homelessness. I know your usual reaction to such requests is to think the person asking for help needs to be more self-sufficient. But in this case, I strongly urge you to give as much help as you comfortably can. Decide on an amount you can give without putting yourself in danger of sharing this person's plight. Also do some research to discover social service agencies which may be able to offer this individual more assistance with housing or medical expenses or whatever his/her needs may be.

Any parties thrown by Snakes during the last two weeks of May are bound to be a success. The planets line up to smile upon your host or hostessing efforts. If your abode is too small to hold many people, consider staging this event at a restaurant. Or why not give a catered picnic in the park to take advantage of fine weather? Another possibility is the progressive pot luck. Recruit some friends in your neighborhood to open their houses and serve aperitifs. Then the crowd moves on to someone else's place for hors d'oeuvres and a glass of bubbly. Next stop will be for the main dish, served with a few very special wines. Then you all move to the dessert house where you sample a variety of chocolaty or fruit treats. Finally you all finish up singing old standards around the piano at your own house. If guests have had a bit too much to drink, hide their car keys and let them sleep on your couch.

## SNAKE June 2014

Another Mercury retrograde period takes place from the 7$^{th}$ of this month until the 1$^{st}$ of July. This one may affect your dealings with people in your immediate environment such as neighbors, roommates and co-workers. You may also notice that brief communications such as text messages and e-mails go awry in some fashion. Mercury retrograde, remember, precludes the signing of binding documents and the making of long term commitments.

Usually you glide confidently through any kind of social occasion. However, around the 8th, you may make a rare social faux pas. Something you say or do will shock those around you - spill champagne on an honored guest, blurt the wrong name at your boss's wife or mistake the head of the department for the janitor. When you realize what you have done or said, you will feel most uncomfortable and wish you could melt out of sight on the spot. Don't let your discomfort show. Maintain aplomb. Panicking will only amplify your mistake. If you did something that requires an apology, make one gracefully. Don't dwell on the incident afterwards. Change the subject, letting others perceive that your elegance is not dimmed by a minor social error.

You may find yourself reminiscing about a discarded friend during the last week of June. In the old days, unless former pals unexpectedly materialized in the present or at least had a listing in your local phone book, these kind of musings rarely resulted in action. These days, Google makes it wonderfully easy to track someone down and send an e-mail or a Facebook poke. As a result, we sometimes re-awaken relationships better left to slumber in our memories. Think very seriously before contacting this sloughed-off former buddy of yours. It's quite possible nostalgia has dimmed your memory of this person's irritating faults. I seem to think they talk too much and are constantly interrupting. Write down everything you remember about how and why the friendship ended. Look at this list every day for at least a week. If, after seven days of remembering the bad as well as the good, you still feel the urge to get in touch, click away into your murky past and see what the renewed acquaintance brings.

**SNAKE July 2014**

You may be hit with a tsunami of fatigue around the 5th. Just making it through the day's basic events requires every ounce of your strength. Before making a doctor's appointment, try revamping your diet. Eschew, at least for the time being, any beer, wine or cocktails. Eat only tiny portions of meat, relying more on fresh vegetables and fruits to round out your diet. Also keep your intake of cheese, bread and pasta to a minimum. Those foods can make Snakes feel more sluggish than usual. Between bouts of work, lie down. Snake people function best when they can be supine after a spurt of hard labor.

At a social event you attend around the 12th, you will witness one of your friends bullying another. The bully is likely to be someone with more social advantages. He or she may hold a more prestigious job or have won the genetic lottery in comparison to the other person who sports ultra plain features. I strongly advise you to intervene on behalf of the bullied one. Make it clear that you do not approve of mockery, even when it is disguised as humor. If the bully doesn't desist, start bullying them in the self-same manner they were denigrating your friend. Bullies back down when confronted with their own weapons.

The last two weeks of the month are an important time to focus on your finances. You may want to make an appointment with your banker or personal financial advisor. If you have a business, you should discuss some crucial matters with those who invested in your venture. If you hold property in common with someone else, review that fiscal relationship carefully. Changes related to important money matters are in the air for Snakes right now. As far as possible, take charge of your own finances. Otherwise, some of the alterations you experience now will stem from other people's (iffy) choices. An investor in your business may withdraw his/her support. A partner may be ready to sell her/his share. If you do not have the funds to buy them out, you may find yourself with a strange new business bed-fellow.

## SNAKE August 2014

The early part of August is likely to prove quite trying for you, Snake. Jealousy, control and manipulation - all three will play a major role in your life this month. Perhaps you and your partner have a quarrel about who has been engaging in mild flirtations lately. If one of you has more control of the purse strings, she or he may attempt to control the other's behavior using financial leverage. If you have an ex who owes you child support or alimony, he or she may try to withhold funds unless you perform a favor that you find distasteful. Don't give in. Insist on being paid your due. Or simply hire someone shady to throw a scare into the debtor.

If you are a parent, you may have to console one of your children about a major disappointment around the 12th of this month. A scholarship, promotion or other honor goes to your child's hated rival. A rejection letter arrives from the university or graduate school of his/her dreams. Your child may be jilted at the altar. He or she may become the subject of vicious gossip. A business venture your offspring poured his or her heart into fails. Offer love and support. Do not reproach your son or daughter by offering any "you should have/could have" comments. Such remarks are disparaging and will only make his/her pain sting more deeply. If you do not have children, you may be called upon to console a niece, a nephew or another young person you know well. Spend extra quality time with the kid. Take them on road trips or hikes where they have the opportunity to come clean about what happened and how they really feel about it. One on one contact with children always pays off both for them and for you.

Your career will take a decided upswing around the 20th. Months or perhaps years of honing your skills will result in some kind of significant reward. However, there may be a catch. Although you will garner some kind of prestige, honor or promotion now, the financial aspect of your advancement will be delayed. The increased income will remain tantalizingly out of reach for at least a few more months.

## SNAKE September 2014

If you have been contemplating a move, early September is an excellent time to look for a new abode. Even if you did not find anything that suited you earlier this year, the stars align now to favor your locating a wonderful new home. Something extra special will come on the market rather suddenly. So check frequently with your real estate agent or whatever website you use for apartment or house-hunting. This new home will meet almost all your requirements in terms of price, location and other considerations. You are likely even to get several advantages that were only on your wish-list: huge closets or a fireplace, hardwood floors or other elegant architectural features. If you aren't thinking of moving, then embark on those home re-decorating plans you had been postponing for financial reasons. They will become more feasible now. Perhaps a wealthy friend gifts you with her nearly new swanky furniture when she decides (once again) to renovate and start from scratch.

Coupled Snakes may find themselves growing bored of their partnership around the middle of this month. Your partner seems unappreciative of you. You feel as if you can predict every word out of your significant other's mouth. As far as lovemaking goes, given how unimaginative the sex has become, — it seems as though is following a script. You'll be arriving at a bit of a crossroads now. Both single and partnered Snakes will find themselves beset with new admirers. Those who are in committed relationships will have to choose whether to re-kindle the old flame or take a chance on new romance. No need to hurry on this decision. Giving up a steady partner in favor of the unknown lover down the road can be daunting. Ponder. Give due consideration to whether you prefer to stick it out with Monsieur or Madame Script - or take a walk.

You're likely to gain a helper of some kind toward the end of this month. Perhaps your boss will decide you deserve an assistant or an additional person in your department to handle the overflow. Or you may decide to hire someone yourself. Someone to handle the gardening or cleaning or other household chores which take you away from the hobbies or cultural activities you really want to pursue.

### SNAKE October 2014

This month presents us with the last of 2014's Mercury retrograde periods. This one a starts on the $4^{th}$ of October and ends on the $25^{th}$. That's nearly a whole month's load of postponements and indecision and electronic breakdowns. Ugh! Given the position of this particular retrograde, I must advise against any major purchases or significant changes regarding to aesthetics. Now is not the time to splurge on that irresistible oil painting you see in a gallery. Nor is this period best for altering your appearance or acquiring expensive new clothing. If you go for it, the change in hair color that your new stylist suggests will seem disastrous to you next month. That designer jacket that tempts you now will not seem quite so elegant in the clear, cool light of the post-Mercury retrograde phase. Stay your hand.

You have nursed a grudge against a certain person for a long time. He or she once sought to actually harm you. They may have gossiped behind your back, maligning your reputation unfairly. Or this individual may have tried to come between you and a lover. Around the 14th of this month you will have a chance to get even. Tempting though it may be, I urge you to refrain from excessive acts of vengeance. The positions of the planets indicate that sweet revenge would come with a hefty price tag. In some way, what you do to this character will come back to haunt you. Find a devious way to subtly embarrass or humiliate them.

Your love life may heat up rather dramatically toward the end of this month. I'm not sure if you and your partner will renew your romantic commitments toward each other. Or if one of those new admirers has become worthy of your affections. At any rate, the planetary positions for the last few days of October for Snakes indicate a 90% chance of receiving extravagant gifts and an 80% chance of sexual fireworks. You will be in your element. Enjoy yourself. Self-denial is neither your style nor your druthers, Snakey.

### SNAKE November 2014

November of this year will be an absolutely fabulous month to be a Snake! For much of this year, you have been feeling that your life smacked too much of the weary old world and all its petty problems. This month you will experience more of the elegance you not-so-secretly crave. Travel is very likely to become prominent in your life again. Fortunately, we're not talking camping or bunking down in a dreary Motel 6. When you go on trips in November, you will be ensconced in the sort of luxurious accommodations you have always preferred. Luckily it looks as though someone else is picking up the tab - your employer? A generous client? Your new or old lover? Or maybe you have a secret admirer.

Your creativity will also be firing on all cylinders throughout this month. It will probably peak around the $14^{th}$. You may wake up from a dream that week filled with a vision for a new project. Make sure you keep a notebook handy by your bed so you can record this dream inspiration while it remains fresh in your mind. A portion of this new idea may involve combining different genres or modalities of expression. This may be a good time to contact that potential collaborator you met earlier in the year. Perhaps the two of you can bring this idea to fruition together.

A friend of yours may come to you with a surprising admission around the 26th. She or he is attracted to one of your exes. You have not been involved with this former lover for a very long time. The two of you are on relatively good terms but there is no longer any attraction between you. Squelch any lingering sense of possessiveness you may feel. That's just silly. Wish your friend well and give him or her your blessing to pursue a relationship with your long-ago ex. You might be tempted to forewarn them of some tiny flaws in manners or tricky sexual habits belonging to the ex. Best to abstain. Let them find out about the lovemaking marching music accompaniment and the occasional flatulence on their own.

**SNAKE December 2014**

You may be contemplating some alteration to your appearance which less astute souls might interpret as vanity. Maybe you're considering laser eye surgery to permanently correct your vision so you can discard glasses and contacts for good. Or maybe you have researched a bit of discreet plastic surgery. Older Snakes may seek to subtly reverse the effects of aging. Or it might be you seek to transform yourself from a 9.7 to a 10. Not to worry. These days nose jobs and eye lifts are as common as Cheerios. The first week of December is especially favorable for aesthetic surgery. However, if you can't schedule the surgery before the 18th, then wait until the start of the Goat year in February of 2015.

There's a risk that some secret of yours will be exposed around the 10th. Behave with extra kindness to everyone around you in the weeks leading up to that time. Give a large donation to a popular charity for children or animals and make sure the local gossip mongers learn of your generosity. People will be more likely to be sympathetic to your predicament if they have recently seen your compassionate side. You may have to put up with some embarrassment for a week or more. But as long as your secret does not involve anything illegal, the incident will soon be obscured by some other unrelated scandal. Gossips have a very short attention span. The hottest new scandals get the most attention from busybodies.

A disagreement with your lover may create a dark cloud over your plans for celebrating the western New Year. Chances are it's a minor tiff - not a major quarrel. I'm afraid, dear Snake, that you may be at fault here. Could it be that something your sweetie said triggered some hidden insecurity of yours? You snapped back defensively. Then the entire incident mushroomed. Send your sweetie a text message taking responsibility for your touchiness. Shrink the argument down to microscopic size with a lighthearted, humorous observation. No use spoiling New Year's Eve over a petty quarrel over who gets to drive which car to the party.

**SNAKE January 2015**

Looks like you are in for a visit from an unexpected foreign guest this month. It is possible this person will be someone you have known for years. However, it is more likely that you will take in a stranger with but a tenuous connection to you. Shortly after the western New Year, you will receive a distress call about this person's need for shelter. Perhaps the child of a friend you made while vacationing years ago comes to your area on an exchange program. The teen's arrangements for lodging with a family will have fallen through at the last minute. Or you may receive a heavily accented message from the sibling of a friend of your college roommate announcing his/her hotel reservations were lost and there isn't a single room left anywhere in town. You will initially extend your hospitality to this person out of a sense of charity and obligation. However you may find that you enjoy the company of your guest and will do whatever you can to keep them around longer.

A close friend of yours may experience bereavement around the 16th of January. This event may happen quite suddenly as the result of a freak accident. This person is likely to lose someone very important in his/her life. It may be a spouse, a parent or even a child. Offer as much support as you can to your pal during this time of emotional distress. The best medicine against grief is distraction. Take your pal to the movies or theater or get concert tickets or go on a trip - just the two of you - somewhere distracting and fun.

Your property may be the target of vandalism toward the end of January. You will not discover the damage until several days after it occurs. Someone may spray paint on the back wall of your house. Perhaps you will find a broken window on your garden shed or garage. Or somebody might scratch the passenger side of your car while it is in a parking garage. Make sure your insurance policies are up-to-date to cover this sort of vandalism.

# HORSE 2014
## OVERVIEW FOR THE WOOD HORSE YEAR

*Hardy Horse,*

*According to Chinese legend, the Horse year is not an excellent one for Horses. Most all other signs benefit from their own years. But not the Horse. This will be a troubled and sometimes even dangerous year for you Horse people. The perils are not your fault. They are simply there . . . like bad luck. The best way for you to handle this situation of course is to exercise caution in all of your activities. Opt out of chancy business deals. Don't go trekking in the Himalayas. Cancel your subscription to the Bungee Cord Club and renege on all plans for ski holidays in avalanche season in the Andes.*

*In other words, keep it simple. Stay around home a lot. Busy yourself with homey projects like baking Christmas cookies or working in the garden – and even then watch out for domestic accidents. You could pierce your palm with a tomato stake or dent someone's car on the way to the market to buy the flour and chocolate for cookies. Just be careful. You are walking on eggs this year. Now, please don't go sulk somewhere and not come out till this year is over. Do understand that the reason for difficult times in your life is always about learning. Obstacles and setbacks are about helping you to see what it's like to be Horse of a different color. sw*

———— ᴇ ᴊᴇ ᴊᴇ ————

## THE CHINESE YEAR AHEAD
## HORSE 2014

### HORSE February 2014

Mercury takes another of its three-week retrograde journeys this month. It will run from February 6th through the 28th. During this period, you may experience minor snafus related to travel plans, missed messages, crossed wires, and just plain glitches. Not disasters. Just mix-ups and snags. Unless you can get things done before February 6, postpone important commitments and major purchases until a day or so after Mercury goes direct.

On January 31, 2014, your very own year began. With it comes a chance for public prominence. Your involvement in some sort of political or spiritual group may bring you to the forefront around February 12$^{th}$. Perhaps you are one of the speakers at a rally related to environmental issues. Your eloquence lands you on the evening news. Impressed both by your forcefulness and by your photogenic appearance, the organizers of the group offer you some kind of leadership position. Or maybe, fired by your concern about some burning issue, you will decide to run for an office. Your campaign gains traction quickly. If you don't go public or seek the limelight, you may decide to start teaching some sort of course related to your spiritual practice.

Money, which you thought was a lost cause, arrives around the 19th. Perhaps a long-disputed insurance matter is finally settled in your favor. Or could be that someone who borrowed money from you years ago makes good on a long-overdue loan. You might very well decide to use these funds to buy some new duds. You have had to deprive yourself of such luxuries for a while, and some of your formerly glorious apparel was beginning to look embarrassingly threadbare. As you hate coming across as shabby, when you have some spare cash, good-looking gear is a first priority. You usually favor the classic look; but this time why not add a vivid scarf or flashy tie to add pizzazz? 2014 is, after all, is your year to shine.

While out for a solo walk during the last few days in February, you may see something amazing - maybe even supernatural or vaguely suspect. Perhaps you will be in the woods and catch a glimpse of an animal. This might be a creature experts say has not lived in your region for decades. Or it may be an animal so rare as to be assumed extinct. Or, if you're strolling in town, you see someone duck very suddenly into a car. Could be you will benefit from a fleeting sighting of a reclusive celebrity. This apparition will come as a huge surprise. And it will mark you and cause you to do some serious thinking.

## HORSE March 2014

An ex-partner may extend an olive branch to you sometime around the 3rd-10th of this month. You and he/she have been at odds for awhile now. Yet you still have lingering romantic feelings for them. Don't let your hopes mislead you. Chances are this former lover has no romantic agenda at all behind these peacemaking efforts. He or she may have decided that since the two of you live in the same town and run in the same circles, it is silly to maintain the hostilities. Or perhaps you and this person are still co-parenting children you had together and your ex wants to wants to declare an armistice for their sake. It could even be that the two of you still own some joint property and your former significant other seeks a truce merely in order to discuss business. The message? Keep your romantic notions in check. You broke up with this person once. Better try to keep it that way.

You may become the target of an attempted crime around the second or third week of this month. You will foil the aims of the thieves. But it can be very scary. Perhaps you will find someone trying to break into your car or home. The criminal will run off when you arrive. Horses of smaller stature and/or an outwardly gentle demeanor may targeted by a mugger. You defend yourself this time too, perhaps using a well-aimed kick you learned in a martial arts class years ago. Keep your eyes open and your ears pricked for a possible scam too. There's a shady bit mid-month you need to be ready for.

Expanding your musical tastes toward the end of March eases some of the inner tension you are experiencing. Explore different genres of music on your favorite online music source. Try listening to a type of music you know nothing about - the mellifluous sounds of the harp-like African kora, the elegance of classical guitar or Tuvan throat singing. Open your mind as well as your ears so you can learn to appreciate many different sound patterns.

## HORSE April 2014

At work, you may chafe under the strictures of some by-the-rules supervisor around the 4th. Or if you are self-employed, you may encounter another strict authority figure or institution - a landlord, bank loan officer or even a tax agent. Keep your head. Continue to interact politely with this person. Do not resort to angry words or actions. Sarcastic rejoinders may make you feel good for about five minutes but will cost you in the long run. Use imagination and humor to help diffuse your tension. Imagine this boss as a cartoon character. Think: "I am interacting with Bugs Bunny or Homer Simpson." That should keep the mood jocular.

You may be tempted by an old bad habit during the second week of April. If you previously smoked, someone might offer you a cigarette when you are feeling stressed. Horses who attend AA meetings may be invited to a party that takes place in a bar. Resist the pull of addiction. Stay away from people and places likely to entice you into breaking your resolve. Instead, head for some neutral place where you feel relaxed and secure. Go to a room in your home which you consider your personal retreat. Or seek out your favorite place in nature. Meditate in this spot. Listen to music on your smart phone or iPod. Chill and continue to abstain.

Your life as a public figure advances. Your campaign or cause gains ground. More people begin to recognize you. They may congratulate you and applaud your work. Finally you feel you are getting some of the respect you deserve. Toward the end of the month, the universe throws you a curve ball. As a result of this new success, you receive an offer of some sort. What is being proffered is highly attractive. But to accept it means betraying your principles. Perhaps you receive a sexual proposition from a political groupie. You know and respect this person's spouse. So you do not even dare. Too, somebody may offer you a bribe of some sort. Say no. Dare to hold on to your integrity.

## HORSE May 2014

Horse people who live with animals may experience some distress early this month. One of your non-human friends may get lost. If you have smaller pets like mice or guinea pigs, they may escape their cage. If you are a dog-owner, you may let your pooch off the leash, turn your back for a moment and then find your canine companion has vanished into thin air. Or one of your cats slips out the back door and does not return the next morning. You walk the area shaking a bowl full of dry cat-food but hear no answering meows. Perhaps one of your horses leaps over a fence and wanders away. Enlist the help of animal-loving friends and neighbors in searching for your lost animal.

You may have an unpleasant brush with the law around the 11th -19th of May. If you fell off the wagon during last month's period of temptation, you may have brought this upon yourself. You might have been driving with a high blood-alcohol level. However some Horses will experience problems arising from the prejudices of a law enforcement officer. You may drive through a small town where the police have set up a speed trap. It is said they don't arrest locals, but they try to increase the city coffers by falsely claiming out-of-town drivers are breaking the law. Or you may receive unwarranted attention from the police due to the color of your skin. Again, don't get huffy and rebel. Call a lawyer who successfully defends people who are discriminated against.

A good friend may fail to express his/her gratitude and appreciation toward the end of the month. Perhaps you put up some closet shelves for a pal who just moved. Or you offer to watch their children so they can go to a health care appointment. This individual will be so caught up in his/her own affairs that the words "Thank you" will neither enter their mind nor come to their lips. Don't lash out with resentful remarks or go somewhere and sulk. Your excessive anger diminishes you just as their ingratitude does them.

## HORSE June 2014

Mercury goes retrograde on the 7th of this month until the 1st of next month. This particular retrograde phase is likely to have the strongest effect on matters relating to home, family, and siblings as well as brief communications and short journeys. Use this time to re-organize your home. You might want to take time to clean out your overloaded e-mail boxes. Exercise extra care and patience when talking with people or sending messages. Also apply meticulous planning to any short journeys you want to take. Until July 1, sign no binding documents, don't buy expensive electronic equipment and expect the devices you do own to dysfunction. Mercury retrograde is best used as a time for planning and attending to details.

You will meet a new person the latter half of this month. This individual may be a new employee at your workplace. Could be a new neighbor. You will take an instant dislike to him or her. He or she possesses none of the qualities you admire. Perhaps he offends your sense of style by neglecting his appearance and grooming. Or she seems unduly shy and withdrawn. You see none of your own strength reflected in this person. Perhaps you see them as spoiled. Of course your distaste for this person does not give you the right to mock him or her. Their failure to live up to your personal tastes does not constitute a moral flaw. Minimize your contact with him or her as much for their sake as for yours.

As compensation, you will also meet another person around this same time. Here you will not be repelled. *Au contraire!* Perhaps this highly attractive individual suddenly contacts you in relation to your campaign or takes the class you are offering. There is instant chemistry between you. He or she may have recently ended a difficult relationship. Their last partner wounded them deeply. That makes this person look upon you as something of a savior. Watch out. Don't do any rescuing. It's always tempting for strong people like Horses to want to boost another's morale by loving them. Rescue usually backfires.

## HORSE July 2014

Your new relationship continues to grow apace. There is strong sexual heat between the two of you. Even in public, you have a hard time keeping your hands off each other. You act like teenagers embroiled in a first romance. Saying goodbye to each other even for small periods, like when one of you goes to work, turns into a long interval of kissing and murmured endearments. Some of your friends find this behavior cute. Others view it as slightly nauseating. I don't want to rain on your garden party, but I advise you attempt to limit your public necking as it may indeed embarrass those who are obliged to witness it.

When you are not whispering x-rated compliments in each other's ears, the two of you spend a lot of time complaining about your respective exes. You each have a former lover in your recent past whom you intensely resent - even hate. Beware of building too much of the foundations of your relationship on sharing hatred. Rancor can serve as an amusing (even fascinating) basis for conversation. But it is not a healthy emotion on which to base a loving relationship.

Around July 14th, you may face a test in this new union. You will meet someone whose opinion your new lover values. Could be his/her family or offspring or just some close friends he introduces you to. Initially these people will dislike you. You will have to use your charm to win them over. Or... if you find them equally unpleasant, you may have to break the news to your sweetheart who might take it amiss. Prepare for your first fight.

You may find yourself in a costume of some sort toward the end of July. Perhaps you attend a Renaissance Faire and get into the spirit of the period. Or else you participate in a play or some other kind of performance. You look resplendent in this outfit. You feel particularly proud of this getup because you designed it yourself. Perhaps you even made part of it with your own hands. The reactions you receive are highly gratifying. Strangers come up and compliment you. Many of them give you longing glances. Your new sweetie finds you even more irresistible than usual. You may even gain mild local fame from this appearance. Perhaps someone photographs you and the image appears in a local paper or magazine. Don't shrink from this surprise renown. Own it.

## HORSE August 2014

Early August could involve you in a substantial property transaction. Perhaps you and your ex will finally agree to sell that land you owned jointly. Or you may decide to purchase an atypical sort of building, either as your own dwelling or for income property. Since this is your year, any property transactions are likely to evolve in your favor. If you sell, you will make considerable money over your original purchase price. If you buy, you will land the best bargain on the market. Perhaps you find an especially motivated seller who is eager to shed this property. He or she is not interested in quibbling after you make your initial offer. This is a time of lucky breaks for Horses. But just because this is your lucky year, don't neglect any crucial details. Go over all paperwork more than once. Make sure you have not overlooked anything before signing the contract.

You may discover around the 17th that the co-worker or neighbor whom you dislike has a surprising connection to someone you want to impress- a sibling or cousin whose favor could advance your cause, campaign or teaching efforts. Or it may emerge that the individual you practically despise is an old friend of those connections of your sweetie whose highest kudos you seek. If you have already backed off on your expressions of contempt as I suggested, then no worries. On the other hand, if you permitted yourself to bully or denigrate the person in question, you may have to apologize - add a dollop of your most vigorous sincerity.

An old friend might ask you to perform an odd favor around the 22nd. You might feel apprehensive and fear that he or she is roping you into something illegal. They may request that you drop off a package at an address in a slightly sketchy part of town. Or they may ask you to call a number at a certain time and pretend to be someone else. Your buddy won't offer any explanation. Don't worry. The matter your friend is involved in is more about hot romance than it is about anything disreputable.

## HORSE September 2014

In September, someone will make the mistake of underestimating your debating skills. This should occur around the 13th of this month. He or she tries to mock you while you are speaking at a public rally in support of your cause or while you are teaching one of your courses. You will effortlessly pull the rug out from under this person, exposing the flaws in their logic. Go ahead. Set a trap which will cause this sarcastic individual to take a verbal pratfall. Everyone present will chuckle at how foolish this guy or gal looks for trying to take you down.

You and your new sweetheart may have a major blow-up as September ends. He or she could have read a flirtatious post on your Facebook wall. The message will be from a very attractive person from your past. Unfortunately, you might panic and try to lie about the matter at first, covering up your true history with this person. When your lover finds out, she or he is angry and tells you the relationship is over. You don't feel ready to let go of this new love. You feel wonderful when the two of you are together. You might decide to get him or her back at any cost. You will call, e-mail and send Facebook messages until she/he blocks you.

Then you may resort to other measures. Try to slow the pace of your galloping frenzy, Horse. Stop and consider if the next, more radical, step in your plan is really wise. Do you really think that having one of your exes call your defected sweetie and plead on your behalf will work? Are you sure you want to create a fake Facebook profile and use that to contact him/her? Is threatening to kill yourself unless she/he returns really a sane idea? Horses are known to fall in love hard. Falling out of love is especially difficult for you. But you are essentially a pragmatist.

You know full well that any outrageous behavior on your part could reflect badly on your reputation. Be mindful of the possible fallout. And ask yourself if the love affair was really about true love after all. It was sexy. But is that all?

## HORSE October 2014

Mercury is retrograde again this month. That means waiting a while on important matters like surgery, contracts and legal matters. Also, from the 4$^{th}$ until the 25$^{th}$, anticipate a few delays and minor mishaps related to communication and travel.

I hope you will have cooled off and let your wiser side prevail. Perhaps you then decided to use intelligent communication to win your lover back. Of course it could be your lost sweetie shares your taste for emotional melodrama and responded to some of your less mature tactics. At any rate, it looks like the two of you get back together around the 12$^{th}$-15$^{th}$ this month. The make-up sex is fantastic, explosive, like fireworks going off in the bedroom every night. The two of you are closer than ever. You lie entwined in each other's arms in between bouts of lovemaking, talking about your future together and apologizing for the giant misunderstanding of last month.

Shortly after this reunion, your lover may accompany you to a big family event. You feel pleased at first to see how well she/he gets along with your relatives. But you may feel a little apprehensive when one of your older relations pulls your sweetie aside and starts blabbing about your wild past. Rescue him or her in a hurry. No use risking more conflict.

You may be tempted to scrap your budget for the sake of a fabulous find on a shopping excursion around the 21$^{st}$. You know you look amazing in a one-of-a-kind item of attire you discover. Although it may mean playing the shell game with the utility companies next month or running up your credit card balance, you feel you simply must own this fashionable elegant basic. No one else could possibly look as good in this raiment as you do. Before you whip out your credit card, call in a level-headed friend for a second opinion. She or he may advise you to look for something similar at a lower price. Or they may say "Go for it!" and once again set your credit card on fire

Schedule an appointment with your doctor before the end of the month. I know you're accustomed to thinking of yourself as strong and physically impervious. But those minor symptoms you've been experiencing might signal something more serious. Make a list of all your symptoms. Go through the list one complaint at a time during the exam. Have a thorough checkup. Make sure your physician runs all of the appropriate tests. But, because of Mercury retrograde, avoid scheduling any surgery unless there is an absolute emergency.

## HORSE November 2014

Between the 2$^{nd}$ and the 8$^{th}$ of November you may hear news of the death of someone who was once very important to you. Although you and this individual had drifted apart, their passing will affect you very deeply. At first, you may find yourself coming up with excuses for not attending the funeral which is but a few hours' drive from you. You will tell yourself you are too busy. Or you might think that some of the people at the funeral will not want to see you. Do try harder to make the time to say goodbye to this old friend.

If you've been driving an older vehicle and hoping to postpone the purchase of a new car, it may be time to start shopping around the 12$^{th}$. Your old car could give up the ghost around now. Problems with the transmission or something else too expensive or too tricky to repair will necessitate a new car. Since your old one won't have much trade-in value, you will have to look carefully at your options. Look into available financing. See if anyone you know and trust is in the process of selling their used car. Shop extensively before you buy.

There's an upcoming get-together with those connections of your sweetie who have always viewed you with suspicion. Think about using your manual skills to make some kind of gift for these people. Nothing amateurish. Whatever you can produce with enough dexterity that it looks almost professional. Present it with flair and style. An expensive bought gift may make it look as though you are trying to win them over. Whereas a hand-crafted gift will convey a simple message of possible friendship.

You may experience some uncomfortable symptoms related to the tail end of your digestive tract around the 29th. Before consulting a doctor, try changing your diet. At least temporarily, cut down on dairy products. Eat only small portions of meat. Add twice as much fresh fruit and an equal amount of vegetables. Confine yourself to only one glass of wine or beer each day. Also minimize your intake of caffeine. The intestine doesn't like to be fed foods which gum up the works.

## HORSE December 2014

Another quarrel with your lover may find you in an anti-social mood as December begins. This time it's less likely to be a major emotional battle. You have reached the stage where you have begun to bicker over small things. Who left toothpaste all over the bathroom sink? Whose turn is it to change the cat litter? Who takes out the recycling and who gets to empty the trash? You may begin to feel chronically irritated at all these mundane matters. If you can, take a short solo trip. Borrow a friend's cabin in the country. Some brief time apart will clear your head. Instead of resenting your sweetie's habit of boiling the coffee, you may even start to miss him or her.

You may find yourself jealous of a friend's success around the 14th of this month. You and this person aren't in direct competition. Your efforts are in vastly different fields. Yet at some level you unconsciously assumed you would find success before this person did. Somewhere, you feel pleased for this pal. Yet, these positive feelings are shadowed by unspoken resentment. Treat these negative feelings as an alarm clock. Think of them as a wake-up call alerting you to whether (or not) your desire to create a wealthier future for yourself is indeed your ultimate goal. Your friend's achievement has nothing to do with you. His or her success has merely reminded you that perhaps you don't really want to accomplish anything similar. Now that you know more about your own goals, you should feel free to congratulate him or her warmly and with sincerity

The holiday season features a happy announcement. Your family is expecting a new member. Perhaps your new partner and you have decided to have a child together. Or if you have grown children, there may be a grandchild on the way. Maybe one of your siblings or cousins is going to give birth or adopt in the approaching New Year. A time for celebration is nigh.

## HORSE January 2015

Your humanitarian side is deeply affected by something you read or see during the first week of 2015. This information actually creates a subtle soul realignment within you. You may start to meditate more frequently. You become able to see more clearly into your consciousness and understand your dreams. You gain new insight which enables you to better discern your own faults as well as recognize your positive attributes. You may feel a bit abashed about some of the things you did or said in the past. Yet you also realize that you have the strength and talent to evolve into a better version of yourself. You feel inspired and excited by the growth you have achieved this year. You can be confident that the innate heroism and brilliance within you will allow you to accomplish great things. Perhaps not monetarily. But from a humanistic point of view.

Your teaching, activism or political career continues to earn you increased respect. People who formerly avoided or even disliked you, seem to regard you with new eyes. One of these former enemies may even open the door to an important appointment or nomination of some sort for you during the latter part of January.

Around the 20th, just as you are so enthusiastically gazing toward the mountain of enlightenment, you suddenly stub your toe. This may happen on either a literal or a metaphoric level. This new awkwardness is sending you a message about paying more attention to the journey than to the destination. Could be a flat tire. Or a day or so of tripping over your own feet as you tread the sidewalk. This spate of clumsiness is the universe's way of reminding you of the hard work and attention to detail necessary for any great personal accomplishment. Your long-term noble goals can only be reached step-by-step. Momentous periods of clarity about ourselves and our goals do not mean that the clouds part and the universe banishes all obstacles from our path. We still have to slog and drudge up two steps and back down one every time.

# GOAT/SHEEP 2014
## OVERVIEW FOR THE WOOD HORSE YEAR

*Gifted Goat,*

*Goats (Some cultures prefer to use Sheep) are fairly comfortable in Horse years because the industrious aura surrounding the Horse keeps you feeling secure and safe. You would do well this year to ensure your position in the structure where you find yourself currently ensconced. Now, you may claim that you are not part of any structure, that you are a freelance magician, a self-employed dog walker or a famous plastic surgeon who operates alone. But if you do work on your own, I'll bet that you are either very married to a solid citizen type who either pays the bills or keeps the books – or both! If you aren't married, then you probably live at home where you can be sure of 3 squares and a warm coverlet. Goats do not very often go it alone.*

*Which brings us back to the Wood Horse year. You enjoy the atmosphere of this year because it cradles your need for dependency. You can count on the Horse. We can all count on our Horses. They are consistent, solid, practical - if headstrong - beings. So in this Wood Horse year, you will continue to sail ahead with Lady Luck by your side. Invest some money in property this year. Get yourself a cottage or a bungalow to restore. You work very well with your hands and this year, handy work is on everybody's docket. sw*

---

## THE CHINESE YEAR AHEAD
### GOAT 2014

**GOAT February 2014**

With the Horse year cantering on in, Goats will be entering passionate new pastures. If you are in an established partnership which has grown a bit stale, you will have the opportunity this month to refresh your relationship. Make new inroads where you two never ventured before. Perhaps go to untried places together and discover new sports or hobbies you both enjoy. You usually like life to be structured from the outside. You don't want to have to supply the schedules or make the rules or (btw) clean up the dishes. You are a free spirit and like it that way. This year, the tables might just be turned.

Mercury goes retrograde from the 6th of this month until the 28th. Lay in an extra store of patience as people tend to become a bit flaky about messages during these periods. Communications go all murky or get lost in the mail. Travel arrangements are similarly subject to confusion and delay now.

If you haven't got that partner I mentioned above and are in the market for a brand new lover, the first couple of weeks of February will offer a fabulous opportunity to meet a scintillating new someone. Single Goats are advised to get out and about as much as possible. Make yourself visible. Attract notice. Dress to look your best. In addition to parties and evenings at clubs with friends, find unusual ways of meeting people. Why not go to a museum alone looking stylishly intriguing in one of your favorite outfits? If you spy a an attractive creature looking at a painting, strike up a conversation. Share your knowledge of art. Or just chat about the weather. It doesn't much matter if you have a "good line" to use or not. Your sexual magnetism will be at its peak.

Although your love life is likely to flourish this month, things may be difficult for you on the work front. The third week of February is likely to be particularly problematic. A boss, or if you are self-employed - a client, publisher or producer will find fault with your work. She or he will be testy about how you completed a project late or didn't meet a deadline. Minimize the potential for confrontation by being especially punctual and careful with details after February 14th. And, while you're at it, perk up your attitude.

Take precautions to protect your health as February draws to a close. The planetary positions signal greater vulnerability to your immune system right now. Don't neglect to wash your hands before eating. You might want to use an herbal remedy designed to boost your immunity such astragalus or a combination of Echinacea and goldenseal. These compounds are available at all health food and vitamin stores.

**GOAT March 2014**

As March begins, your sex life continues to flourish, lustful Goat mine. You and your partner enjoy trying new positions as well as zany locations for lovemaking. Was that you and your honey ululating loudly in the women's restroom at that club last night? Why not make a trip to your local sex toy store? There are some new developments which will offer exceptional thrills.

You might get a chance to live the lush life (at least temporarily) around the middle of the month. A wealthy friend, perhaps a Monkey or a Dragon, may invite you to housesit. This gig will give you access to amenities you lack at home. You and your sweetie will have some real fun relaxing in your friend's home theatre or game room with the latest model technology. Or you can prepare gourmet meals for each other in a palatial kitchen equipped with all of the most expensive chef gadgetry. Maybe you and your honey can unwind together in the whirlpool or loll about in the swimming pool. Perhaps, in exchange for watering plants, walking dogs, feeding cats or whatever, your pal will even give you the keys to one of his/her luxury cars. Leave everything better than you find it. That's the best way to get asked back.

Did you have a messy break-up or unpleasant altercation with someone recently? It looks like there's an individual lurking around the corners of your life who resents you. He or she might try to make trouble for you in some way around the 28th. The trouble in question may be something relatively minor like the time-tested (boring) calling your phone and hanging up repeatedly. You might notice some spiteful text messages or nasty notes on Facebook. Things could escalate from there. This person may seek to damage your property. They could stoop to slashing the tires of your vehicle or badmouthing you to mutual friends. If this ex of yours or resentful acquaintance still has a key to your home, get the locks changed right away. If the difficulties continue and/or escalate, don't hesitate to take out a restraining order.

**GOAT April 2014**

An influential person, perhaps a contact referred by the person you house-sat for last month, offers you some kind of work. If you have handyman/woman skills, perhaps you'll be doing some repairs or renovations around this buddy's home. Or she/he may hire you to use your creative talent in some way, like painting a mural in their living room. You may be asked to re-organize the person's entire wardrobe or straighten up their kitchen cupboards. Never mind if the job is menial. It pays. Things are likely to be a bit tight for you financially now. The extra income will be a boon.

Meanwhile, at your primary job, things may go from bad to worse this month. Around the 17th, that boss or client who complained about you back in February may start delivering ultimata. You are dealing here with a very complex individual who has poor communication skills. It's also possible this individual behaves unreasonably with most of the people he/she works with. Their behavior is so erratic and their approach so weird that they may well be in need of psychiatric help. But don't use this unstable person's problems as a justification for shooting yourself in the foot financially. Unless you have another job lined up, try to mollify the person. Don't let them get your Goat or set your temper alight. Acknowledge your errors or tardiness as though you meant it. Apologize. Promise you will do better in future. Flying off the handle could be a grave misstep. The brief satisfaction you might derive from telling off the client or boss and slamming out, won't count for much if you end up unemployed with no money to pay the bills.

Around the 22nd, your brain will be tingling and alive with creative inspiration. Ideas for new projects will arrive fast and thick. Make sure to note ALL these ideas down, whenever and wherever you receive them. Choose just one to start with right away. Attend to one project after the other.. Starting too many projects at once might prevent you from gaining the momentum you need to fulfill your vision.

## GOAT May 2014

Brace yourself, my dear Goat. I'm afraid you will have to exercise patience again in early May. Your part-time employer is quite likely to complain about the work you are doing for her/him. Perhaps the stress from your job has rendered you insomniac and you're arriving later than promised to complete that job for your benefactor. I think the best course here will be to acquiesce. Goats are masters at working long hours - sometimes days on end. You will catch up on sleep when the job's done. Listen to your friend's complaints and criticisms in silence, nodding your head here and there to indicate you are paying attention. Even if she/he rants a bit, remain diplomatic. I know that behaving meekly in the face of criticism may go against the grain with you. However, if you handle things gently your friend will cease the ravings sooner. Avoid arguments or the two of you might not be able to declare a truce for months. Hang in there. You really need the money.

The good news for this month of May comes around the 18th. Your lover is likely to offer you a gift. In fact, multiple gifts are a distinct possibility. Your sweetie realizes you have been going through a rough time and take you to your favorite store and treat you to several items. Don't be surprised when your honey also picks up the tab for a meal at the restaurant of your choice.

The end of the month, be prepared to be snubbed by an old friend. You might run into this person in public somewhere and greet him/her warmly. And you will receive a rather cold response. Or you might send an e-mail to this person and not hear back for a week. Is there a possibility a former lover has been spreading poison about you? One tricky revenge tactic of exes is to spread nasty rumors about those who have thrown them over for someone better. Contact the old friend who snubbed you directly and find out the scoop.

## GOAT June 2014

June should bring you a surprise offer of new employment. Take this opportunity to start over with a clean slate. Resist the temptation to insult your old boss on the way out the door. Maintain the high ground rather than sinking to his/her level. Display your best qualities at your new job. Arrive on time, or even a little bit early every day. Try not to be the first one out the door at the end of the workday. Ask questions when your duties are explained to you. This will help you not only meet but exceed expectations. Whatever you do, don't embody the new broom who sweeps clean. Keep on sweeping clean no matter what.

If you are planning an important meeting or other event, check and double-check to make sure the details don't somehow get garbled. The caterer you hire may think the 12pm lunch meeting is meant to be an 8pm dinner buffet. Mercury is retrograde from the 7th of June until the 1st of July. That inevitably means at least a few delays and some extra confusion. You know by now that you mustn't sign any irrevocable documents during a Mercury retrograde. But during this one, refrain from buying appliances or electronic devices.

You and your sweetie are still quite passionate about each other. You find her/his mere presence in a room sexually exciting. You hold hands when you walk down the street together. You gaze deeply into each other's eyes even when at a party with other people. Unfortunately, your sweetie's needs and desires may run counter to the demands of your new job around the 23rd. Perhaps they want you to come to a late-night concert at a club when you have to get up early for work the next morning. Or could be your honey asks you to leave work early to drive him/her to a health care appointment. Explain how important it is that you impress your boss with your work ethic right now. If this relationship is meant to last, she/he will understand.

Around the 29th, you may have uncomfortable time at a gathering with your partner's friends. This circle of your sweetheart's pals all share a certain interest. Could be anything from shooting skeet to dominoes. Unfortunately, it is a hobby you don't share with them all. Instead of trying to broaden the conversation to include you, these people keep talking about this arcane topic you know nothing about. You feel excluded. As much as you hate spending time apart from your lover, perhaps it is better to urge them to go to events involving this group on their own.

**GOAT July 2014**

Your good taste will lead you unerringly to a fabulous treasure around the 7th of July. Not only that, this gorgeous item will have a very low price-tag—or might even be free. If you see a sign for an estate, yard or garage sale around this period, hang a detour to check it out and see what's on offer. Make the rounds of your local thrift shops. There's a strong possibility you will find whatever it is sitting next to a trash can or dumpster, discarded by someone who lacks your discerning eye for value. Your friends will be amazed by your story of how you came across this enviable new possession. Enjoy your gloating rights. You came by them honestly.

You may finally resolve a minor mystery related to your own health the second or third week of this month. Whether through a generalist doctor's visit or simply by reading an article, you will learn about an underlying chronic condition which has been affecting you. Diverse puzzling physical symptoms that you thought were unrelated to each other can all be traced to this previously undiagnosed health issue. You may even gain insight into certain emotional concerns you have had or behavioral traits you have tried unsuccessfully to stem. Do not worry. See a competent specialist or alternative medical practitioner who will provide the proper remedies. This matter doesn't involve anything fatal. You may, however, be more than surprised when you first learn this information. Rest assured. This discovery will help you manage the problem and the symptoms will occur less frequently.

A revelation of another sort will probably take place toward the end of the month. A close friend of yours may confide a secret to you. What your pal reveals will probably relate to his/her past. She/he will likely swear you to secrecy. If you can't keep a secret, say so before the person relates their story. If it's too late and they have spilled the beans, make it your business not to share what he/she tells you with anyone - not even your most trusted intimates.

## GOAT August 2014

August brings a major crossroads for Goats. Your partner is offered an exciting opportunity in another state. Perhaps she/he has a scholarship to go back to school or it might be a spanking new job. They ask you to move with him/her. You will have to weigh the pros and cons on each side. On the one hand, you would be leaving your job as well as your support system of friends and family. This means you could end up relying completely on your significant other while living in a place entirely unfamiliar to you. This could result in a similar situation to the one where you felt uncomfortable and out of place with your honey's group of friends. Why not try living apart and visiting each other frequently for the first few months?

On the other hand, you are strongly attached to your lover. You fear that long-distance relationships rarely last long. But leaving your current home would put you out of reach of that stalker ex. Also, if that vengeful former lover has put a strain on your other social relationships, it may be best to start fresh somewhere else. Investigate what opportunities are available for you in this new location. Are there jobs in your field? Do you have contacts in the creative community there? In other words, if you decide to move away to live with your main squeeze, do so in stages.

If you quarreled with that wealthy friend of yours back in May, the two of you are likely to reconcile around the 20ᵗʰ. He/she will extend an olive branch but will not offer a complete *mea culpa*. You will both have to make concessions in order to revive the friendship. Don't let your surly side get the better of you. Compromise is the engine that drives longevity in any type of relationship.

The last four to five days of this month may bring you a series of unusual dreams. While in a deep REM state, you might find yourself having sex with someone you can't stand in real life. Or you may be standing at the altar with a dead celebrity. Perhaps that bullying ex-boss will serve you a dish of ice cream topped with grasshoppers. Dreams exist so our subconscious can express itself while we are not awake to quash it. The notions which rise to the surface are always fanciful and sometimes terrifying as well.

## GOAT September 2014

Whether it is only your sweetie who is moving or both of you, there are liable to be some surprises and/or confusion involved in this transition. Perhaps you will find something you thought you lost years ago while you are packing. If it is only your partner who is departing, she/he may accidentally take something along which belongs to you. The movers may arrive a day late at either end of the move. This could necessitate last minute arrangements for remaining in your old abode a bit longer. Or you may have to camp out in your new home for a while. Critical items like checkbooks or phones might, by a fluke, end up packed in a box beneath out-of-season clothing.

You will hear unhappy news about an older person around the 11ᵗʰ. She or he may be entering the final months or even last weeks of life. Hearing this will sadden you. You will also find that it falls to you to comfort and support a relative or friend directly impacted by the impending loss. Perhaps your mother is losing one of her parents. Or possibly your aunt or uncle's spouse has been diagnosed with a deadly ailment. Time to put aside family grievances. Offer kindness and compassion.

Another period of peak Goat sexual energy arrives around the 24th. If you moved, it may be that you and your partner are giving a sexual inauguration to every room in your new home. Maybe you're having fun unpacking those sex toys you purchased together a few months ago? If you remained behind while he/she moved, perhaps you pay a sultry visit. Or if you stayed behind, maybe you will find someone new to partake of your urge to relieve the sexual pressure as frequently as possible during this period. Wherever your current Goatly rutting takes place, do take time out to nourish yourself and get your chores done.

## GOAT October 2014

Mercury is retrograde throughout most of October (the 4th to the 25th). When mailing bill payments, allow extra time for possible postal delays. If you make a payment by telephone or online, be sure to record the confirmation number in case a computer hiccup results in some confusion. These kind of snags are more liable to occur when the planet which rules communication and transport heads. backwards. Don't be too chagrined either when electronic devices glitch and household appliances choose to go on the blink. It's all Mercury's fault.

You will have the opportunity to form several new friendships during the first ten days of October. Depending on which fork of your August crossroads you chose, these new pals could be local or maybe they are acquaintances in your new location. If that is the case, I strongly urge you to make some solo friends as well as couple friends. It's important for you not to become an appendage of your partner in this new locale. On the other hand, if you elected to remain in your old home, determine, as you form new relationships, whether or not you are open to new romance. If you and your recently moved away sweetie have decided to maintain a long distance relationship, be careful not to give the wrong signals to new pals.

No matter where you are, the third week of this month is likely to usher in a few new creative opportunities. Perhaps someone will see that mural you painted in your wealthy friend's living room and hire you to decorate the walls of their home or business. Or maybe that dress you designed and sewed for a good friend's wedding brings in tons of new orders. Maybe the photographs you displayed in a local coffeehouse earn you an invitation to participate in a group show at a gallery. Whatever you crave as a hobby or activity outside of work, this period is fertile for Goat creativity.

You will be asked to accompany someone, perhaps your partner or a close friend, to an event around the 28th. At this gathering you will have to do some fancy social footwork. A boorish individual will express some views you find abhorrent. Perhaps she/he will say something rankly bigoted. Unfortunately, this horrible person will turn out to be the spouse of someone very important to your friend or partner—maybe a boss or academic superior. You will have to place your words very deftly in order to stand up for your beliefs without causing a controversy that wreaks havoc in the life of the person who brought you to the party. Don't chicken out on your principles. But if the tone starts to mount, excuse yourself from the conversation to attend to an urgent call of nature.

## GOAT November 2014

That relative or acquaintance whose impending death was announced back in September is likely to pass away early this month. Make attending the funeral a priority. Even if you have moved house, try to go back and be there for the service. Your absence would make the loss even harder to bear for your mother, aunt or friend. If you are short of funds, the bereaved person will probably be willing to pay for your plane ticket.

Your partner is likely to be very busy right now adjusting to his/her new job or academic responsibilities. You may feel a bit neglected, especially if the two of you are now separated by thousands of miles. These feelings, combined with a sense of depression about other events in your life, might put you on edge. Some kind of blow-up between the two of you is possible around the 14th. Try to steer clear of a battle royal. Instead of letting tension build up, try to burn it off through physical activity. Sign up for some kind of movement class—anything from kickboxing to yoga.

If you can't afford a series of classes or a gym, go for long walks. Take your sketch pad with you and hike to a park a mile or more away from your home. Sit and draw something you see there. Nature is a tranquilizer.

Those pesky chronic symptoms may also recur now. Pressure can trigger them. It's important to follow the advice of your medical person and remember to take those medications regularly - not sporadically. Exercise and the right concoctions will quell the pains and stiffness promptly.

The name of someone you dated years ago may come up in a surprising way around the 29th. He or she is not exactly famous, but it is somehow connected to prominent people. Perhaps you will notice his/her name on the credits of a movie, listed as one of the crew members. Or an article you read about a well-known politician might contain a reference to the pol's aide who just happens to be your college boy or girlfriend. You wonder if you ought to contact that person to see if they remember you.

**GOAT December 2014**

Your attempts to placate your lover after your minor falling out may backfire around the 12th. Perhaps you paint the words "I'm sorry/I love you" on the sidewalk in front of the house, only to learn that city ordinance prohibits sidewalk painting and you get a fine. Maybe you will decide to send your sweetie a video apology via smart phone of you reciting a love poem while standing on your head naked. Unfortunately, your sweetie's boss is standing next to him/her when the message appears on the screen. Try to avoid this kind of snafu by balancing creativity with discretion.

You may receive a windfall toward the middle of this month. Possibly that recently deceased relative or acquaintance left you a small behest. Or maybe you get another commission for one of your creative projects. I know you might be tempted to spend all of this sum on holiday gifts as well as a few tasteful trinkets, toys and baubles for yourself. I suggest you use at least a portion of the money to establish more of a beachhead on financial security.

Around the 20th, you may notice some strange goings-on involving your neighbors. Something you see out of your window or while walking your dog may seem quite out-of-the-usual. You may feel tempted to check into the matter. You don't want to appear nosy. But perhaps you'll want to slap a bow on a box of cookies as a holiday gift, then ring the doorbell so you can ask a few questions. Or maybe you'll think about turning out your lights at night so you can more easily observe what is taking place in the brightly lit windows across the way. It's possible you will try to discuss what you see with other neighbors. Avoid letting your curiosity lead you to jump to conclusions. Unless you think someone is in real danger, do not interfere. If, however, your worst suspicions appear to be coming true - an abused child or spouse or even a pet being mistreated - don't be afraid to go to the authorities. Social services are there for a reason.

## GOAT January 2015

Does your partner have a habit that drives you crazy? Perhaps she/he squeezes the toothpaste tube from the middle. Or maybe your otherwise perfect lover consistently leaves the task of making the bed to you. It's possible some little thing she or he does unconsciously, like aimlessly humming a tuneless hum while sitting on the toilet, irritates you. On a day early in January when you are already feeling vexed, you might snap at your significant other about these little habits.

Considering the ways the stars are aligned right now, your critical remark could precipitate a major relationship battle. My advice, dear Goat, is to develop your own counter-habit to prevent an argument. Whenever you feel bothered by some minute aspect of your lover's personality, pull on a strand of your hair or bite your lip or twirl your fingers. Let this action serve as a reminder to you to pause before speaking. During that brief pause, decide whether the problem is really worth discussing. It's pick your battles time. If you must bring it up, choose a means of addressing the annoying habit that won't make your partner feel rejected or overly criticized.

January 2015 is a good month for taking a hard look at your wardrobe. Early in the month assess the strong parts of your wearing apparel and decide to chuck out the weaker elements. Accessories are often impulse buys and don't really go with anything you frequently wear. Get rid of that dumb tie with the eagle painted on it. Throw out those patterned stockings which make your legs look fat. Rid yourself of frivolous excess now so you can make room for a few good things to enter the closet. Take your time, but plan to acquire some quality new clothes.

There's some kind of class or workshop around the 18th of this month that is very important for you to take. This learning opportunity will benefit you a great deal. Both the content of the class and the contacts you make through it will prove invaluable to you in the coming months. Even if you are experiencing a period of financial scarcity, try to come up with the funds to participate in this course. Sell some old books or CD's. Sign up to be a paid research subject at a university or clinic in your area. Worse comes to worst, borrow the money. What you gain from the course will allow you to broaden your scope and increase your income considerably.

# MONKEY 2014
## OVERVIEW FOR THE WOOD HORSE YEAR

*Merry Monkey,*

*Your notorious problem-solving talent appeals strongly to the practical Horse. So nothing much stands in the way of Monkey progress this year. On the contrary, Monkeys will be encouraged the ply their variety of trades and manage things in their own clever way. Do not interfere with any Horse's trajectory. Do not take the wheel. When the car starts sliding toward the ditch, shut your eyes and whistle a happy tune. Horses do not like to be helped or corralled, hemmed in or criticized. And neither do you, Monkey mine. Obviously this is a big order for Monkey people who can see through almost any situation and always want to help out in a pinch. Horses get themselves into many a scrape.*

*My advice Monkeys? Stay out of it. Unless the Horse year begins reeling and staggering and threatening to bring down your very own house, stay the hell away from giving any advice or sticking your nose into complex situations. (If you are an in-law this advice is especially targeted to you) Let this year sort out its own difficulties. Go to all the parties you are asked to. Entertain your head off. But don't steal any scenes or try to take over where others have gotten there first (deals, relationships, business projects, inventions etc. as well). Your job this year is to ride in tandem at the hasty circuitous Horse year's hectic pace and not fall off the planet. sw*

━━━ ℯ ℯ℄ ℯ ℯ ━━━

## THE CHINESE YEAR AHEAD
## MONKEY 2014

### MONKEY February 2014

Mercury retrograde alert! I advise against making any life-changing commitments this month. Most of February—from the 6th until the 28th—is dominated by a Mercury retrograde period. Steer clear of signing contracts, or even making a lasting verbal "handshake" agreement". Wait to firm up contracts or pop the question to a sweetheart until at least the beginning of March.

You may experience an unusual encounter with some kind of critter around the 10th of this month. Perhaps your pet gerbil escapes its habitat and goes scampering across your bed. Or you encounter a snake slithering out of your toilet. Or maybe you'll walk out the door in the morning and discover a wild animal on your porch. Depending on where you live, it could be an alligator, a bear or a giant buck deer with huge horns. Even if you are a tad alarmed when you come upon this intruder, you will manage to contrive a witty adventure tale about its visit to entertain your friends. You are a Monkey after all. You know how to turn even the most harrowing experiences into lively stories.

You're likely to meet a fascinating person around the 17th. Could even be another Monkey. He or she may hail from a foreign country. Or maybe this scintillating individual simply lived abroad for several years. He/she has many fascinating anecdotes to share. If you are currently between partners, do snap this catch off the market immediately. You may have found the perfect companion who, although they might get under your skin and sometimes irritate you, they will never bore you.

You may become the target of a phone stalker around the 22nd. The calls are neither violent nor are they distasteful or lewd. Whoever it is calls you repeatedly and then hangs up. You have a strong suspicion about the source of these calls - that ex you dumped a while back wants your attention. The calls are not illegal or dangerous. However they are a nuisance, which is precisely what the caller intends. Could it be this person just wants some kind of closure? Use caller ID to confirm your suspicions. Then when you finally get them on the line, explain that you valued your time together. Gently make clear that it is best for both of you to move forward now. If the calls don't stop after this, you may be obliged to change your phone number - an even bigger nuisance perhaps. But sometimes necessary in dire cases.

## MONKEY March 2014

Another meeting of a group whose activities you enjoy is coming up around the 4th of this month. A person you dislike recently joined this group. You have tried subtly dissuading this individual from participating. You have attempted to exclude him/her from conversations. You may even have hosted private events where you invited everyone but this annoying character. Yet she/he just won't take the hint. Let go of your aversion. Consider this quote: "Every person you meet knows something you don't. Learn from them." Take this information as your personal challenge. Make an effort to discover this individual's hidden area of expertise or charm. Try actually listening to them, drawing them out. As disagreeable as it may seem at first, you may actually grow to like and appreciate this previously annoying person.

Around the 18th, you may purchase something at a thrift shop or a moving sale. It may be a jewelry box, a jacket or a book. Later you make a discovery about this item. Within a hidden compartment, or tucked inside a pocket or lodged between the pages, you find something of value. What will you do? Will you try to trace the original owner? If you purchased it at a charity shop, will you give the item back to them to sell and use the profits for their cause? Will you keep it for yourself? Give it as a gift? Ethics is a personal issue. Monkeys are not known for theirs.

You continue to spend time with your fascinating new friend/lover. Around the 23rd, the two of you may go on a brief journey together. It may be but a day trip. Or perhaps you spend a weekend out of town. During this excursion, you share an adventure which involves breaking rules in some way. Could be you will sneak into a place which is officially closed. Or you will park in a no parking zone - just to tempt the local cops into giving you a ticket. Whatever you do, your relationship should continue to be amusing and sexy.

## MONKEY April 2014

Your new main squeeze may ask a significant favor of you around the beginning of April. Perhaps she/he is experiencing a financial crisis and asks to borrow some money. Or maybe an emergency involving this individual's home necessitates them finding new digs for a while. Since the two of you spend so much time together, your place seems like the natural choice. Consider the upheaval a move-in would create in your current existence before accepting to share your digs. If you are tempted to help your sweetie with money, give rather than lend it. Better not to create obligations which can cause tension between you.

Around the 12th of this month, you will be moved to take up a new hobby or creative pursuit of some sort. Oddly enough, it will be an activity which formerly did not appeal to you. Perhaps you begin gardening or start writing poetry. Your enthusiasm for this new pastime grows rapidly. You may begin checking books about gardening out of the library. Or maybe you will attend a monthly poetry reading event at a local coffeehouse. This new sideline will soon become a passion. Remember to stick at it. Practice makes perfect.

A close friend you haven't seen in years returns to town around the 16th. The two of you renew your friendship. You go out for dinner together or perhaps meet for drinks. The two of you spend hours catching up with each other. Even though you have not been in touch for years, you feel immediately comfortable confiding in this person. She or he has had some surprising experiences since last time you met. You may discover that some of this person's creative projects dovetail with yours. You two may eventually collaborate on a brilliant new business scheme or web project.

At work there is an exciting new project on the docket the last week of this month. This assignment proves to be intellectually invigorating. Your co-workers cannot understand your enthusiasm. They find this project weird or even somewhat boring. Ignore their opinions. Continue to apply yourself to this effort. Its success may eventually point the way to a wholly new job or even enhance your new business venture.

## MONKEY May 2014

The beginning of May offers Monkeys the karmic equivalent of a double coupon day at the grocery store. Whatever good deeds you perform this month carry extra weight. For maximum karmic benefit, assist people geographically close to you. Look around and see which of your friends and neighbors could use a hand. Offer aid in whatever mode seems suitable. Perhaps a single mother in your area hasn't had any time off for months because she can't afford child care. Offer to pay for a sitter. Or go over and take care of the kids yourself. Give generously to a local charity. If there is a low-income family behind you in the checkout line, tell the cashier you want to pay for their purchases as well as your own. Or send an anonymous donation to someone you know who is ill but cannot afford a doctor.

After watching a movie around the 17th of May, you may be inspired to alter your appearance in some major way. Perhaps the protagonist's haircut, tattoos or piercings will appeal to you very strongly. Without waiting to consult anyone, you make an appointment at a hair salon or a piercing/tattooing parlor to emulate this character's style choices. The change is fairly dramatic. Some of the more conservative people at your office (not to mention your sweetheart) may do a double or triple take the first time they get a gander at your new look. Ultimately though, your boss values your intelligence enough to overlook this new statement of eccentricity. Your good friends offer enthusiastic compliments. And your honey? Let's hope he or she will not get snagged on the silver ring in your tongue.

Two people in your social or work circle may announce their impending nuptials this month. Unfortunately, you consider at least one of these people to be a bit of a pain in the posterior. Contribute generously to a pitch-in gift to be given by the gang. But arrange to be out of town the day of the wedding. Let everyone think your trip stems a longstanding commitment or family obligation.

## MONKEY June 2014

Mercury goes retrograde again this month (June 7 until July 1). That often means re-thinking - particularly with regard to relationships. During the first week of June, you may learn something unpleasant about that delightful new friend/lover of yours. Perhaps a whispered conversation reveals that he or she misrepresented the reasons for needing that loan or a place to stay. Or could be this individual reacts angrily when you refer to the two of you as a couple. Suddenly you perceive your lover or friend in a new and rather negative light. You feel hurt and betrayed. Look back carefully at previous interactions with them. What signals or red flags did miss? Examine your reasons for choosing to ignore some aspects of your paramour's behavior. Love is often blind. Until we are brutally frank with ourselves about our misconceptions, we may repeat certain self-deluding patterns over and over again.

A friend of yours may host a big bash around the 20th of the month. At this party, you are likely to meet someone who makes his/her admiration for you very evident. This person may be a generation older or younger than you. You are flattered by the compliments this attractive individual gives you. He or she clearly has a crush. You may decide to indulge in a fling with her or him. Be careful, though. There's also a strong possibility you will overdo things at this party. Obviously, if you faint and/or get sick during the shindig, this person's interest in you will be significantly diminished.

You may hear news around the 29th of June that your childhood home has been involved in a damaging incident. Could be fire or flood or even a break-in with vandalism. You will feel saddened and perhaps bit shaken up by this news. It doesn't look like anyone will be hurt. You may however lose a few family photographs and keepsakes.

Northern hemisphere residents will be enjoying backyard picnics and barbecues at this time. Caution is advised around bodies of water. Those of you in the Southern climes are in the middle of winter sports and experiencing chilly days and nights. The planets are aligned in such a way now that Monkeys may experience accidents due to extreme weather patterns. Keep your eyes peeled on local meteorological reports so as not to fall victim to the unexpected.

**MONKEY July 2014**

Early July may find you contemplating the purchase of a new vehicle, perhaps after a long period of driving an old car or relying on public transportation. Determine in advance how much you can afford to spend. If you belong to a credit union, that institution may be your best choice for financing. Do your research online to choose the best car or van for you. Consult independent consumer advice websites, not just auto manufacturers' information. Narrow your choices to three or four well-reviewed vehicles before visiting any dealerships. When you go in for some test drives, don't hesitate to haggle a bit about price. With the right kind of persuasive Monkey dialogue, you will be in for a very pleasant surprise.

Your car shopping trip may yield more than a new vehicle. There's a good chance you will meet another new admirer. Perhaps another client looking for a new car will strike up a conversation. Could be a car salesman/woman will ask for your e-mail address or phone number. Give out your e-mail willingly. But until you know this person better, don't relinquish your cell or home number. Certain phone stalkers and even excessive phone talkers can become huge bothers.

Your new hobby or creative pastime continues to reward and delight you. Perhaps the first crops from your garden will blossom. Or you recite some of your poems at that monthly event, receiving praise from other poets. Your mild success encourages you to delve deeper into this activity around the middle of July. You may decide to create a raised bed in your yard for growing different kinds of plants. Or maybe you submit one or two of your poems to an anthology editor and hear positive news about publication.

An elderly relative needs your help again. He or she may be at risk for some kind of health problem due to prescription medicines. Could be that multiple physicians have prescribed pills for this person without knowledge of the other medications she/he is taking. A nefarious reaction could result. Make sure you have a family practice doctor thoroughly review your family member's health picture before the end of the month.

## MONKEY August 2014

Be prepared for a slightly awkward encounter early this month. Looks like you might run into an ex. This individual may be someone you parted from on rather unpleasant terms. He or she will be accompanied by someone whose presence will render the chance meeting even more uncomfortable. If your ex left you for another lover, it may just be that person. Or if your relationship with this ex began with him/her leaving a partner for you, he or she may have reunited with that person. If you are gay or bisexual, there's also a possibility that two of your exes are now a couple. Don't show your discomfort. Smile politely. Keep your greetings brief and diplomatic. Resist any temptation to indulge in snide comments or remarks about who is now with whom. Put the incident behind you as quickly as you can.

Your visit with your elderly kin last month may have clued you in to another potential problem in his/her life. Is someone trying to take advantage of this older person in some way? Perhaps a sweet young thing in his/her 50s is trying to wiggle into matrimony with your 80-something relative. Or could be a social worker or elder-care volunteer has been going through your aged relative's things scouting for valuables to sell. Your elderly relative's feelings of isolation and loneliness make him/her vulnerable. Dig into the details and attempt to put a stop to this situation. Getting to the bottom of the real story may prove difficult. The senior citizen in question may actually enjoy the company of this gold digger. If possible, arrange to make more frequent surprise visits to the person's home. Perhaps enlist another relative to assist you by popping in from time to time as well.

At work, that unusual assignment you completed earlier in the year reaps you an unusual reward. Perhaps the client involved calls and tries to hire you away from your employer. Or maybe one of your colleagues plans to leave the firm and wants you to come along to their new company. You will definitely have some major decision-making to do at the end of August.

## MONKEY September 2014

Looks like you'll meet a new (serious) romantic partner this month. This person promises to be much more than another casual fling. Coincidences and similarities will abound in your connection. The two of you may discover you went to the same concert years ago and sat three rows apart. Your sister may have dated your new sweetie's neighbor back in high school. Perhaps the two of you went to the same summer camp as children. Maybe you both named your first pet after the same TV character. The serial serendipity you register together will bring you rapidly closer to one another and create an environment of more than just passion. Friendship is a great way to start a love affair.

Your relationship with this new love interest is likely to progress very rapidly. You may adjourn to the bedroom after flirting over coffee for two or three hours. After the simmering heat of your first lovemaking, one of you may even want to suggest a commitment or at least moving in together very soon. This new lover may have a job which involves children in some way. Or this person may be a parent of young children. Monkeys are known to love romping with children. There is much promise in this new bond. Don't take it lightly.

The last week of the month provides a propitious time to introduce this new romantic partner of yours to friends. Host some kind of get-together so your pals get to meet him/her. Don't bother making it fancy or posh. Have a potluck supper to keep the work load minimal. Why not invite everyone over to watch a favorite old movie you all love? You will be heartened if your new lover gets along swimmingly with your gang. If they don't, you should take a step backwards and look more carefully at what you are about to get involved in. If our friends like the new person as much as we do, it's a positive sign. If they don't, it could be a wake-up call.

### MONKEY October 2014

You may begin to sense a slowdown during the last week of September. After October 4th, that molasses-like pace will become even more pronounced as Mercury goes retrograde. You Monkeys prefer the company of quick-witted people and fast, easy travel. Mercury retrograde periods are often especially frustrating for you. Use your sense of humor to see the comical side of this slow-motion period. Not to worry. Mercury goes direct again on the 25th.

Someone in your social circle may seek your advice around the 8th. This person confides in you about an awkward dilemma he or she is in. You may be strongly tempted to share this news as it's a juicy piece of gossip. This would be a bad idea. Your friends who enjoy gossip will only spread the news. After all, the person who told you about the problem did "confide" in you. That means they expect you to keep their business quiet. Don't be tempted to lack discretion now. Otherwise, people who do not share your proclivity for telling tales will be more shocked by your loose-lipped impropriety than at the news you impart.

Toward the 15th, your new honey asks you to make some kind of physical change in yourself to please her/him. Perhaps your lover suggests that you lose or gain a few pounds. Maybe she/he asks you to wax your pubic hair. Or else your lover wants the two of you to get tattoos of each other's names. You will have to decide whether the alteration your sweetheart wants is something you want to do. Or if perhaps the relationship is not strong enough to warrant such a gesture.

A good friend of yours has been less vivacious than usual. She or he has been behaving in an almost anti-social manner. They're turning down invitations, not picking up phone messages or returning e-mails. You sincerely wonder if this old pal is becoming too remote to remain part of your inner circle. You will certainly feel a bit sheepish when they announce the reason for their odd behavior in the last week of this month. It might be that your buddy has a serious illness or a member of their family has one. Could be cancer or another potentially fatal disease. Offer this friend as much moral support as you can. And perhaps you can drive him or her to and from treatments or find them a reputable specialist for a second opinion. Rally a group of friends who can help this person with the everyday life chores such as house cleaning and pet care.

### MONKEY November 2014

You may find it difficult to focus on work the first week of November. Your projects seem tedious. People at the office grate on your nerves. They are petty and irritating. You wonder how they manage to keep on living such stultifying lives. Everything seems to repeat on an endless loop. You feel like one of those hamsters riding on a perpetual wheel. Perhaps it's time to give more serious consideration to that offer you received a few months ago. You would, of course, lose the security of the current job. But the challenge of a change would certainly be less tiresome. If you are up to it, create your own challenge. Start a whole new business.

A neighborhood gathering around the 12th could be a bit of a trial for you. Most of the people present have diametrically opposite political viewpoints from yours. They express their opinions openly and tactlessly. They have no consideration for the fact that others present may have a different point of view. They use negative expressions to characterize everyone who disagrees with them. They obviously think none of "those people" are present. Use your wit and intelligence to express your own views clearly and succinctly. Demolish their misinformed notions with a few well-placed truths. Then change the subject, offering a conversational olive branch. Hand out a few insincere compliments to make amends. After all, these folks are your neighbors. You may have to mince a few words so as not to alienate them. In future, you will know from whom to keep your distance.

Some worrisome financial news comes to you around the 20th. You may hear that a legal or insurance matter failed to go your way. You had assumed this decision was in the bag and have already mentally earmarked the funds you thought were coming in for sure. Will you have to re-think that dream purchase or trip you had planned? Maybe not. All is not lost. Turns out the legal matter or insurance claim issue has not been closed - just postponed.

## MONKEY December 2014

You could be in for a pinch of embarrassment around the 11th. A while back, you formed a strong dislike for someone you knew socially. You decided this person must be a phony. Perhaps you even took it upon yourself to unmask him or her. This individual may have casually mentioned something in passing about his/her past. Or they boasted about graduating from a particular university or serving in the military. You attempted to check up on this information and subsequently told several people that the educational institution or military branch in question knew nothing of this individual. Now the very same person you dubbed "phony" has rung you up to offer you a gift or a new job or some kind of unusually kind favor. Do you feel like a fool? I'll bet you do.

Many Monkeys will find themselves surrounded by a powerful force field of luck around the 15th-18th of December. If you buy any lottery tickets, you are likely to win. If not the jackpot, you will garner at least a small amount. You may want to schedule a trip to a nearby racetrack or casino. Just be sure not to bet more than you can afford to lose. The planets are providing you with an opportunity, not a guarantee.

Thoughts of mortality may dominate your thoughts around the 27th. Perhaps it is the illness of a friend, or just your awareness of the passage of time. Either way, you may find yourself dwelling on thoughts about the brevity of life and the constant proximity of death. You may express these gloomy thoughts to others through joshing quips. Your tone however betrays an underlying sense of uncharacteristic gloominess as 2015 approaches.

One thing you haven't been working on enough of late is the state of your health and well-being. Because you are preoccupied with dark thoughts of late, I invite you to take up a spiritual pursuit or at least start yoga or tai chi classes. You need to empty your Monkey mind for awhile. Take a holiday from your anxieties by embracing activities which increase calm, quiet your nerves and teach you to concentrate on gaining peace of mind.

## MONKEY January 2015

You may discover by accident early this month that a recent gift you received was colored by some ambivalence on the part of the giver. Perhaps the giver re-gifted an unwanted present they got from someone else. Maybe you learn the designer perfume or "authentic" artwork you were given is actually a cheap knockoff. This discovery, although not serious, is infuriating. You do not fancy being taken for a simpleton. Of course you can't say anything to the person who offered you the poisoned present. But you can throw is in the dustbin and forget you ever held it in your hand.

Around the 17$^{th}$, you will feel itchy for some sort of change in your abode. Choose your favorite color and paint one wall of your bedroom that shade. Buy sheets and pillowcases in a hue which matches or even contrasts with the paint. Visit an antique store or thrift shop and look for some delightful item which will enhance the room. Perhaps a vase or a small framed print. If you're handy, why not make some curtains or hang just the right amount of framed drawings, prints or paintings? The effort will be worth it. You will once again have made your house your home.

You may still be mulling over that career move you contemplated last month. In the meantime, the miasma of boredom you faced then may linger on, possibly even obscuring your judgment. Sternly resist any temptation you may feel to "liven up" the office with practical jokes. Your Monkey business could backfire on you. The same goes for the kind of subtle-insults-embedded-in-compliments you pride yourself on delivering with your engaging smile. If you persist in indulging in prankish behavior, you may leave this dull job under a cloud. Recognize your boredom and your desire to raise a little office hell as symptoms of stress. Schedule an extra yoga class during your lunch break. Take a mental health day away from the office. Spend time doing whatever makes you feel relaxed and content. As the Goat year approaches, true peace of mind is a goal you must earnestly pursue.

# ROOSTER 2014
## OVERVIEW FOR THE WOOD HORSE YEAR

*Resilient Rooster,*

*By this time, with all that went down over the past few months, your love life ought to be back on its feet (and you up off your knees). One thing Roosters tend not to do is listen. You act and manage and run things efficiently. You remain alert and on schedule. But you sometimes miss out because you think you know it all and you don't want to hear any new stuff which might clutter up your synapses and/or cause you to have to change your ways. Listen up. The Horse year is a workaholic's dream. You are a labor intensive person. Even if you were retired, you would be Doing something. Cooking, reading three books at once, gardening, jogging, building or . . . shopping. You are a kind of renaissance person who likes to have a finger in every pie and an iron in all the fires.*

*Your active nature suits the Horse's temperament down to the ground. If you continue to forge so avidly ahead on all your projects, you will meet with no obstacles to progress this year. Family squabbles crop up here and there during Horse years. You can't sort them out so don't tire yourself trying. Illness may strike a loved one. Hold hands and speak soothing words of comfort. Nothing like solid support from a sturdy Rooster pal to boost one's morale. Eat more protein. Cut back on sugar. Take longer walks in leafier places. Being one with nature calms the harried Rooster spirit. sw*

———————— ꞏꞏ·ꞏ ————————

## THE CHINESE YEAR AHEAD
## ROOSTER 2014

### ROOSTER February 2014

The Chinese New Year may find you newly unemployed. You might have disputed your boss's unfair policies toward workers. Your employer retaliated by summarily firing you - on a very slim pretext. Looks like you might be consulting with attorneys about suing the firm. Make sure they kicked in for your unemployment insurance as well. In the meantime, keep working on your podcast, book or blog. Fortunately your significant other makes enough money to support the household right now. They can hold the fort financially - at least for awhile. In return, you can pitch in with household duties and take care of grocery shopping - even cooking.

Eager though you are to crusade against your evil former employer, avoid going to court this month. Mercury, the planet of communication, is retrograde from the 6th until the 28th. This planetary glitch could cause your lawyer to miss some crucial point in presenting your case. Or it could turn out the judge is in favor of the big corporations and not for the little guy - you!. Stay out of court till Mercury goes direct.

You want to earn money again, but you find the job hunt stultifying. Maybe your resume isn't conveying your true level of talent. Try not to be discouraged by the frequent rejections. The few job offers you do receive are simply not up your alley. You will spend too much time watching movies and television as well as reading political news online and listening to the vast, diverse selection of music on your iPod. You frequently hold forth about your opinions on all of these subjects on your Facebook page. Not to worry. This period of stasis is temporary. The job search may be redundant by April.

I know you usually pooh-pooh the sentimentality of Valentine's Day. But this year make an effort. Do something romantic to show your appreciation for your partner's patience and support. He or she finds you fascinating and sexy. But let's face it. It's not easy to carry the financial load for both of you. On February 14, find an opportunity to pamper your sweetie. Cook their favorite meal. Give them a foot massage. Instead of imposing your listening and watching tastes, put on your honey's favorite music or watch their favorite show with them.

## ROOSTER March 2014

The good news is that your creative project will likely gain support of some sort around the 5th. Perhaps your blog or podcast receives a favorable mention on an important website. Or a friend may help you find an agent for your book. You feel encouraged. You have always wanted work that showcased your true talent and allowed you to focus on your personal interests. Because you are not really interested in a JOB per se, your employment history has been a series of unfulfilling slaveries. Most of them paid too little. Many of them ended acrimoniously. Keep focusing on your own projects. Visualize a positive outcome.

You may land in a bit of social hot water around the 13th of March. You will express one of your controversial opinions either too strongly or in the wrong context. Perhaps one of your Facebook posts irks people. Even some of your close friends, who usually admire your candor, think you behaved boorishly. Your partner advises you to pour oil on the waters. But you stubbornly persist giving everyone a piece of your mind. As far as you are concerned, you are doing them a favor by enlightening them. You know that attitude smacks of arrogance. But you can't help yourself. You're a Rooster.

After the 22nd of the month, you could be scheming how to purchase yourself a new toy. Perhaps you have your eye on a new version of the iPhone or some other shiny techno gadget. Or maybe the latest gear for your favorite hobby or sport. Your significant other refuses to pay for it, arguing that she/he is already shouldering all the major expenses. You dream up myriad schemes for moneymaking but thus far, none of them gain traction.

Toward the end of the month you may become involved in aiding someone else. A friend or former co-worker may be experiencing some kind of crisis related to paying for health care. Perhaps this person has been diagnosed with a serious ailment, but has no health insurance. Or this individual may have recently taken in a disabled relative, but lacks the funds to convert their home to wheelchair friendly status. You are moved by this person's plight. It looks like you might initiate a Facebook page or a Kickstarter program to raise funds to help out your pal. You may find that you are gifted for fund raising. Could it be a new career path?

## ROOSTER April 2014

Your partner may be miffed with you around the 6th. She or he took you to a function related to her/his workplace. You made a few sarcastic remarks on the way to this event about the lack of physical appeal among your sweetie's co-workers. Then when you arrived, you struck up a conversation with the boss's spouse. You virtually trapped this poor person in a corner while you raved about one of your passions. The spouse, a gentle soul, nodded politely which misled you into believing she actually cared about whichever of your current enthusiasms you expounded upon—the films of Quentin Tarantino, or Dr. Who or the French Revolution or atheism. Maybe you should cease arguing that your pet subject is something everyone should know about. Roosters have a tendency to want to share their enthusiasms when they should button their lips.

Apologize to your miffed partner. And next time you attend an official DO, promise to think before you gush.

Your creative project, which you hope will eventually evolve into a stream of income, may stall again around the 16th. Is it possible you have been too wrapped up in your own concerns to oil the gears of networking? Open up your storehouse of compliments. Spread praise and thanks all around. The friend-of-a-friend agent who is taking time to look at your book is not obligated to do so. Send an e-mail expressing your appreciation. Nor are your friends required to listen to your podcast or post favorable comments on your blog. Take the time to ask about the progress of their own projects. Develop a strong network. Weave a web of mutual support.

There's a strong probability you'll be plagued by headaches around the 25th. This may be more than just the stress of unemployment. Get your eyes checked. You might need glasses. If you already wear glasses, your prescription may have to be changed. Perhaps you need bifocals or progressives. The latter will correct both distance and close vision. The former will eventually cause you neck problems from raising and lowering your head every two seconds. Consult an up-to-date ophthalmologist before buying new prescription glasses. With the right correction, your headaches will disappear.

## ROOSTER May 2014

Your partner feels the need for a change of scenery around the 10th. He/she proposes a trip. Although your significant other is willing to foot the bill so the two of you can enjoy a getaway together, you may feel a bit cranky at first. You don't want to take time away from job-hunting. The truth is your partner's largesse makes you uncomfortably aware of your financially dependent situation. Now that you do not have a job to go to everyday, you are free to spend your hours on your creative project. Yet now you feel a bit trapped in your relationship. You cannot afford to break up with your significant other. This realization makes you antsy. You appreciate your partner supporting you. But you also find yourself more drawn to casual flirtations. I suggest you go on this vacation with your partner. Concentrate on appreciating your sweetie's best qualities. Set aside any regrets about not being able to participate financially. Any edginess you feel is due to your current, rather dismal, economic situation. It has little or nothing to do with your partner's faults.

Around the 17th, you may get good news in your battle against your former employer. Perhaps the authorities at the unemployment office have agreed with you that you are entitled to unemployment benefits. Or maybe your lawyer has some good news for you as well in your wrongful termination suit.

You may run into an old friend while you are out with your partner around the 24th. The two of you were buddies years ago when you were a different person than the one you have become. Unfortunately, unlike you, your old pal has not matured. He or she may say something offensive to or about your significant other. Then and there, you want to point out the very good reason why the two of you are no longer friends. He or she thinks being bluntly critical is funny. You do not. They like to mock others and you no longer engage in such petty cruelty. Once you have made your position clear, shake hands with your old pal and be on your merry way.

## ROOSTER June 2014

Your fundraising efforts for that sick or disabled friend were highly successful. You are pleased that your efforts have truly aided this person. You realize that this friend is going through a most difficult time. You feel genuinely glad that you have helped make this person's life will be a little bit easier. Unfortunately, when she/he calls to thank you the first week in June, you may put your foot in your mouth. Perhaps you imply something dumb such as that people "give themselves cancer". Or you thoughtlessly use the word "lame" to mean "weak" or "unintelligent." This person may not upbraid you because he/she feels grateful for the money you helped raise. But someone who overhears the conversation, perhaps your partner, points out your lapse. Don't go all defensive. Remember that life is a learning experience. Resolve, once again, to watch your words more carefully in future.

These foot-in-mouth situations are one of the hazards of Mercury retrograde. In addition to cautioning my clients against signing contracts or undergoing surgery at these times, I also remind them to hold their tongues in check. This is especially true for signs as prone to bluntness as yours, Rooster mine. This month's Mercury retrograde begins on the 7th of June, Mercury does not go direct again until the 1$^{st}$ of July.

During the second week of June, you are likely to get some good news about your creative project. Perhaps that agent has decided to submit your book to a publisher. Maybe your blog, podcast or video is nominated for some type of award.

The following week, however, your partner may start to gently nag you about job-hunting. You have been unemployed for several months now. You have not had any job interviews in a while. Your partner might not realize it, but the stream of resumes you started sending out in February has slowed to a trickle. You haven't even told him/her about the couple of job offers you turned down just after you were fired. Those potential jobs seemed too demeaning. You will have to get serious now about finding new employment. You can't pin all your hopes on the possible success of your book, blog or podcast. Perhaps the solution is to leverage that creative project to find a real job.

Trying not to sound too motherly, I strongly advise that change your attitude and take a job. Not just any job. But almost. The routine of getting up and out in the morning, working for your money and being in a situation where there is hope for promotion is key to your equilibrium and that of your couple. Re-entering a work environment will give you back some of the self-confidence you lost when you lost your job.

## ROOSTER July 2014

A close friend confides a secret in you around the 7$^{th}$ of June. It turns out she/he is cheating on a longtime lover. You have mixed reactions. Part of you disapproves of your friend's deceitful behavior. But another side feels a bit envious. The jealousy you feel of your friend's sexual adventures may be heightened by the fact that you have been offered one or two opportunities to cheat recently. So far, you have turned down these chances. But you feel tempted because the people who offer you these dalliances heap compliments upon you. They may be fans of your blog or podcast. Or perhaps they are Facebook friends who have taken to posting flirtatious comments on your page. You are not sure you want to give up the security of your relationship. Yet compliments, for you, are like a drink of water to someone crossing the desert. Praise is key now. But you worry. Is it merited?

You are a practical person. And you like to do things right. As much as your ego is boosted by the praise and kudos you are receiving from outsiders, you know the path to personal security lies in the real world where people work hard for their money and don't cat around cheating on their lovers. So you get back to sending out piles of resumes and by month's end you receive a pleasant surprise.

A resume you sent out last month nets you a job interview for a not-so-bad position. You secretly feel a bit surprised they even called you. You didn't think you were really qualified for the position. This might not be precisely your dream job but it's only one or two ladder rungs shy of it. Prepare for this interview as if you were a star athlete training for the Olympics. Make sure you have the perfect clothes. Beg or borrow better duds if everything in your closet makes you look like a minimum wage worker. Get a haircut. Practice answering some tough interview questions so that you don't have to hem and haw. Call your references to make sure they feel ready to rave about your skills.

### ROOSTER August 2014

The second or third week of August you will probably re-join the ranks of the gainfully employed. You clinched that interview last month. The salary is much better than your last job. You make enough that you can finally buy that toy whose purchase you've been postponing since early this year. However, this new position also demands a higher degree of professionalism than that dead-end job you held last year. You will probably have to invest some of your paycheck in more impressive work attire. You are also likely to discover that in return for your higher salary, you are expected to put in longer hours than at your last job. Even good news often requires a few adjustments.

Your partner is delighted that you have landed a job more suited to your skills. He/she is also relieved not to be the sole breadwinner in the household any longer. Your unemployment may have been harder for your significant other than you realize. Your sweetie may have foregone a few personal luxuries in order to keep the household ship afloat. Now that you have a regular paycheck again, plan something special for your partner. Perhaps you can treat her/him to dinner at an elegant restaurant. Buy them a gift certificate to his/her favorite store or, now that you are feeling more confident about yourself, share an extra snuggle or two.

Around the 25th, you are likely to get some family news. You have been estranged from one of your close relatives for a while. Now that person is dying. This individual hurt you very deeply. You still bear the scars of the words and actions he/she inflicted upon you when you were too young to protect yourself. Other relatives try to persuade you to visit the hospital. You angrily refuse, claiming that the dying person is evil. Secretly, you fear that old wounds will re-open and bleed uncontrollably if you so much as see this individual. Without inventing some huge lie, bow out of that death bed scene. Just say NO. Unless you would get pleasure out of watching them suffer, let the person die without you. This person only ever did you harm. No need to inflict more pain on yourself by renewing acquaintance at the end of their life.

### ROOSTER September 2014

Your partner may strongly suggest that the two of you find a new home around the beginning of September. He or she may feel that your old place is too small or too far from work. Go hunting with your significant other for a new house or apartment. You will enjoy looking at possible new abodes. You will likely find the prospect of this change exciting. Deciding on a new place to live together will re-cement the bond you two have created over the years. These forays into the world of real estate will definitely bring you two closer together.

By the middle of September you have developed an awareness of the key players in your new workplace. You have, so to speak, gotten to know the lay of the land at your new job. Some degree of patience will be in order. A co-worker is confident to the point of boastfulness. Yet they do possess a great deal of charisma that makes their bold behavior seem appealing. Although this individual is too arrogant to stoop to sexual harassment, he or she has clearly conveyed their strong attraction to you. You know you should remain faithful to your partner who supported you through unemployment. Yet at times you feel an almost magnetic attraction to this co-worker. Don't act on these feelings just yet. Further acquaintance with this person may reveal an unpleasant layer to her/his personality.

On the other hand, you and another co-worker loathed each other at first sight. This person's voice affects you like nails on chalkboard. He or she criticizes every idea you propose. Unfortunately, you might have to depend on this individual in some way. Possibly he or she is assigned to bring you up to speed on some of your assignments. You may even have to share an office with him/her. Avoid letting things descend into open hostility between the two of you. But protect your privacy. Don't make any personal phone calls when he or she is within earshot. Make sure this character doesn't learn the pass code for your laptop or smartphone. Beware office politics - especially the beginning of a new job. You may not know it, but you are being tested. Keep your nose in the air, get your work done and be as agreeable as possible.

**ROOSTER October 2014**

Mercury retrograde again! It starts on October 4th. Please do not sign any binding documents or legal papers until after the 25th. Wait until the first or even second week of November. Anything you sign now is likely to require revision at a later date. Expect delays in transport and glitches with electronic devices.

Children will occupy much of your time away from the office this month. If you have offspring, perhaps you throw yourself with renewed enthusiasm into your parenting duties. Or a busy friend or neighbor may ask you to help out by watching their kids. You may find these babysitting responsibilities less onerous than you expect. Perhaps you discover that you and one of these children share an enthusiasm for a particular video game or action movie series.

Take a new approach with that detractor at your office the week of the 11th. Try killing him/her with kindness. When you go out for coffee, bring one back for them. If she/he forgets to bring an umbrella on a rainy day, offer yours. You can make this person understand that you know they have been testing you. Thank them (sarcastically) for giving you dirty looks every time you pass in the halls and for snitching on you when you took an extra half hour for lunch. Every time you do them a favor, mention how much you appreciate how they have annoyed you. Soon, they will share the joke and join the ranks of your allies.

A friend of yours who had been joyfully anticipating a new arrival will experience disappointment around October 18th. It may be either a miscarriage or a stillbirth. This individual and their partner both want very much to become parents. This sad event shakes them to the core emotionally. Express support and sympathy. Avoid suggesting that they try again. Give them time to grieve this loss. This couple has been trying to become parents for several years. This is not the first time life has dealt them this kind of blow.

You and your partner may find the perfect new home around the 22nd. Your partner is very excited. You also feel happy yet you also have some reservations. You realize this move represents a kind of re-commitment to your partnership. You aren't sure you want to close off other options. A new house to share represents a huge mutual decision. It can cause untold trouble in a couple's life. Many of the basic new house decisions which arise will be dicey. He likes red wallpaper. You prefer sky blue. She wants a real staircase. You prefer a simple ladder-like affair. Think long and hard before agreeing to move house.

## ROOSTER November 2014

Despite your differences of opinion, simple economics dictate that your and you companion are likely to move during the first half of this month. On moving day, the two of you will be exhausted. You may order some kind of take-out food and dine amidst piles of boxes. Something about the novelty of being in a new place may put you in an amorous mood. You and your partner have sex on the floor of every room in your new abode. Then you leave body-prints on the walls of the shower. You arrive slightly late to work the next day with your cheeks flushed and your eyes glittering. Both your rival and that seductive co-worker examine you more closely than usual.

Your cheating friend gets caught around the 21$^{st}$ of November. Perhaps his/her significant other actually discovers the cheaters mid-coitus. Or your pal may just caught in an egregious lie. This could well turn into one of those feces hitting the fan situations. Your buddy and his/her spouse will stage a bitter argument. Other people in your social circle will take sides. You may even come in for a share of the blame for knowing about your friend's deceit and failing to tell her/his partner. Whatever they say, you did the right thing by keeping mum. No real friend rats on a pal. You knew, of course, that sooner or later the truth would out and the culprit would be caught. But at least their getting busted was not of your doing.

A casual exchange of e-mails between you and a sibling, cousin or other relative could turn into a political disagreement around the 29$^{th}$. This person will may send you a link to an article in the news. At first the two of you find common ground, seeing something humorous in this story. Then your relative will say something you find offensive. You will respond by making it clear you are on the opposite side of the issue. Try not to let the discussion escalate into an angry exchange of words. Rather than openly castigating the other person for having different views than yours, you can agree to disagree. Nonetheless, you are never going to feel quite the same way about this relative whose ideas are not really ideas, but rank prejudices.

## ROOSTER December 2014

A workplace holiday party could get out of hand around the middle of this month. The addition of alcohol to the tricky interactions between you and your co-workers may have some surprising results. You won't be entirely surprised when that arrogant yet seductive individual has one too many glasses of champagne and finally makes her/his overture to you more explicit. What may rock you back on your heels is an odd expression of some kind of hate-lust from your rival. Remember that workplace affairs are messy even at the best of times. If one or both parties involved are already in committed relationships, the potential for negative consequences increases exponentially. Steer clear.

A further complication may result from this party. There is a strong possibility your direct supervisor will make an ill-considered joke after a few drinks. The wording of her/his clumsy attempt at humor may rub you the wrong way. You might be itching to lash out with a sharp retort. Refuse to give in to this impulse lest you find yourself unemployed again very soon. Keep smiling - no matter what. And remember which side your bread is buttered on.

You and your partner may attend another holiday gathering together shortly after this office party. You will head for a dinner party at the home of someone who lives outside of your town. There's a strong chance that the drive to this destination will be characterized by some sort of confusion. You or your mate may mix up the dates. It's also highly possible you'll get the address wrong. You could end up lost on some lonely country road. Weather conditions such as fog or snow could worsen this situation. The frustration of getting off-course could cause you and your significant other to bicker. Plan the trip carefully in advance to avoid this possibility. Double-check the time of the event as well as the address. Bring a GPS or at least a good map.

As the western calendar year draws to a close, you will be in a much better position than you were when 2014 began. The Horse has made you jump through a few hoops. But you made it. Safe and sound in your new digs with a healthy new attitude about your future.

## ROOSTER January 2015

So long as you didn't throw caution to the winds at last month's office party, this should be an excellent month for you career-wise. An idea you present gains the support of your superiors. You are invited to lunch with people a few rungs above you on the ladder. You seem to be on the inside track. That rival of yours seems to be occupied with some crisis in her/his personal life. She or he has no energy to spend on trying to trip you up. Your rejection of that boldly confident superior of yours seems to have knocked the wind out of him/her. Instead of appearing resentful, this formerly cocky person is even a bit abashed.

Someone may come to you around the 9th with an offer related to that creative project you nurtured last year. The proposal will come wrapped in flattery, which always tends to open your ears. Caution is advised here however. This individual may be a con artist of some kind. Possibly he/she is trying to ride on the coattails of your talent. Perhaps this person is offering to publish your book in exchange for a fee. Is this really a service you need? Writers can self-publish e-books these days without resorting to vanity presses. Or maybe he or she wants to become your partner on that blog or podcast. Find out what talents or connections he or she brings to the table. Investigate the terms carefully. Ask to speak with his or her former associates. Ask searching questions.

Your friend who cheated on his/her partner may come to you seeking a place under your roof during the last week of the Year of the Horse. He or she has been thrown out by the betrayed spouse. Although you may feel sympathetic, having this person live with you even temporarily will put a strain on your relationship with your significant other. Help this buddy find a roommate to share an apartment. Or advise them about buying something of their own. Best not to keep too close company with someone whose reputation has been besmirched by sneaky behavior. Your partner is not wrong to want the person gone. With them around, the vibes at home are not terrific.

# DOG 2014
## OVERVIEW FOR THE WOOD HORSE YEAR

*Doubting Dog,*

*Oh lucky you! Horses can't enough of Dog company. They are already mighty energetic people who never stop working and building and painting and writing and dancing. Horses are, in fact, a tad frenzied. Your presence is positively tranquilizing to the Horse. You are a person of reason, logic and good sense. Your calculating (somewhat paranoid) way of thinking impresses the hasty Horse and may even influence him or her to change certain major things about his or her lifestyle. Where you see wasted effort or extreme behavior, you do not hesitate to remark on it. You Dogs can make spontaneous pejorative comments which really sting. And you are terminally critical.*

*But you can also be constructively critical to help out a friend who is making a big mistake. The Horse (who just about never takes advice from anyone) will heed your counsel and even thank you for having more horse-sense even than they. Conversely, when the Horse is in power, the general ambiance can be somewhat tense and laden with free floating anxiety. This antsy atmosphere is not your favorite. Why? Because you were born anxious and disquiet. You certainly don't need extra reasons to fret. Try working off some of that nervousness with meditation or yoga. Or . . . if eastern practices don't appeal to you, try scrubbing your floor, washing the car or running around the block 111 times. sw*

---

## THE CHINESE YEAR AHEAD
### DOG 2014

**DOG February 2014**

You may be tempted to do something underhanded the first week of this month. You took a look at the world around you and decided that as everyone else is merrily treading the grassy path of dishonesty, you should not continue to stumble down the rocky road of integrity. Perhaps you'll imagine cheating on your taxes. Or contemplate completing that advanced degree by paying someone to write your thesis or dissertation. You might decide to keep some money that isn't really yours. Don't do it. Don't cross that line. The moral consequences will be more costly than any money is worth. If all of your friends are double dealing, replace them with a better class of people. Seek the company of friends who will inspire you to be your shining best. Join another crowd which recognizes and reinforces your nobler tendencies.

Mercury goes retrograde on the 6th of this month and remains on its seeming backwards course until the 28th. Don't let this become yet another cause for worry, Doggie. Just remember not to sign any irrevocable documents or make any life-changing decisions. And don't go berserk when your computer and your smartphone die on the same day. These kinds of kinks are typical of the influence of Mercury retrograde.

Around the 17th, you may receive a request for help from a friend or family member. This person may ask you to come to their aid in a situation involving their offspring. Naturally, with your usual devotion and loyalty, you will do what you can to assist your pal. Perhaps your friend's teenager will stay in your home for a month or more to cool down after a family quarrel. Or you might loan your friend bail money to get the youngster out of jail. Whatever the help entails, you can be sure the person will be sincerely grateful and will one day return the favor.

A health problem may concern you toward the end of February. Headaches or back spasms or strange shooting pains in your arms and legs. All of those could very well be related to stress. You have a tendency to worry a lot. Make an appointment with your doctor. Take along a list of your symptoms so the doctor has something concrete to go on. Also, take measures to mitigate the tension in your life. Relieve yourself of irksome people who pump the very air out of you whenever they are around. Excuse them from your life. Start protecting yourself by meditating on a regular basis. If sitting meditation bores you, develop a walking meditation practice. Sign up for a class in tai chi or yoga. Schedule weekly massages to prevent tension from building up.

**DOG March 2014**

An ex will probably play a prominent role in the events of the first week of March. You are dealing here with someone who has become a fixture in your life. Perhaps the two of you still share child-raising responsibilities or own property together. This former lover may be at the end of a relationship and suddenly seek to re-ignite your passion for him or her. Be wary of what she or he says. They may attempt to use underhanded means concerning money or manipulation of the kids to get you back. Keep your thinking cap on. Don't give in to their ploys. What she or he really wants from you is not love. Rather they are interested in holding some power over you. Try to put yourself out of reach of this ex's stratagems. You might be willing to respect her or him as a co-parent or business partner, but show no hint of any willingness to reunite with them.

Someone in your family may become involved in a minor scandal. He or she probably did not do anything wrong or immoral. Nonetheless, judgmental people may seek to cast aspersions. Defend your family member to those who might critics him or her out of hand. Consider your relative's feelings as well. Do not allow your defensive actions to make the situation more visible. This relative is a younger person or a highly sensitive adult. Boost his or her self-esteem by assuring them of your support through this difficult time.

You are usually dubious about new things and unfamiliar people. But on or about the 19th, your cautious behavior will win over someone who initially disliked you. One of your previous detractors may offer a surprising gesture or token of friendship. Perhaps she or he will ask you out to lunch or offer you a small gift. Make the most of this gesture as it has the potential to serve you in your professional life. The detractor in question was all wrong about you and seeks now to make it up to you. That can only be a good thing as they have the both finances and influence galore to share with you.

You are feeling pinched in the pocketbook these days. Take heart Doggie. In the next few months, the fiscal picture will vastly improve. You may not earn more money per se. But some kind of windfall of extra bonus will befall you and you will begin once again to be able to put butter on your mashed potatoes.

**DOG April 2014**

You may quarrel with somebody dear to you around the 5th of April. He or she will say something you interpret an insult. Re-examine the events carefully. You may have snapped at this person for no reason. Has misfortune caused you to develop a chip on your shoulder? The real source of your anger stems no doubt from a hidden resentment you harbor toward people who treated you badly in the past. Your friend's words may have innocently touched on a painful memory. Recognize that your pal did not mean to brush those bruised places on your ego. Offer an apology for growling. You may also want to examine the roots of your emotions. . Begin your research by journaling about your feelings. If that doesn't relieve some of the residual anger, you can work things out with a reliable therapist.

Mid-April is likely to bring excellent financial news. Perhaps you get a raise or even an offer of a promotion. Perhaps you will be offered a new job. Maybe a stream of income you have been trying to develop suddenly takes a leap in profits. Use the money wisely. I mean put some of it away as soon as it becomes available. Stash it in a place where you cannot touch one cent. Think first in terms of savings and sound investments. Then buy yourself and your sweetheart some luxury items you couldn't afford for too long.

The last ten days of this month offer Dogs a special opportunity. If there is a project you have been hesitating about, now is the time to take the leap. The planets are lined up to support you. Expand that short story into a novel. Look for an agent for your voice-over work. Start painting that triptych you envisioned months ago. Just remember that the universe has a sense of humor. The agent you find may think you do marvelous funny voices and send you on those types of auditions rather than the sexy-voiced commercials you initially dreamed of. The romance story you planned to develop into a film may be hijacked by your characters who decide it should be a science fiction book. Never mind. The important thing is that you have taken your creativity to the next step.

### DOG May 2014

As May begins you may get a very challenging assignment at work or school. At first this task might seem a bit daunting. You could find yourself wondering if you can complete it all successfully by yourself. Don't let your anxiety get the best of you. Do not despair and/or throw in the towel. Break this big project down into small, manageable sections. Make a plan for attacking each section individually. As you complete each part, you will gain confidence. By the time you near completion of this major project, you will feel as if you have completed a marathon. You will be exhausted - and mighty proud of yourself.

You many wonder if it isn't time to call it quits with your current lover around the 17th of May. She or he will unwittingly reveal some pernicious form of narrow-mindedness. Perhaps this he or she reacts with shock and horror when you reveal an unconventional yet harmless escapade of your youth. Or could be he or she is horribly rude to a server in a restaurant. Or their reaction to a story on the news may reveal a previously undetected form of bigotry. Do not make excuses for bad behavior on your lover's part. Take the issue up with them. If they don't relent, think about all those other fish in the sea. Dogs must take care to attach their loyalty to those who truly deserve it.

A neighbor may become troublesome around the 27th, hosting rowdy parties with loud music playing late into the night. Or they let their dog crap in your yard. Worse they park on your lawn. You can avoid escalating the tension and try to remain cordial. But do define your boundaries. In other words, before you call the police, have a conciliatory chat with them. Make certain they understand that that their aggressive behavior simply will not do. If it continues, call the police.

## DOG June 2014

You may have to put up with rudeness from someone in a position of authority around June 11th. A tax official, a loan officer at a bank or one of your work supervisors or teachers. This person will use rules and regulations to make you jump through unnecessary hoops. You will be galled at being put in a position of groveling subservience. Unfortunately there is not much you can do to dissuade this character from attempting to reduce you to a pulp. Technically, they have done nothing wrong - just abused their power. You will have to keep your temper on a tight leash. Snarling at this person could result in him or her using their power to retaliate - big time!

Your home could use a bit of sprucing up. Why not invite some pals around for a painting party? Liven up the ambiance in that living room with brighter walls. Or make your bedroom walls red and dim the lighting to enhance to sensual atmosphere. Get new drapes and shades for the windows. Then mid-June, throw a party and invite all the folks who helped with the redecorating.

An opportunity for travel may arise around the third week of June. It is likely to be something of a gift. Perhaps a good friend offers to take you on a trip using her/his bonus miles from frequent business travel. Or maybe a relative asks you to house sit for a couple of weeks, giving you a free place to stay in the heart of one of your favorite cities. By all means, accept this offer. Use your time away from home to de-compress.

Enjoy your trip, but pack both your patience and your sense of humor. Mercury, planet of communications and transportation, is headed on another of its retrograde journeys this month. Starting on the 7th of this month, anticipate a few extra wrenches to tumble into the works. Sign no papers. Make no promises. Stay away from courts and resist the urge to ask someone to marry you. Mercury will go direct again on July 1.

An old friend you lost touch with years ago may contact you around the 26th. At first, you feel a bit wary. You wonder what this person's motives are for trying to resume a dead friendship after so long. You examine each word in every e-mail or phone conversation expecting to be hit up for a loan or asked to perform some arduous favor. It could be that an honest attempt to resurrect the relationship is being hindered by your suspicions. You are always on your guard. Try to relax and enjoy the renewed association.

## DOG July 2014

A new romantic interest enters your life in the first week of July. There will be a whopper of a physical attraction between you and this person. You may find yourselves skipping dinner reservations in favor of multiple sexual romps. You may even find yourselves stealing away from a theatre performance or concert in order to slake your desires in a conveniently located restroom or broom closet. This one is an authentic hot ticket!

You may be tempted to skip a mandatory social event around the 19th. Be careful. This shindig promises to boost one of your sources of income in a curious roundabout manner. A connection you make there will turn out to be very useful. You will have to be patient, however. This new contact is not about to tap you on the shoulder and hand you a sack of cash. The route between meeting this person and augmenting your income will involve more than a few twists and turns. But the booty will prove well worth it.

Dogs who are parents of young adults may be met with some disturbing news toward the end of the month. This is not about doing chores and obeying rules. It looks like it's about personal choices. Perhaps one of your offspring expresses political or religious views diametrically opposite to yours. Maybe your son or daughter announces future plans which differ drastically from your hopes. Instead of going to medical school, your child announces plans to become a tattoo artist. Perhaps your son or daughter introduces you to a fiancé who has a prison record. Whatever it is, your first reaction may be anger and horror. Resist the temptation to deliver a lecture. Don't go ballistic. Forbidding their stated choice may have the opposite effect and see them jumping into their folly with both feet. Show your displeasure mildly. Then change the subject. Sometimes youngsters are just testing the waters.

What is making you so paranoid these days? You suspect everything and everybody of harboring ulterior motives. Make a vow not to worry so much about where the people who love you are coming from. Take their compliments and messages of friendship and love at face value. Quell that skeptical Doggie instinct of yours and just have yourself some good old-fashioned fun - especially in the royal bed chamber with you know whom.

## DOG August 2014

Your relationship with your new lover builds in intensity as August begins. The two of you enter the phase where your friends and relatives find it slightly embarrassing to dine with the two of you. Looks as though you can't keep your hands off each other. One of you lolls on the other's lap while the rest of the group twitches and wishes you'd cut it out. If you play footsie under the table at restaurants or hold hands in public places, try to do so discreetly. People find it sweet when you gaze into each other's eyes or gently stroke one another's hair as you pass by. Do try to keep the sexual side of your affair private. Gestures of tenderness in public should remain unobtrusive.

You may encounter jealousy around the 17th of this month. Someone in your life who did not know about your new romance discovers it and is miffed. Could be one of your exes. Or someone who was a casual sex partner before you met your new sweetie. For some reason, the nature of your relationship with this jealous person was clandestine. Perhaps he or she was married or still involved with someone else. Or maybe the two of you work together at a place where interoffice affairs are grounds for dismissal. Worse - maybe this jealous individual is your therapist or clergyperson. At any rate, the hidden nature of this old affair makes the ex's jealousy even more toxic. Under the influence of the green-eyed monster, people do some wacky things. Let's hope you aren't stalked and that they don't play that ring-your-number-and-hang-up trick that just about all rejected lovers get up to sooner or later.

The investment you made in yourself back in May is going to pay off in some small way toward the end of August. Your agent may get you a recurring gig somewhere. The chapters you wrote of your big novel receive laudatory comments from your teacher in a writing workshop. You show your paintings to a gallery owner who asks you to participate in a group show. Some kind of kudos for your creativity are in order at the end of August. Please don't think the praise is phony. It is not.

## DOG September 2014

Around the 5th of September, you will receive some misguided advice. Someone you have relied upon and turned to for sound counsel for years lets you down. It will be a shock to realize that your mentor is, in fact, not perfect. You have been accustomed to seeing them as infallible. This character might be an older sibling, an aunt or a kindly uncle. Might be a teacher or even your spiritual guide. You will discover that the suggestions you get this time have been shaped by his/her prejudices or for a selfish motive. Get at least one second opinion.

Your new sweetie may make a misstep with you around the 19th. He or she offers you a gift which reveals a total failure to understand your tastes and personality. You feel thoroughly baffled. The present seems almost like it was meant for someone else. It appears to have been hastily chosen at the last minute. If you formerly thought of this person as a potential serious romance, you may have to re-classify him or her to the friends-with-benefits category. Good sex is a wicked blindfold. It can successfully conceal character flaws. Beware.

Shortly after this incident, that jealous individual from last month may very well appear on your doorstep. Resist the temptation to console yourself by hopping into bed with Mr. or Ms. Green Eyes. Someone who is capable of overt jealousy is likely to be controlling and even dangerous. Why not hang in with the sexy lover till something better (more serious) comes along?

The last four or five days of the month you will be putting out petty fires and dealing with other people's messes. Suddenly everybody you know on this earth seems to need your help, advice, consolation or money. You will be fielding calls from several friends and relatives at once. Racing neighbors' kids to the emergency room, rescuing soaking wet stray animals and cooking dinner for your best friend's family while he or she is out of town. Not to mention fielding multiple pleas for some of your ready cash. It may be almost impossible to maintain your equilibrium. No growling please. Remember. It takes many good deeds to build a good reputation, and only one bad one to lose it.

**DOG October 2014**

You may discover a previously hidden talent this month. Try some skill you have always felt curious about but never attempted. You may find out you are a natural at anything from in line dancing to wind surfing. You might pick up a pair of knitting needles for the first time and turn out a beautiful cap for a friend's baby. Or maybe a techie friend will show you how to build a computer. You will copycat their efforts and end up finding it surprisingly easy. Even if you aren't a whiz at this new field immediately, if you enjoy it, continue to apply yourself. Dogs are often hesitant to try new things for fear of appearing ridiculous. But they just as often have a huge cache of skills which lie dormant for years. Early October is a great time to awaken one of your untapped abilities.

This kind of reappraisal of your personal skill set is a perfect way to make the best of this month's snafu-laden Mercury retrograde period (October 4th till the 25th). Take the usual precautionary measures with regard to not signing contracts and avoiding surgery. Electronic glitches are common now too.

Feeling a bit off lately? Lower energy? Poor digestion? Perhaps you have an allergy. Have a physician test you. People often develop allergies - even in adulthood. You may have a previously undetected sensitivity to dairy or gluten. Modifying your diet to eliminate whatever it is could restore your energy.

An old lover whom you have kept in touch over the years may call you around the 21st. He or she feels dissatisfied with a current partner. This ex still idealizes the past romance with you. He or she may want to re-kindle that old relationship. Steer clear. That old sock is not the serious relationship I spoke about above. Don't lengthen the affair with your sex object. Enjoy it while it lasts. But do keep your eyes open for a fresh romantic partner who has the kind of depth and loyalty you value.

The end of the month of October affords you a professional opportunity arising from the contact you made back in July. I warned you it would not be simple. Turns out this character needs you to take a plane somewhere or join them for a road trip to a distant city. They are being sincerely friendly and mean well. But you - being mistrustful you - wonder what the heck they have up their sleeve. Relax Doggie. They just want your companionship for the trip. Nothing underhanded or hidden lurks behind their request for your presence. Take this chance to build a friendship with them. The time spent will pay off in the long run.

## DOG November 2014

In early November, your opinion of someone in politics or government rubs a good friend the wrong way. In this instance, the pal becomes vehement and even seems to take your point of view personally. You simply want to agree to disagree. But your chum is having none of it. He or she is determined to change your mind and persists in arguing with you every time you see each other. Their unrelenting quarreling will embarrass you and grate on your nerves. Growl. But don't bite. Turns out the person is thinking of running for office and is merely practicing their campaign speeches on their good friend - you.

Jealousy may worm its way back into your life early this month. The auguries for this one are a bit ambiguous. It may be that same person from a couple of months ago displays green-eyed monster tendencies again. Or there could be a third party involved—another man or woman who resents your past or present claim on someone. Could it be you whose eyes are looking rather green around the edges? There's a strong possibility that some annoyance will be involved. If you have a garage, park your car indoors, lest someone slash the tires. If someone vandalizes your property or threatens you, don't wait. Contact the police immediately. However the stalking could also be of the cyber variety. Could be one party learns another individual's password in order to access private e-mail or phone messages. Change your passwords if you haven't already. If it's you who is spying on someone else, there may be stronger consequences than you imagine. Karma will come back to bite you hard within the next year.

A celebration or party of some sort may have to be cancelled due to a health care emergency for a member of your family. It could be that someone goes to the hospital in severe pain from kidney stones, heart attack or appendicitis. There's also the possibility of injury due to some kind of accident. Be especially careful when going up or down stairs. Look first to see if the steps are wet or strewn with small objects. If you have children at home, take extra precautions for their safety this month. Put safety covers on electrical outlets. Make sure drawers containing sharp objects have childproof latches. Watch all little ones (pets included) with extra care.

## DOG December 2014

Your actions may result in others hailing you as a hero early this month. Perhaps you witness a child fall through the ice on a lake. You rush to the save the boy or girl from frigid waters. Or maybe you lead a campaign to shut down a puppy mill. The rescued dogs all go to no-kill shelters or forever homes. Maybe you will hear a kitten crying from the boarded-up basement of an abandoned building and free it. At the very least, you will receive cheers from onlookers. Your circle of friends lauds your efforts. The story might make the local news. It may even become viral on the internet. Enjoy your time in the spotlight. But don't let it go to your head, Doggie.

An appeal you receive from a charity group around the 12th of December may prove to be bogus. Investigate and do intensive research before giving your money to any organization unfamiliar to you. If they are legitimate, they will not mind waiting while you research them.

A shady acquaintance from your past may try to take advantage of your holiday good mood around the 20th. If someone with a history of sketchy behavior reappears unexpectedly around this time, avoid letting them into your home or sharing any personal information with them. Be especially cautious around anyone you know with a criminal record. Horses and Roosters in particular may behave in slippery ways during this period.

Divergence from your usual eating and drinking habits may wreak havoc on your digestion the last few days of December. If you are a usually a teetotaler but decide to indulge in a single glass of champagne for New Year's Eve, you could experience the same ill-effects as if you drank two bottles of wine. If you are a vegan or vegetarian and give in to family pleas to eat a serving of Grandma's roast turkey or juicy roast beef, the meal may choose exit your body sooner rather than later. Be kinder to your body. It's a fragile machine.

## DOG January 2015

That risk you took last May, investing in your own talent, begins to pay glorious dividends this month. Perhaps you get an offer to do the voice-overs in a well-known cartoon television show. Or the query and first chapters of your book have netted you a contract and a handsome advance check. Or maybe those gallery owners will contact you, asking about a show. Use this time to celebrate your achievement. Take at least a brief trip. Visit one of your favorite cities for an extended weekend. Buy yourself some new clothes. Invest in a comfortable, stylish pair of shoes. Get a good haircut. After all, you want to project the cleaned-up version of yourself which bespeaks a certain degree of confidence and success.

Save at least part of the money you earn. You will need to attend to a problem with your home that will likely arise around the 16th. The planetary portents indicate some kind of leakage. Perhaps heavy ice will create a hole going from your roof to your bedroom ceiling. It's definitely to do with water. A plumbing problem or a sewer backup. Be especially careful during this period that you do not leave water running for too long. Untended sinks and bathtubs can and do overflow. Each time you run the water anywhere, put on your kitchen timer. When it dings, run and shut off the faucet.

While out with friends around the 22nd, you may meet an intriguing new love interest. This person will exert a magnetic effect on you. You will recognize this individual by his or her mesmerizing eyes; and will probably find yourself gazing into them as if hypnotized. Enjoy the flirtation. However, people do have baggage. On your first date, ask a few pertinent questions relating to marital status, health history, family background etc. Baggage is one thing. But some people hide secrets inside their valises and trunks from the past. No matter the attraction, don't set up housekeeping with this character - or anybody else until you have been "going steady" for at least 18 months. It takes 18 months for the warts to show up. Give you new couple a chance. But do take it slow.

# PIG 2014
## OVERVIEW FOR THE WOOD HORSE YEAR

*Provident Pig,*

*As you most likely will be in recovery mode after the year of the devious-minded Snake has wrenched the last of your gold coins from your hot little trotter, I must remind you to stop beating yourself up. Whatever happened to you last year was fate. Destiny for Pigs in Snake years means to be duped and hornswoggled and often to lose some of that native Pig innocence you so cherish and cling to. Snakes often take Pigs for a bumpy ride. This Horse year will be one of recuperation and re-centering for Pigs. You will have to work excessively hard. You won't be able to relax the way you like to.*

*No bonbons whilst reclining on your favorite moiré chaise longue, leafing casually through the catalogues from antique auction houses in splendid venues. No caviar at those intimate gourmet suppers you are so famous for giving at your charming abode. Nope. Piggy, this year is shoulder to the grindstone and nose to the elbow grease year. You won't be slaving for nothing. There is an objective. You need to rebuild your emotional and material self. Nothing like turning over the soil in 2 acres of garden or spackling the whole upstairs ceiling to help restore one's confidence. Keep yourself occupied with practical chores. The Horse smiles on a busy Pig. sw*

―――――― ℮ ℯℂ ℯℯ ――――――

## THE CHINESE YEAR AHEAD
## PIG 2014

### PIG February 2014

Pigs are likely to feel drawn to projects related to family and the past as the Year of the Horse trots on in. You might take up genealogy in order to research your ancestors. Maybe you'll gather information by visiting a graveyard or a dusty records office in the small town where your great-grandparents once lived. Or you might interview an elderly relative in order to ask questions about his/her childhood memories or about the early years of the last century. Perhaps you'll be arranging family photos in an album or scanning them to create digital versions for posterity. You might even decide to combine photos and interviews in a family history book. Whatever method you choose to use for this research, you will be a busy camper in February.

From the 6th until the 28th of this month, Mercury, the planet ruling communication and transportation, goes retrograde. Confusion and delays become more common themes in most people's lives during these periods. This particular retrograde phase is likely to have an especially strong impact on matters related to technology and group dynamics. Remember to maintain your best level of patience and your sense of humor for these little backward trips of the planet named for the messenger of the gods.

Have you been carrying over your holiday season indulgence in rich foods past Valentine's Day? If so, now is a good time to pull in the reins on your diet. The planetary omens indicate you could face health consequences later in this year for throwing dietary cautions to the wind. Those bacon sandwiches and chocolate chip cookies could come back to haunt you in a few months' time in the form of diabetes, gout or some other nasty illness related to unrestricted gourmandizing. You still have time to head off these potential health problems if you start transferring your dining affections from cream and butter to kale and blueberries.

## PIG March 2014

Beware little Piggy! There is someone in your life who does not wish you well. This character is a bit of a social predator and sees you as fair game for either mockery or malicious gossip. He or she may be a participant in a religious group you belong to or do volunteer work with you. You have probably sensed something a bit dark about them. With your usual optimism and desire to think well of everyone, you have been giving them the benefit of the doubt , telling yourself they have no reason to harm you. Your instinct about this person's so-called "jokes" is not mere paranoia. This unpleasant interloper could be a Monkey or a Rat. Ask a Tiger or Horse friend of yours to help you 1) To understand the troublemaker's motives. 2) To put a stop to their games.

The third week of this month may present you with the temptation to spend more than you can afford. Knowing your weakness for culture, it's likely to involve either books or art. You might discover a bookstore stocked with hundreds of tomes about all the subjects which most fascinate you. You could emerge from this vortex of literary temptation laden with several pounds of fascinating tomes on your favorite topics. You may try to justify your expenditure to yourself - after all, these kinds of books are extremely rare or aren't available in a less expensive electronic format.

Look as though you may very well stumble across an antique shop selling precisely the kind of beautiful items you love. One can run up quite a hefty bill purchasing old oil paintings of mythological figures or elegant art deco tables. Take some time before the 15$^{th}$ to draw up a budget showing yourself exactly how much you can splurge when you find this fabulous store. Then stick to the figure like super glue. Do not overspend now.

Cut back even further on those dietary indiscretions. Whether you are guilty of eating the ears off that chocolate rabbit someone gave you for Easter or you have been sneak-eating ice cream in the night, you simply must cut down on treats. If you deny yourself the kinds of sneaky snacks which seem to eliminate anxiety, you will avoid a far more noxious anxiety when you find out you have contracted a lifelong chronic illness.

## PIG April 2014

Some gallant action of yours could be misinterpreted around the 1$^{st}$ of this month. You might pull a small child out of the path of a speeding car only to see the child's parent assume you somehow caused the frightened youngster's tears. Or you might return a lost pooch to its owner who will mistakenly accuse you of dog-napping. Everything will come out right in the end, but before it does, you may have to endure someone delivering a tongue-lashing you don't deserve. I'm afraid that even when the confused individual discovers his/her error, you may only expect a rather truculent, insincere apology. People are weird. Let's just agree for now that doing a good deed is its own reward. If it isn't, why bother?

How are you fixed for cash? I hope you took my advice last month and didn't overspend. A wonderful investment opportunity is likely to come your way. You won't want to be noodling around in the couch cushions and digging out change from your coat pockets in order to take advantage of this chance. News of this venture comes to you via unusual channels. Keep your ears open for investment opportunities that are being discussed in your work entourage.

There may be some awkwardness between you and a friend of yours around the 20$^{th}$. He or she will accidentally let slip some personal secret. Perhaps your pal confides this information to you while inebriated or when he/she is feeling highly emotional. Afterwards, your buddy will be embarrassed about sharing this information. Don't be hurt if they suddenly seem a bit distant or curt with you. Pride is in the way of their affection for you just now. They will recover soon. In the meantime, give your friend space. Don't mention the embarrassing secret. Don't even say you won't tell a soul. Drop it.

Making life work smoothly for you now is largely dependent on your taking action. If you want to go on a trip, plan it yourself and go. Taking a course? Do the research, find the school and go do it by yourself. The stars are not shining on relationship issues for you at this time. Your motto for now? DO IT YOURSELF.

## PIG May 2014

The first week of May finds you feeling particularly amorous. If you have a partner, the two of you will spend hours together alternating between making love and feeding each other restorative snacks for the next round of vigorous sex. If you have been single, your pheromones now cast a spell on whomever you desire. Even if you consider yourself average-looking, you now have the ability to fascinate someone who looks like Brad Pitt or Angelina Jolie. Just don't invest too much emotionally in any new dalliance which commences under this influence. A romance which commences during this period is unlikely to have staying power. That, of course, doesn't mean you can't have fun while it lasts. Take the roller coaster ride. If the union has staying power, it will be revealed on the first curve.

That unpleasant individual with the snarky insults may intentionally condescend to you at a gathering around the 14$^{th}$. He or she seeks to undermine you in the eyes of the rest of the group. Don't let yourself go all tongue-tied because of this person's verbal sleight-of-hand. You know the situation well by now. You know their motives. Answer with a remark which floors them. "I know you want me to lose my job. But I won't. So clam up!" or something of that ilk. Hit them with what you know is behind all this gabble.

A friend may ask you to do something slightly unorthodox this month. It's not actually illegal, but it might involve a white lie or two. Perhaps your buddy is cheating on a lover and asks you to give him or her an alibi. Maybe your pal wants you to fake a job reference so help him/her get a job after being unemployed. Or maybe they are being evicted and need you to lie to their landlord about their income. If the friend is long-term and you trust them, go ahead and fib. But if you fear the outrage of the cuckolded lover, the wrath of the landlord or the loss of reputation *vis a vis* the potential employer, beg off. I know it's hard for you to say no. But you must protect yourself against reprisal.

## PIG June 2014

This month features another of those irksome Mercury retrogrades. This one stretches from the 7$^{th}$ of this month until the 1$^{st}$ of July. Its effects are likely to be strongest in matters related to home, family, siblings and neighbors. Since short journeys will also be affected by this phase, this is not the best time to make that quick getaway you've been contemplating. Those born in the western zodiac sign of Gemini are likely to be the most discombobulated this Mercury retrograde. If your natal Sun is in Gemini, practice deep breathing regularly (I'm serious.) until after the retrograde period ends. If you have friends with this sign, be patient if they seem scatty and a bit ditzy.

How open-minded are you? If you made up your mind about most issues years or even decades ago, the events of this month could be particularly trying for you. Even if you consider yourself very open and accepting of unusual people and circumstances, the universe may throw you a curve ball now. Instead of letting this situation make you angry, upset or defensive, try shifting your perspective. Think of what comes your way during the last two weeks of June as a major test you're being given before moving up to a new level.

Fair warning: You are liable to appear a bit foolish at some point mid-June. Unfortunately, the sudden ridicule which will visit you is most likely to occur when you are trying to look your best. If, for example, you are taking part in a June wedding, check your shoe for dog poop or a strand of stray toilet paper before leaving the restroom. A pigeon might paint your windshield just before you pick up your highly critical in-laws. Some devilment is afoot which wants you to look silly. In this case, forewarned is unfortunately not necessarily forearmed. This is about happenstance. Not something you can plan for or against.

A change at work toward the end of this month will probably result in you having a new boss. She or he is the kind of person who voices too much criticism. Don't let their lack of appreciation upset you. If this boss did not approve of your work, they would not hesitate to can you without a New York millisecond's notice. You simply have to learn how to get on their right side. Try ego-boosting compliments.

**PIG July 2014**

Does your wardrobe give people the wrong idea about you? Perhaps you used to be a Goth girl or boy and still have a lot of vampire attire even though you work at a law firm now? Or maybe you recently gained or lost weight and now your clothing all looks like ill-fitting hand-me-downs. This month is an excellent time for you to refresh your items in your closet. Shop wisely, buying pieces which really suit you, both in terms of style and fit. It might be best to update other aspects of your appearance such as your hair style, make-up or facial hair. Try to make your current appearance match the lifestyle you have chosen. You don't have to have those tattoos removed. But do camouflage them during serious business meetings.

You will have to exercise your integrity to prevent a friend from doing something rankly dishonest. This event will probably occur when the two of you go out together the third week of this month. You and your buddy might stumble on something of value. It might be an expensive watch, or the hottest newly released smartphone. Perhaps it will be a wallet full of cash containing the owner's ID. Your friend might want to keep this find. Or they may propose doing a "dine and ditch" when a server takes too long to deliver the bill. Steer your pal away from doing anything shady that involves you. Keeping your own nose clean is your own business. Don't be swayed.

A good friend may experience some kind of major tragedy or upheaval in his/her life toward the end of July. It could be anything from a messy divorce to a death to a loss of employment. He or she will need a lot of emotional support. You may notice that some of the other people in your group are not as sympathetic to this situation as they might be. You are the compassionate Pig. So you will step in and offer the kindness and empathy your pal so desperately needs during this period - kindness and empathy they won't necessarily receive from the other, less merciful people.

**PIG August 2014**

Are you up for a trip? Your partner or perhaps a good friend may propose a spur-of-the-moment weekend jaunt early this month. Go ahead. Say yes. Being in an unfamiliar location will help disperse any feelings of stasis or boredom you may have experienced recently. Don't consult guidebooks for this trip. Just improvise, letting Lady Luck direct your choice of accommodations restaurants, etc. You need more spontaneity in your life right now. There's an excellent chance that the pleasant sense of disorientation you experience on this short journey will give you the inspiration you need for a new creative project.

You may receive news of a death in the family around the 16th. The deceased person is unlikely to be a close relative. It probably won't be anyone who has been important in your life. Most likely, a relative you haven't seen in years may reach the end of his/her life. This person's passing might shake loose a family secret or two. The startling information will throw light on some odd behavior exhibited by your older relatives. You might discover that your rich great-aunt started her fortune by running a house of ill repute or through some form of smuggling. Or you might discover your cousin was a bigamist with a hidden second family. The surprise will not be a tiny one.

A sardonic comment slipping out of your mouth at an inopportune moment could land you in hot water around the 24th. Perhaps at a party you remark that the term "criminal lawyer" is redundant only to discover the person you're chatting with is head of the local bar association. Or maybe you make a wisecrack about greedy physicians only to arouse the ire of your host whose son works for Doctors Without Borders. Save any sarcasm for private conversations where you know your audience well.

Your reputation as 'The good guy" often reaps you negative benefits. This season coming up will be rife with scammy people who have not other goal than you relieve you of some of your hard-earned money. Right now, set your mind to being careful who you take up with from now till the end of 2014. Sometimes when people are being a tad too nice, it's because they want something from you.

## PIG September 2014

Your bank account is likely to grow significantly this month. It might be that the investment you made this spring starts to pay some dividends. Or that cranky boss of yours, whom you have won over by commenting on their lipstick shade or admiring their Gucci loafers, surprises you with a bonus check. You might get an unexpected offer on a piece of real estate you've had on the market for ages. Whatever it is, your wisest course is to allocate most of it to savings. Don't forget you also have to give the tax authorities their cut. Spend just a little bit, perhaps treating your partner or a close friend to a special treat dinner at the most elegant restaurant in town.

A friend of yours might make a horrible relationship decision around the 21st. Perhaps he falls madly in love with someone who makes horrible racist remarks, offending everyone in your circle. Maybe she plans to marry a man 22 years her senior who has six children by four different women, none of whom he supports. Or it's possible your well-off pal leaves a devoted spouse of 15 years for a gold-digger just out of school. Hard as it may be, I advise you to bite your lip and remain silent. No matter how wise your counsel is right now, your pal will refuse to listen. She or he is even likely to end the friendship if you speak up now. There will be plenty of time later on, when the house of cards collapses, to say, "I did try to warn you."

How do you feel about children? I hope you like them because you may experience a sudden influx of pint-sized humans in your immediate vicinity around the 27th. Perhaps your next-door neighbor opens a day care business? Or maybe a friend experiences some kind of housing emergency and moves in to your house with a pack of offspring. If you are single, you might become romantically involved with someone who has a few kids. Whatever it is, your will become extremely familiar with the co-mingled scents of apple juice and diapers.

## PIG October 2014

This month's Mercury retrograde period may prove to be a serious pain in your posterior. With no consideration to your feelings, needs or schedule, the planet ruling communication and transportation will again make one of those irritating make-believe-backwards trips through the skies. (Of course the planets never actually move in reverse, it's just how they appear from our perspective on Earth.) From the commencement of this phase on October 4th through its conclusion on the 28th, you will no doubt experience a few hassles. Try to avoid scheduling any surgery or other health procedures until at least a week after Mercury goes direct. This time around, Mercury may prove especially troublesome in matters pertaining to food and cleaning or organizing. Household woes and family deadlines will be affected.

Where have you been applying your creative energies lately? Whatever project has most excited your imagination the past few months will garner you some sort of recognition now. If you came up with a clever new solution to some problem at work, you may get a promotion now. If you have been bubbling over with new ideas for delicious dishes, a recipe you enter in a contest might win you a prize. Or if you wrote a short story, it will be accepted for publication in an anthology. Yippeee.

Mid-October may see you mistakenly involved in someone else's drama. Perhaps two of your co-workers are having an affair. The spouse of one of these people gets wind of this dalliance, but mistakenly casts you in the role of home-wrecker. Or maybe you receive a slew of e-mails meant for someone with a similar address to yours. The sender keeps urgently demanding funds owed to him or her. You try writing back explaining the error, but the person who sent the e-mails assumes you're just trying to wiggle out of a debt.

Where your creative project is concerned, don't let the recent success slow you down. Sometimes when we have a victory, we give ourselves permission to slack off. If you are a writer. Write. A painter? Paint. A musician? Practice. Whatever pursuit you have taken up, practice practice practice. Grit brings success faster than mere talent.

## PIG November 2014

How well do you deal with last minute changes? A family emergency is likely to put the kibosh on a long-anticipated trip or excursion around the 12th. You might receive a call while you are in the car at the very beginning your journey. It's possible that you'll have to come to a relative's rescue in some way. The matter is likely to be related to health, or legalities. Maybe your mother calls you from the hospital where she just passed a kidney stone. She wants someone to stay with her while she recuperates at home from the ordeal. Perhaps your grownup son or daughter has been accused of breaking the law and needs you to post bail. Or it might be that one of your siblings is stranded on a country road, his/her car un-drivable after hitting a deer. These dratted rescue efforts will be rewarded by a star on your crown in heaven.

A close friend whom you have known a long time may surprise you by announcing she or he has always had a crush on you. This unexpected turn of events is likely to take place around the 23rd. We could be talking here about someone whose secret attraction to you means that he or she has always had a different sexual orientation than you assumed. The omens I'm seeing indicate you probably don't feel the same way about him or her. Try to remember sometime in the past when this friend or another close pal was harshly rejected by someone else. Remember and be your best compassionate self. If you cannot react to this sensitive person's advances with any sexual enthusiasm, let them down easy.

A young adult or teenager you know will experience some kind of crisis around the 26th. He or she needs advice from someone older and wiser. However in order to counsel this individual, you may have to reveal something about yourself you usually keep quiet. On this occasion compassion matters more than discretion. If you tell the kid that you too smoked dope or shoplifted or blew up mailboxes, it won't ruin your grownup reputation. But it will relieve his or her mind and let them that although you regret those stupidities, you did them. All young people do dumb things.

## PIG December 2014

If you feel run-down and sluggish as this month begins, the solution is not to spend the weekend in bed. You need more exercise. As you well know by now, exercise gives us energy. It doesn't make us tired. Come up with a realistic plan to become more physically active. Don't join that gym across town just because they are offering discounts on membership now. You know full well that the prospect of driving that far will discourage you from going regularly. If December weather where you live is warm, why not plan on regular walks or bike rides? Or if the weather is cold in your locale this time of year, maybe a series of hot yoga classes will entice you to move your body more often. If there's a physical activity you used to love as a child, perhaps you can take it up again. Find a class in figure skating or gymnastics or whatever it is that excited you years ago. Motivation is the key to maintaining any program of vigorous exercise.

Holiday gift time is liable to be a trifle awkward this year. A friend will give you something she/he expects you to adore. But you will actually feel puzzled about your pal's choice. It might be an amateurish homemade art project too ugly to display anywhere in your home. Yet your friend beams with pride when presenting it to you. Or it could be some item of clothing which clashes violently with your tastes. You might receive an item that has nothing to do with your interests—a book about baseball even though you abhor sports, a coffee table book about snakes with full color illustrations, a monthly delivery of luxury chocolates when the giver knows perfectly well you are on a draconian diet. Try not to let your disappointment show. Decide if the gift was merely a lapse in taste or if it reveals a previously unsuspected chasm between you and your buddy. If you decide to continue the friendship, you can subtly hint about how to improve their gift-giving skills.

## PIG January 2015

Financial problems may rear their hydra-heads in early January. You could receive some unpleasant correspondence from the tax officials, dunning you for monies you didn't know you owed. They may threaten to siphon funds from your paycheck or your bank accounts - or worse put you in jail. At the same time, either your car or your home (or possibly both) will require expensive repairs. Somebody who owes you money and promised to pay this month suddenly pleads bankruptcy. Your partner or one of your children is diagnosed with a medical problem necessitating a very costly course of treatment. This month is going to break your bank account and then some. Relax. It's only money.

After the ten-day spate of financial strain, you may develop some unusual mental quirk. Perhaps some old song constantly runs through your head. You even sometimes find yourself humming this tune, even though you don't particularly like it. Or maybe you compulsively re-arrange the letters of every name or phrase you see on a sign, screen or page, seeking as many anagrams as possible. Maybe you find yourself analyzing the numerological significance of the figures in every address you read or the sums in your checkbook. Or you could become obsessed with some kind of conspiracy theory. You are anxious. These obsessive manifestations are frequent when we are super stressed. Don't worry. This phase won't last very long. The New Chinese Year (Goat) is due Feb 19. Your life is in for a big boost.

Try not to let the final week of the Year of the Horse drain away in useless anxiety or mental fidgeting. There's an opportunity around this time for you to experience some kind of major emotional or spiritual breakthrough. Perhaps you will suddenly feel a sense of dropping the weight of some pain you have carried around for years. Maybe a concatenation of unusual circumstances permits you finally to heal an insecurity you've felt since childhood. If you meditate, you may experience some kind of vision which shifts your spirituality to a new level. Something very positive is imminent for Pigs in the last week of January.

# CHINESE CALENDAR

(Capricorn and Aquarius Find Dates for Your Year Here)

## THE CHINESE CALENDAR

*Year | Sign | Element | Year begins | Year ends*

1900 | Rat | Metal | 1/31/1900 | 2/18/1901
1901 | Ox | Metal | 2/19/1901 | 2/7/1902
1902 | Tiger | Water | 2/8/1902 | 1/28/1903
1903 | Cat | Water | 1/29/1903 | 2/15/1904
1904 | Dragon | Wood | 2/16/1904 | 2/3/1905
1905 | Snake | Wood | 2/4/1905 | 1/24/1906
1906 | Horse | Fire | 1/25/1906 | 2/12/1907
1907 | Goat | Fire | 2/13/1907 | 2/1/1908
1908 | Monkey | Earth | 2/2/1908 | 1/21/1909
1909 | Rooster | Earth | 1/22/1909 | 2/9/1910
1910 | Dog | Metal | 2/10/1910 | 1/29/1911
1911 | Pig | Metal | 1/30/1911 | 2/17/1912
1912 | Rat | Water | 2/18/1912 | 2/5/1913
1913 | Ox | Water | 2/6/1913 | 1/25/1914
1914 | Tiger | Wood | 1/26/1914 | 2/13/1915
1915 | Cat | Wood | 2/14/1915 | 2/2/1916
1916 | Dragon | Fire | 2/3/1916 | 1/22/1917
1917 | Snake | Fire | 1/23/1917 | 2/10/1918
1918 | Horse | Earth | 2/11/1918 | 1/31/1919
1919 | Goat | Earth | 2/1/1919 | 2/19/1920
1920 | Monkey | Metal | 2/20/1920 | 2/7/1921
1921 | Rooster | Metal | 2/8/1921 | 1/27/1922
1922 | Dog | Water | 1/28/1922 | 2/15/1923
1923 | Pig | Water | 2/16/1923 | 2/4/1924
1924 | Rat | Wood | 2/5/1924 | 1/23/1925
1925 | Ox | Wood | 1/24/1925 | 2/12/1926

1926 | Tiger | Fire | 2/13/1926 | 2/1/1927

1927 | Cat | Fire | 2/2/1927 | 1/22/1928

**Year | *Sign | Element | Year begins | Year ends***

1928 | Dragon | Earth | 1/23/1928 | 2/9/1929

1929 | Snake | Earth | 2/10/1929 | 1/29/1930

1930 | Horse | Metal | 1/30/1930 | 2/16/1931

1931 | Goat | Metal | 2/17/1931 | 2/5/1932

1932 | Monkey | Water | 2/6/1932 | 1/25/1933

1933 | Rooster | Water | 1/26/1933 | 2/13/1934

1934 | Dog | Wood | 2/14/1934 | 2/3/1935

1935 | Pig | Wood | 2/4/1935 | 1/23/1936

1936 | Rat | Fire | 1/24/1936 | 2/10/1937

1937 | Ox | Fire | 2/11/1937 | 1/30/1938

1938 | Tiger | Earth | 1/31/1938 | 2/18/1939

1939 | Cat | Earth | 2/19/1939 | 2/7/1940

1940 | Dragon | Metal | 2/8/1940 | 1/26/1941

1941 | Snake | Metal | 1/27/1941 | 2/14/1942

1942 | Horse | Water | 2/15/1942 | 2/4/1943

1943 | Goat | Water | 2/5/1943 | 1/24/1944

1944 | Monkey | Wood | 1/25/1944 | 2/12/1945

1945 | Rooster | Wood | 2/13/1945 | 2/1/1946

1946 | Dog | Fire | 2/2/1946 | 1/21/1947

1947 | Pig | Fire | 1/22/1947 | 2/9/1948

1948 | Rat | Earth | 2/10/1948 | 1/28/1949

1949 | Ox | Earth | 1/29/1949 | 2/16/1950

1950 | Tiger | Metal | 2/17/1950 | 2/5/1951

1951 | Cat | Metal | 2/6/1951 | 1/26/1952

1952 | Dragon | Water | 1/27/1952 | 2/13/1953

1953 | Snake | Water | 2/14/1953 | 2/2/1954

1954 | Horse | Wood | 2/3/1954 | 1/23/1955

1955 | Goat | Wood | 1/24/1955 | 2/11/1956

1956 | Monkey | Fire | 2/12/1956 | 1/30/1957

1957 | Rooster | Fire | 1/31/1957 | 2/17/1958

1958 | Dog | Earth | 2/18/1958 | 2/7/1959
1959 | Pig | Earth | 2/8/1959 | 1/27/1960
1960 | Rat | Metal | 1/28/1960 | 2/14/1961
1961 | Ox | Metal | 2/15/1961 | 2/4/1962
1962 | Tiger | Water | 2/5/1962 | 1/24/1963
1963 | Cat | Water | 1/25/1963 | 2/12/1964
1964 | Dragon | Wood | 2/13/1964 | 2/1/1965
**Year | *Sign | Element | Year begins | Year ends***
1965 | Snake | Wood | 2/2/1965 | 1/20/1966
1966 | Horse | Fire | 1/21/1966 | 2/8/1967
1967 | Goat | Fire | 2/9/1967 | 1/29/1968
1968 | Monkey | Earth | 1/30/1968 | 2/16/1969
1969 | Rooster | Earth | 2/17/1969 | 2/5/1970
1970 | Dog | Metal | 2/6/1970 | 1/26/1971
1971 | Pig | Metal | 1/27/1971 | 2/14/1972
1972 | Rat | Water | 2/15/1972 | 2/2/1973
1973 | Ox | Water | 2/3/1973 | 1/22/1974
1974 | Tiger | Wood | 1/23/1974 | 2/10/1975
1975 | Cat | Wood | 2/11/1975 | 1/30/1976
1976 | Dragon | Fire | 1/31/1976 | 2/17/1977
1977 | Snake | Fire | 2/18/1977 | 2/6/1978
1978 | Horse | Earth | 2/7/1978 | 1/27/1979
1979 | Goat | Earth | 1/28/1979 | 2/15/1980
1980 | Monkey | Metal | 2/16/1980 | 2/4/1981
1981 | Rooster | Metal | 2/5/1981 | 1/24/1982
1982 | Dog | Water | 1/25/1982 | 2/12/1983
1983 | Pig | Water | 2/13/1983 | 2/1/1984
1984 | Rat | Wood | 2/2/1984 | 2/19/1985
1985 | Ox | Wood | 2/20/1985 | 2/8/1986
1986 | Tiger | Fire | 2/9/1986 | 1/28/1987
1987 | Cat | Fire | 1/29/1987 | 2/16/1988
1988 | Dragon | Earth | 2/17/1988 | 2/5/1989
1989 | Snake | Earth | 2/6/1989 | 1/26/1990

1990 | Horse | Metal | 1/27/1990 | 2/14/1991

1991 | Goat | Metal | 2/15/1991 | 2/3/1992

1992 | Monkey | Water | 2/4/1992 | 1/22/1993

1993 | Rooster | Water | 1/23/1993 | 2/9/1994

1994 | Dog | Wood | 2/10/1994 | 1/30/1995

1995 | Pig | Wood | 1/31/1995 | 2/18/1996

1996 | Rat | Fire | 2/19/1996 | 2/6/1997

1997 | Ox | Fire | 2/7/1997 | 1/27/1998

1998 | Tiger | Earth | 1/28/1998 | 2/15/1999

1999 | Cat | Earth | 2/16/1999 | 2/4/2000

2000 | Dragon | Metal | 2/5/2000 | 1/23/2001

2001 | Snake | Metal | 1/24/2001 | 2/11/2002

2002 | Horse | Water | 2/12/2002 | 1/31/2003

**Year | *Sign | Element | Year ends | Year begins***

2003 | Goat | Water | 2/1/2003 | 1/21/2004

2004 | Monkey | Wood | 1/22/2004 | 2/8/2005

2005 | Rooster | Wood | 2/9/2005 | 1/28/2006

2006 | Dog | Fire | 1/29/2006 | 2/17/2007

2007 | Pig | Fire | 2/18/2007 | 2/6/2008

2008 | Rat | Earth | 2/7/2008 | 1/25/2009

2009 | Ox | Earth | 1/26/2009 | 2/13/2010

2010 | Tiger | Metal | 2/14/2010 | 2/2/2011

2011 | Cat | Metal | 2/3/2011 | 1/22/2012

2012 | Dragon | Water | 1/23/2012 | 2/9/2013

2013 | Snake | Water | 2/10/2013 | 1/30/2014

2014 | Horse | Wood | 1/31/2014 | 2/18/2015

2015 | Goat | Wood | 2/19/2015 | 2/7/2016

2016 | Monkey | Fire | 2/8/2016 | 1/27/2017

2017 | Rooster | Fire | 1/28/2017 | 2/15/2018

2018 | Dog | Earth | 2/16/2018 | 2/4/2019

2019 | Pig | Earth | 2/5/2019 | 1/24//2020

## Books by Suzanne White

 CHINESE ASTROLOGY PLAIN AND SIMPLE

 THE NEW ASTROLOGY™

 THE NEW CHINESE ASTROLOGY

 THE ASTROLOGY OF LOVE

 THE NEW ASTROLOGY BY SUN SIGN SERIES

 THE NEW ASTROLOGY POCKET GUIDE

*Available on Paper From all Booksellers online and off*
*and*

http://suzannewhite.com

and

http://www.smashwords.com

http://www.suzannewhite.com/chinese-astrology/yearindex.html

Get Your Copy of **New Astrology Full Year of Horoscopes** Book *http://suzannewhite.com/astrology/newAstrology.html*

Visit **http://suzannewhite.com** for Personal Chart Readings
Books, Horoscopes & Lifestyle Advice

## ABOUT THE AUTHOR

Best Selling author Suzanne White is American. She lives in France. In Provence. Suzanne speaks and writes both French and English. She has been a college professor, a fashion model, a journalist, an interpreter, a novelist, a fireworks salesperson, director of a Parisian Couture boutique, an elevator operator, a shoe salesperson, a single mother and a simultaneous translator. She came to writing late at age 33. By age 38, she had written her first best seller. THE NEW ASTROLOGY™, A savvy fusion of Chinese and Western astrological signs creating 144 NEW SIGNS. Suzanne White's fans and readers have dubbed her: "The High Priestess" of Chinese and Western Astrologies. Suzanne's books are on every best seller list worldwide. She does Private Chart Readings and answers all e-mail personally. suzanwhite@aol.com

###

Made in the USA
Lexington, KY
24 February 2014